HOW TO READ A
SHAKESPEAREAN PLAY TEXT

This is an invaluable introductory guide for the English student who needs to decipher a page from a play, or a facsimile equivalent, from the Shakespearean period. The original quartos and folios of early play texts are increasingly subject to editorial and critical scrutiny, and electronic facsimiles are making the originals accessible to undergraduate and graduate students. Giddens provides a practical 'how to' guide to the original printed texts of Shakespeare and his contemporaries. He explains how the features of the play text came about, what the different elements mean, and who created them. The book provides that important first step towards bibliography and critical editing, presenting a detailed account of how to read these early texts and how they have been turned into the modern editions we are accustomed to.

EUGENE GIDDENS is Skinner-Young Professor in Shakespeare and Renaissance Literature at Anglia Ruskin University, Cambridge. He is an associate editor of *The Cambridge Edition of the Works of Ben Jonson* and a general editor of *The Complete Works of James Shirley*.

HOW TO READ A
SHAKESPEAREAN PLAY TEXT

EUGENE GIDDENS

CAMBRIDGE
UNIVERSITY PRESS

CAMBRIDGE UNIVERSITY PRESS

Cambridge, New York, Melbourne, Madrid, Cape Town, Singapore,
São Paulo, Delhi, Dubai, Tokyo, Mexico City

Cambridge University Press
The Edinburgh Building, Cambridge CB2 8RU, UK

Published in the United States of America by Cambridge University Press, New York

www.cambridge.org
Information on this title: www.cambridge.org/9780521713979

First published 2011

Printed in the United Kingdom at the University Press, Cambridge

A catalogue record for this publication is available from the British Library

Library of Congress Cataloguing in Publication data
Giddens, Eugene.
How to read a Shakespearean play text / Eugene Giddens.
p.   cm.
Includes bibliographical references and index.
ISBN 978-0-521-88640-6 (hardback)
1. Shakespeare, William, 1564–1616 – Criticism, Textual.
2. Shakespeare, William, 1564–1616 – Authorship.   I. Title.
PR2976.G49   2011
822.3′3 – dc22   2010048071

ISBN 978-0-521-88640-6 Hardback
ISBN 978-0-521-71397-9 Paperback

Contents

Illustrations

Acknowledgments

I am very grateful for early and continued bibliographical training and encouragement from Martin Wiggins, John Jowett, and Stanley Wells, who taught me as a PhD student at the Shakespeare Institute, University of Birmingham, and for many years thereafter. David Bevington, Martin Butler, Ian Donaldson, and David Gants, the general editors and electronic editor of *The Cambridge Edition of the Works of Ben Jonson*, greatly enhanced my knowledge of early texts. Under their tutelage, as an Arts and Humanities Research Board research associate, I learned how to collate for stop-press variants, perform headline analysis, and deploy a host of other bibliographical techniques as discussed in this book. The 'Guidelines' for the *Cambridge Jonson* are probably the best 'How to...' manual in existence for beginning editors, and I am fortunate to have heard many conversations and exchanges that refined and tested those instructions. Research towards this book, and especially towards those sections that concern James Shirley, was supported by a Clark–Huntington Joint Bibliographical Fellowship to the Clark Library, UCLA, and Huntington Library, San Marino. Research in the Meisei University Library, Tokyo, was funded by an Anglo–Daiwa Japanese Foundation grant, and facilitated by the generosity of Noriko Sumimoto, Hitoshi Honda, and Chiaki Hanabusa. Bibliographical work on the forthcoming *Complete Works of James Shirley* has been supported by the Arts and Humanities Research Council. I am particularly grateful to Teresa Grant, one of the general editors of the *Complete Shirley*, and Alison Searle, postdoctoral researcher, for countless discussions about textual difficulties. Dr Searle has also been a keen reader of drafts of this book. My institution, Anglia Ruskin University, has been very generous in providing time to conduct this research. Special thanks go to Cambridge University Press's anonymous final reader, whose keen insights vastly improved this book in its last stages. Zoe Jaques also deserves my gratitude for reading drafts at every stage, for constructing the line drawings, and for boundless support. Any faults that remain are my own.

The illustrations have been supported through the generosity of a British Academy Smaller Research Grant. Stephen Tabor at the Huntington Library, Noriko Sumimoto of Meisei University Library, and the Syndics and Imaging Services department at Cambridge University Library have been most helpful and generous in supplying rights to use images from their collections.

Introduction

This book offers a detailed consideration of how Shakespearean play texts
came about, including the material constraints and cultures of performance,
publishing, printing, and reading that produced them. It then considers
how these conditions impact upon reading early printed play texts. This is
not a book for trained bibliographers. Instead, it outlines bibliographical
insights and techniques to those who have engaged in the study of early
printed play texts without having yet undertaken a course on bibliography.
Jerome McGann pointed out in 1985 that 'textual/bibliographical studies,
already conceived as "preliminary operations," are all but removed from
the programme of literary studies' (McGann 1985: 181). McGann's claim
is still true today, as bibliography is infrequently taught in undergraduate,
masters, and PhD programmes in English. Although Ann Thompson and
Gordon McMullan argue that 'the recent explosion of work' in 'editing and
textual criticism' has brought them 'from the periphery of English studies
to the much-debated centre' (Thompson and McMullan 2003: xvi–xvii),
this enhanced critical interest has not been matched by increases in training
for those not already entrenched within the profession.

In some respects, this lack of attention is understandable. Bibliography
is a discrete field of enquiry, and as a discipline it takes years to master.
Therefore this book makes no attempt to cover everything. Instead it is
deliberately selective of the bibliographical, textual, and literary techniques
that it outlines, and this selection is based upon those techniques that
are most suited to early dramatic texts. Lengthier guides to bibliography
have long been available, and even the much earlier work of McKerrow,
Pollard, Greg, and Bowers is still largely unsurpassed in explaining the
wider field of bibliographical research. There are currently no introductory
guides to reading early modern dramatic texts, although there are very
helpful and up-to-date introductions to the wider field of bibliography,
including Philip Gaskell's *A New Introduction to Bibliography* (Gaskell 1972;
revised 1995) and D. C. Greetham's *Textual Scholarship: An Introduction*

(Greetham 1994). These titles deal with the history of the book from the origins of writing to the present, and the monumental efforts of both, although exemplary in achieving their aims, do not have full relevance or give much theatrically inflected information for those interested primarily in early modern printed drama. As Harry Sellers put it in an early review of McKerrow's *An Introduction to Bibliography for Literary Students*: 'In its immense wealth of curious detail there is a good deal of course that the ordinary "literary student" is not likely to need very often.' (Sellers 1927: 360.) This book is intended to outline the kinds of information that students and scholars of early modern drama do need.

Whilst the printed formats of prose narratives have changed little in the past four hundred years, Renaissance play texts can at first appear alien. Printing conventions for drama have changed, and so have conceptions of what makes an effective dramatic text. Early texts have looser deployments of scene breaks, speech headings, character names, and stage directions, for instance, and these differences can lead to a much altered sense of the meaning of a play. Plays were also subject to different censorship, mechanisms of revision, and markets, and they tended to be at a greater remove from their authors by the time they reached the printing house. As the typographical features and layout of a dramatic text differ so greatly from those of a non-dramatic text of the period, this book complements other introductions to bibliography.

Facsimiles of the early play texts are making the originals increasingly accessible for undergraduate and graduate students. Detailed digital photographs of Shakespeare are freely available through library websites like the 'Shakespeare in Quarto' site of the British Library; while *Early English Books Online* (EEBO) contains low-resolution reproductions of every printed Renaissance play. Whereas in past decades only professional scholars might access the rare books of restricted archives, now they are available for students at all levels. Bibliographical training becomes more and more necessary alongside the proliferation of the early texts.

The point of this book is to explain to the student (of English or drama or bibliography), faced with a page from a play written *c.*1588–1642, or a facsimile or EEBO equivalent, how it works, how it came about, what the different elements mean, and who created them. This book assumes that readers will be very familiar with early modern drama in modernised editions, but it assumes no familiarity with the original printed texts. A handful of plays by Shakespeare and his contemporaries are subject to frequent discussion, but many more are mentioned only in passing. The term 'Shakespearean play text' is used throughout this book to indicate plays by both Shakespeare and his contemporaries – the general period of coverage ends in 1642, with the closure of the theatres, but some plays were performed in the period and published slightly later. Unless otherwise stated, all dates in this book refer to the dates of publication, and all cited copies are those found in EEBO. The complexities of negotiating texts from EEBO are discussed further in Chapter 3. Titles are usually modernised unless a specific point about their spelling or layout is being made.

Chapter 1 considers how theatrical companies acquired plays, and how those works received further revision in the process of being censored and adapted over time. Various states of the text might find their way to the printing house, and it is important to understand theories (from the straightforward to the entangled) of the possible origins of the manuscripts that underlie printed plays. The chapter further discusses theories of why plays came to be printed, and the various possibilities that might shape their production, including variations in format, author input, and alterations that might have emerged over the course of printing. Equally important are considerations of what extant dramatic manuscripts tell us about the type of documents encountered by printers. The mechanics of printing and producing books are briefly addressed. Although much is known about the production of specific plays, there are few such facts that can in turn become generalisations. Bibliographical work requires frequent recourse to words that express degrees of probability and conjecture. Many assertions about the processes and agents who brought about published play texts must remain speculative, but this chapter will make clear what is known, and what might be guessed at.

Chapter 2 considers the physical parts of early printed play texts and their functions. The features discussed include: title pages; dedications; illustrations; dramatis personae; arguments and scenes; act and scene divisions; stage directions; speech prefixes; verse and prose; individual characters; headlines and running titles; marginalia; signatures and page numbers; catchwords; and other paratext, such as ornaments, colophons, advertisements, errata. The chapter outlines how these different parts of the play text might or might not be present, and how they vary across plays. Specific examples are included alongside illustrations. Importantly, this chapter does more than just identify these locations and how they function. It also considers how a reading of original play texts must in part be shaped by the specific concerns of the early printers and publishers. By breaking down play texts into their constituent parts, this chapter offers a greater understanding of how printers dealt with the texts as a whole.

Chapter 3 addresses how the experience of reading the original quartos and folios shapes perceptions of plays. It considers at greater length the impact of missing or brief stage directions, and how misattributed speeches, uncorrected errors, and textual variants both within and across editions might be negotiated. In other words, the features that are *not* apparent to the reader at first glance are discussed, using specific examples. Of obvious relevance here is the printing of stage directions, many of which were regularised or expanded by scribes, theatre companies, or printing houses, while others were not supplied. Other features considered include the rendering of verse as prose and vice versa, the squeezing of lines because of space requirements, mistaken catchwords, and insertion of act and scene divisions. I discuss differences between reading texts intended for different markets, such as the larger collections (in folio) of Shakespeare's and Jonson's works, the smaller collections of James Shirley (1653), and quartos or octavos of single plays. The final part of this chapter describes techniques that can be used towards a bibliographical understanding of specific play texts.

Chapter 4 shows how the conventions of reproducing and editing Renaissance drama shape readings of the plays. The bulk of the chapter is devoted to modernised editions and how editorial policy affects the texts. The chapter focuses on the policies of the Arden, New Cambridge, and Oxford Shakespeare series. Important series of Renaissance drama not authored by Shakespeare are also touched upon. Most of these editions have a remarkable consistency in aiming to enhance the reader's awareness of performance, so I especially consider alterations and additions to stage directions. But I also examine other ways in which editions differ, especially on issues of emendation, insertions of act and scene divisions and locations, and commentary. Collation lines and how they can be negotiated are briefly discussed. The chapter ends with a consideration of electronic editions.

How to Read a Shakespearean Play Text shows many ways in which such texts can be read. Whether in originals, facsimiles, modernised editions, or e-texts, Shakespeare's works have thrived in a variety of reading contexts. Each of these contexts in various ways remains subservient to the published originals. The originals do not necessarily bring the reader closer to the 'true' plays, but they do form the basis, however remote, of a lengthy history of revision, adaptation, and modernisation. Therefore they must be a focus of attention for serious students of early modern drama.

CHAPTER I

The creation and circulation of play texts

This book is primarily concerned with the reading of printed play texts. But in order to understand such texts fully, it is necessary to understand how they came into being in the first place. This chapter considers how Shakespearean theatrical companies commissioned and shaped plays, how those works were further revised through censorship, rehearsal, touring, and revision, and how authors subsequently revised their own works. Any of these various states of a text might find its way to the printing house, leading to entangled subsequent theories as to its possible origins. Equally important will be considerations of what surviving dramatic manuscripts tell us about the type of documents encountered by printers, with the proviso that such determinations are difficult to make: 'whether or not we can accurately distinguish one from another, any kind of manuscript playbook that can conceivably have existed could conceivably have found its way into print' (Blayney 1997: 393). As Peter Blayney's statement implies, it is difficult to generalise about the movement of plays from the theatre to the printing press. Shakespeare's contemporaries, like John Heminges and Henry Condell, might categorise texts as deriving from 'true original' or 'stolen and surreptitious' copies, but the truth must often lie somewhere in between those poles. A play could certainly be 'stolen' from its author or theatre company, but copyright functioned very differently in the sixteenth and seventeenth centuries, where entries into the *Stationers' Register* usually established ownership for the purposes of printing a play, whether that ownership was rightfully obtained or not. More complex still is the issue of what might constitute an 'original' copy. Is it the draft first submitted by an isolated author to the theatre company? Or perhaps the text as first performed? As no examples of these types of texts can be said beyond doubt to survive, they remain Platonic ideals. But we can be more certain about the variety of processes that might lead to the printing of dramatic texts, and this chapter's primary function is to outline the various possible

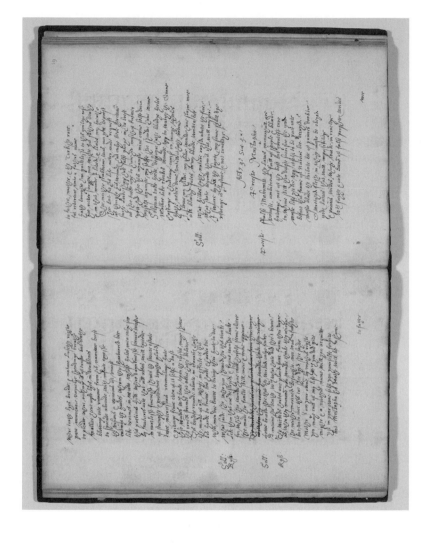

Fig. 1. An opening of the Cambridge University Library *Mustapha*, MS ff. ll. 35 – a fair copy
of a closet drama.

permutations that might affect the transmission of a play from author(s) to page.

WRITING PLAYS

The iconographic picture of Shakespeare sitting in his study, quill in hand and surrounded by books, has a powerful impact upon a conception of early modern play authorship. The long-standing exhibit of Shakespeare's 'desk' at his birthplace supports this image, as does the film *Shakespeare in Love* and even the recent *Dr Who* episode, 'The Shakespeare Code'. In fact, we know little about Shakespeare's compositional practices, or the practices of most other dramatic authors. Thanks to scholars interested in authorship, and particularly to the recent work of MacDonald P. Jackson and Brian Vickers, we can be fairly certain that Shakespeare did not compose all of his forty or so plays in isolation. At least in the versions that survive, *The Two Noble Kinsmen, Henry VIII, Titus Andronicus, Timon of Athens, Pericles,* and *Sir Thomas More* were collaborative efforts. Collaboration of at least this frequency (if not more) was the norm for theatre of the period. It is traditional to see Shakespeare's plays as the products of individual genius. The practice of theatre companies in the early modern period, however, highlights a more collaborative possibility: that plays were 'written' by authors, actors, and others towards the goal of putting them on stage. The title page of the first quarto of *Titus Andronicus* (1594) offers a fairly typical example of this view of authorship: 'THE MOST LA- | mentable Romaine Tragedie of Titus Andronicus: | As it was Plaide by the Right Ho- | nourable the Earle of *Darbie*, Earle of *Pembrooke*, | and Earle of *Sussex* their Seruants.' There is no mention of Shakespeare in this quarto, and his name does not appear on any of his plays' title pages until 1598. Instead, the theatrical companies that performed the play occupy the space of 'author'. Such companies never fully relinquished their status as the original producers of the play, but over the period playwrights increasingly asserted their rights as named authors. Shakespeare himself never, as far as surviving evidence discloses, attempted to have his plays published. But other authors certainly did, and in doing so they made claims towards sole authorship of their works.

The 'author' of an early modern play is more likely to be part of a collaborative theatrical enterprise than an isolated genius. One of the purposes of this chapter is to outline all of the people who could have a hand in dramatic and textual production in the early modern period. I will spell out their possible influences, using surviving examples where available, and more speculative claims where not.

COMMISSIONING PLAYS

Philip Henslowe's *Diary*, a collection of accounts and asset lists for a variety of businesses including the Admiral's Men, offers some of the most comprehensive information about how plays were commissioned in Shakespeare's day. Henslowe was part owner of the Rose, Fortune, and Hope playhouses, and his business dealings with the players tell us much about the composition histories of plays performed in public theatres. (Unfortunately, there is no mention in the *Diary* of either Shakespeare or a play known to be by Shakespeare.) Henslowe importantly shows that most of the plays put on by his company were written collaboratively, and that these plays, when revived for later audiences, were subject to further subsequent additions and revisions. The accounts from 1598 and beyond offer a particularly detailed outline of playbook acquisition for the various companies playing at the Rose. They disclose that 'Normally the conception for a play originated with the playwright' (Carson 1988: 55), but a variety of collaborators might contribute towards the final text. Further, collaboration might come through complex interactions, including:

(1) Theatre company approval of a draft 'plot' for a playwright to complete in full.
(2) Theatre company accepting parts or acts of a play from a given playwright so that remaining parts might be written by another author.
(3) Theatre company instigating revision by the original author or another collaborator.

Ben Jonson, more widely known for his sole-authored pieces, provides an interesting case of someone who participated in multiple modes of authorship. In December 1597 he showed the company the plot of an unnamed play which they approved for completion:

Lent vnto Bengemen Johnsone the [2]3 of desemb*er*
1597 vpon a Bocke wch he was to writte for vs
befor crysmas next after the date herof wch he
showed th*e* plotte vnto the company I saye
lente in Redy money vnto hime the some of xxs.
                                        (Henslowe 1961: 73)

Here Jonson approaches 'the company' with the plot of a play he intended to write in full, and the loan of 20 shillings presumably would be used to cover his expenses while writing. We know from Jonson's 1630s play fragments, *Mortimer* and *The Sad Shepherd*, that his compositional method included writing out a plot, a fairly lengthy prose description of each act, before constructing his plays. In this sense his method of composing plays might have been shaped early in his career by the economic necessity of compiling an outline quickly as collateral for a loan. On 23 October 1598, this, or possibly another, plot by Jonson was selected to be finished by George Chapman:

Lent . . . vnto m^r Chapman*e* one his playe
boocke & ij ectes of A traged*ie* of bengemens plott*e*
th*e* some of　　　　　　　　　　　　　　　　　iij^{li}.
(Henslowe 1961: 100)

From what we know of Jonson's career, he could not have been happy about having someone else write two acts of his play. He notoriously excised his collaborative plays from those he collected in his *Workes* of 1616, and in the case of *Sejanus* he deleted and rewrote the shares of his collaborator (probably George Chapman). He was also apparently teased about being slow to produce work, as he alludes in the Prologue to *Volpone* (A4v). Henslowe's company might have become fed up with waiting for Jonson to deliver the final manuscript. Yet they continued to pay him for various authorial duties concerning plays first written by others. Jonson received payment for 'new adicyons' to Kyd's *The Spanish Tragedy* on 25 September 1601 and 22 June 1602 (Henslowe 1961: 182, 203). Kyd's play had been composed over a decade earlier, and clearly the company felt that it needed updating.

These three sets of business arrangements between Jonson and the actor–managers of the Rose disclose that the playwright patched together income from a variety of composition practices. Jonson carefully erased this early part of his career by ignoring these works in his subsequent publications. Instead, he constructed an image of a single, if not overbearing, authority for his texts (Giddens 2010). He grew to disdain collaboration, and like Shakespeare, has become known as a poet of individual genius. But these efforts at singular self-promotion by Jonson, or apparent self-suppression (or at least silence) by Shakespeare (as in the *Titus Andronicus* title page), disguise more typical modes of script production. At the Rose Theatre, 'collaborated plays accounted for 60 per cent of the plays completed in Fall–Winter 1598, and an astonishing 82 per cent in Spring–Summer 1598' (Carson 1988: 57). Such collaborations needed to be seamless in order to be successful. These figures substantiate a claim that joint authorship was more common than the forms of sole authority we ascribe to authors traditionally given 'complete works'. The most famous theatrical collaboration from the period was that of Francis Beaumont and John Fletcher, whose works, alongside those of their collaborators, were collected in folio in 1647. As George Lisle's dedication in that volume attests: '*For still your fancies are so wov'n and knit,* | *'Twas* FRANCIS-FLETCHER, *or* IOHN BEAUMONT *writ*' (b1). Scholars today invest much time in discerning the authorship divisions of plays, but clearly such divisions were of less concern to the early modern play-going and -reading public.

The Henslowe papers disclose several varieties of collaborative authorship, whereby seemingly haphazard and disjointed methods of arriving at a single script point to some complex possibilities for establishing the 'origins' of a given text. Collaboration could be based upon act-division, sub-plot, or genre, or could be divided between one writer who worked on plots and another who versified. And as Neil Carson argues, 'it is likely that in some cases collaboration was more complicated than these theories allow' (Carson 1988: 58). As many as six authors might unite in the effort towards producing a single play. With so many hands available, it is likely that a variety of practices might have stitched their ideas and lines together. Importantly, even single authorship was subject to collaborative negotiation with actor–managers, premised upon very commercial concerns about the possible success of subject material.

It is also difficult, in the absence of comparable records, to determine how far the activities recorded by Henslowe reflect the practices of other acting companies. For instance, Henslowe's *Diary* in part suggests that the entire company would receive, and therefore approve, a draft of a play, yet Tiffany Stern asserts that the role of dealing with a play manuscript would properly devolve only to the prompter, who not only supplied forgotten lines during a production, but generally acted as stage-manager and book-keeper: 'He did not expect anyone else to have dealings with his book' (Stern 2004: 144). Another caveat emerges because Henslowe's records are almost certainly incomplete, so statements about the proportionality of a given activity could be somewhat inaccurate. Yet, as Neil Carson asserts, 'Until new evidence is forthcoming we must conclude that the working conditions of dramatists writing for the Admiral's Men were probably typical of the time' (Carson 1988: 55). The Henslowe papers, as our most substantive evidence about early theatrical practices, suggest that early play manuscripts have their origins in messy and difficult-to-determine circumstances of authorship.[1]

---

[1] The Henslowe papers can now be subject to wider scrutiny, as they are available online (www. henslowe-alleyn.org.uk).

PAPERS FOUL AND FAIR

Another source of evidence towards the composition of plays is surviving playhouse manuscripts, which, as Grace Ioppolo's seminal study of *Dramatists and their Manuscripts in the Age of Shakespeare, Jonson, Middleton and Heywood* (2006) has shown, are a neglected resource for those studying early modern drama. A few polished drafts of play texts do survive (including Ben Jonson's lavishly annotated manuscript of the privately performed *Masque of Queens*), but most extant play manuscripts are 'foul papers' or the working drafts of authors. These drafts do not form a consistent or easy-to-classify body of material. They range from the almost illegibly messy to the polish of the *Mustapha* manuscript illustrated in Figure 1. Further, determining the exact nature of a surviving manuscript can be difficult: 'it is nearly impossible to distinguish which of the extant manuscripts . . . were used in the playhouse and which were not' (Ioppolo 2006: 8). New Bibliography was exercised to determine the status of the manuscript behind the text, and editors still generally draw distinctions between working with a 'clean' quarto (with presumably a 'clean' manuscript behind it) or with a 'bad' one, whereby either the manuscript or the printers (or some combination of the two) might have caused textual corruption.

The reasons for delving into manuscript complexities in a book about *printed* play texts are two-fold:

(1) Manuscripts highlight how the authority of a text might be compromised from its very inception.

(2) They show that the material remains of a given text are unlikely to have origins in the polished draft of a single author.

The main consideration here is the kind of texts that early modern publishers received from the theatre. As Grace Ioppolo notes: 'Simply stated, it is impossible to study, interpret or define the transmission of an early modern printed dramatic text, or its use in the theatre before publication, without studying, interpreting or defining the role of manuscripts in those processes' (Ioppolo 2006: 4). All printed play texts had their origins in these largely lost manuscripts.

Ioppolo's invaluable *Dramatists and their Manuscripts* is backed by reference to nearly all of the surviving play-text manuscripts from the period. Ioppolo confirms, or relies upon, the terms that underpin traditional assumptions about the manuscripts 'behind' the printed texts of the period: 'Most, if not all, of these texts can be described as one of the following types of manuscript copy: *foul papers, authorial fair copy,* or *non-authorial fair copy*' (Ioppolo 2006: 7). Yet as Ioppolo has also convincingly argued, a theatre company would be interested only in a clearly legible or 'fair' copy, whether that came from an author or a scribe. This fact highlights an additional phase of mediation, whereby the draft of a play text would be rewritten, either by a scribe or author, for final submission to the theatrical company. In either case, one might expect additional changes, through error, deliberate tidying, or last-minute revision. Importantly, many of the surviving dramatic manuscripts have little or no direct relationship to the public theatres. Jonson's *Masque of Queens*, mentioned above, was a private entertainment. The fair copy of *Mustapha* in Figure 1 is a closet drama never intended for performance. Working theatrical manuscripts have only very rarely survived and are difficult to identify with certainty (Greg 1931; Howard-Hill 1988). Theatrical companies must have been reluctant to release their promptbooks directly to the public, as such promptbooks were their only working copies. Many of the manuscripts that survive, in fact, might bring a reader no closer to a theatrical promptbook than early print exemplars.

With these facts and processes in mind, it is clear that a theatrical script undergoes an elaborate series of modifications by a number of potential hands before it makes it to the actors, the publisher, or even the archive. Any hopes of a return to a pre-theatrical, authorial text are likely to be quashed by these processes (and the effects of time). Certainly, no such text exists for Shakespeare or Jonson, and only approximations of them exist for Thomas Middleton, who underwent wide manuscript circulation. The processes of dramatic composition are nonetheless significant, because the idealised state of a play being delivered to a printing house by an author (or on behalf of an author by someone else in possession of his manuscript) did sometimes occur. Humphrey Moseley's 'The Stationer to the Readers' in the Beaumont and Fletcher folio of 1647 notes that 'What ever I have seene of Mr. *Fletchers* owne hand, is free from interlining; and his friends affirme he never writ any one thing twice' (A4v). Although such printers' advertisements cannot necessarily be taken at face value, Moseley probably did see fairly polished authorial drafts, even though he implies here that the Fletcher's drafts did not need to be made 'fair' in the first place. It was the holy grail of New Bibliography – the emerging near-scientific study of material texts, led by R. B. McKerrow, W. W. Greg, A. W. Pollard, and others in the first half of the twentieth century – to discover a text as close to an author's (usually Shakespeare's) intention as possible, and to excise any interfering 'corruption' from that text. Knowledge about how plays were written makes that authorial text seem especially difficult to recover, but further insight into the various stages of revision that a play might undergo elevates that difficulty to fantasy. That is not to say that the efforts of the New Bibliographers were entirely futile. Between them, they introduced most of the bibliographical techniques still used today (see Werstine 2009). But the conclusions based upon those techniques, many of which are discussed in Chapter 3, were sometimes overstated.

ALTERATION

So far, I have considered the construction of play manuscripts up to the point at which they are released by the author(s). Between that point and first (or indeed subsequent) performance there are several further considerations that might alter the text of a play. It is important to outline these possible modes of alteration, because they impact upon the surviving printed play texts.

Once a play script was bought by a theatrical company, it became the legal property of that company, and the author, unless a sharer, had no more stake in the theatrical text (although he might be asked to modify it, or could have it printed himself, and on occasion might provide it to another company, as John Marston seems to have done with *The Malcontent*). Several pressures shaped revisions to that text, with or without the author's knowledge or consent. An Act of 1581 granted powers of censorship over all public plays to the Master of the Revels, Edmund Tilney. A further Star Chamber decree of 1586 gave powers to the Archbishop of Canterbury and the Bishop of London to censor all printed material, including printed plays. The censors dealt with theatrical companies or stationers (i.e., publishers) directly, so authors would have no say in censorship decisions, although they could modify plays in response to censorship.

Of the censors, the Master of the Revels is the more relevant, as every play from this period had to undergo direct authorisation by him before it was performed. This act of licensing seems to have been far more stringent than the relatively light touch of print censorship on play texts. There was remarkable consistency in the office of Master of the Revels in this period, as only four men held the position from 1579, when Tilney was appointed, to 1642, when the theatres closed with Sir Henry Herbert in post. Nonetheless, it is difficult to pin down the period's (or even a particular Master's) approach to censorship, which ranged from the heavy-handed to the negligent. Richard Burt summarises scholarship on censorship by noting that 'some critics have argued that censorship was a systematic and fully conscious contractual agreement; others have argued that it was capricious and arbitrary . . . Some have concluded that theatre censorship was severely repressive, while others have argued that it was enlightened, tolerant, and virtually non-existent' (Burt 2007: 182). In order to give a sense of this range, it is useful briefly to consider five examples of censored plays from the period: *Sir Thomas More*, *The Isle of Dogs*, *A Game at Chess*, *Richard II*, and *The Second Maiden's Tragedy*.

Sir Thomas More is perhaps the most famous example of play-text censorship, because the surviving manuscript possibly offers the sole literary exemplar of Shakespeare's handwriting. It is also the only surviving play manuscript with Tilney's marks as censor upon it. Tilney's cuts were intense, so much so that the joint authors, including Anthony Munday as lead playwright, and Chettle, Dekker, Heywood, and Shakespeare as revisers, seem to have abandoned any attempt to bring the play to the stage. Most forcibly, at the beginning of the play, Tilney insists that the authors should 'Leaue out . . . | ye insurrection | wholly w^t | ye Cause ther off . . . ' (fol. 3v; transcribed in Gabrieli and Melchiori 1990: 17). The play represents citizen revolt against foreign labour, a topical issue in 1593–4, when Tilney probably read the play. Tilney also objected to the staging of More's resistance to the authority of the crown. As many plays from the period, including Shakespeare's history plays, stage rebellion, it is difficult to know why the play was not further revised according to Tilney's wishes, but the fate of *Sir Thomas More* demonstrates the censor's power at its height, as he could prevent a play from being released at all. Unfortunately, without further records we have no way of knowing how frequently Tilney used such powers or if he was generally so censorious as to shape the ways that plays might have been constructed before they reached him. It seems unlikely that theatre companies would take the risk of investing in the composition of a play for it to be rejected, so there must have been a carefully managed working relationship with the censor.

What survives far more frequently in the records are instances of minor censorship, or of the Master of the Revels missing material that he should have caught, or possibly of material that was added by the actors subsequently to licensing. A notorious example occurred in 1597 with *The Isle of Dogs*. Thomas Nashe left the play uncompleted, but Pembroke's Men took enough interest in his draft to have it finished by Ben Jonson, then just starting his career as a playwright. Trouble began when the Privy Council took offence at the play, and instructed Richard Topcliffe as follows:

Vppon Informac*i*on given vs of a lewd plaie that was plaied in one of the plaie howses on the Bancke side, contanynge very seditious & sclanderous matter, wee caused some of the Players to be apprehended and comytted to pryson, whereof one of them was not only an Actor, but a maker of *parte* of the said Plaie; For as moche as yt ys thought meete that the rest of the Players or Actors in that matter shalbe apprehended to receave soche punyshment as theire leude and mutynous behavior doth deserve; These shalbe therefore to Re*qui*r you to exami*ne* those of the plaiers that are comytted, whose names are knowne to you, mr Topclyfe, whatys becom*e* of the rest of their Fellowes that either had theire *partes* in the devysinge of that sedytious matter, or that were Actors or plaiers in the same, what copies they have given forth of the said playe, and to whome, and soch other pointes as you shall thincke meete to be demaunded of them (*Privy Council Register for the Reign of Elizabeth*, National Archive, PC 2/22, 15 August 1597, 346)

Richard Topcliffe served in various roles for the state, including a special commission to seek out Jesuits living in England. He was infamous as a torturer of suspected perpetrators of treason, so the prospect of being 'examine[d]' by him must have been frightening. A later report to the Privy Council explains who was involved by specifying:

8. October 1597 A warrant to the Keeper of the Marshalsea to release Gabriell Spencer and Robert Shaa, Stage players out of prison, who were of lat comitted to his custodie. The like warrant for the releasing of Beniamin Iohnson. (*Privy Council Register for the Reign of Elizabeth*, National Archive, PC 2/23, 13)

Jonson and his fellow actors (including Gabriel Spencer, whom Jonson would stab to death in the following year) were imprisoned, and presumably examined, for nearly two months. As *The Isle of Dogs* is a lost play, the exact nature of the offence cannot be determined, but a wide net was cast to find the author of it. Interestingly, the records do not suggest that the Master of the Revels was included in this blame. It is also of note that the authorities sought to destroy all copies of the play and used considerable resources to do so. In this extreme case of censorship, all traces of the play have been lost.

Luckily, such state-imposed erasure is uncommon, but it importantly points to the fact that censorship could impact heavily upon a text, even after it was first performed. *A Game at Chess* by Thomas Middleton is the period's most infamous example of a play that escaped the censor's pen but caused political controversy in subsequent performance. The play, performed for nine straight days by the King's Men, is often cited as one of the most popular in the period. Although it had been licensed by Henry Herbert on 12 June 1624, it directly represented senior members of the English court, a circumstance usually prohibited on the public stage. Yet more problems arose from the play's representation of the Spanish. The play baldly supports a radical Protestant cause against the Catholic

Spanish, with Prince Charles in the heroic role of the White Knight, while senior members of the Spanish court, including the Spanish Ambassador to the English, were ridiculed. Spanish diplomats, and in particular, Ambassador Count Gondomar, were offended, and the play was quickly removed from the stage, even though (or perhaps because) English relations with Spain were not amicable at the time owing to the failed match between the Spanish Infanta and Prince Charles. Because of the play's notoriety, there was a great demand for reading copies, but equally, it could not be printed without incurring severe punishment from the Crown. Six manuscript copies survive, however, and there seems to have been a small factory of scribes producing them for clients. Middleton himself substantially participated in this production line, as one of the copies, now held in Trinity College, Cambridge (MS O.2.66), is in his hand, and another, the Bridgewater–Huntington (Huntington MS EL 34.B.17) copy, was partially written by him. By 1625, things had settled down enough to permit widespread circulation of the play in print (Taylor 2007: 2.718). That seven contemporary versions of the play survive raises questions about which one might be taken as the most authoritative. So in this instance, censorship led not to the suppression (or loss) of text, but to its destabilising proliferation.

A less invasive case of censorship relates to Shakespeare's *Richard II*. Famously, the deposition episode of 4.1 was not printed in the earliest quartos. It first appears in a deficient version in the fourth quarto (1608), and later in a more coherent version in the first folio (1623). Although Richard Dutton notes that we cannot know for certain if the stage or press censor cut this scene (Dutton 1991: 124–7), Charles Forker argues that 'there is some reason, given the slightly clumsy transition in Q from the point where the deposition begins in F and where it ends, to believe that it had been played all along as originally conceived' (Forker 2002: 517). Forker implies that the censorship of the scene was print-based, and not theatrical, and therefore is owing to the powers of the Bishop of London or Archbishop of Canterbury or the self-censorship of the publisher, Andrew Wise. On the other hand, Janet Clare points out that there would be no reason for the printer to exclude a scene that had been licensed for the theatre, so the scene must not have been present in the printer's manuscript (Clare 1990). It now seems common consensus that Q1 was set from a MS that contained the deposition scene in some form – but a clear explanation for the scene's exclusion has not been found. Censorship could impact upon the point at which a play was printed as much as any point before or after it was performed.

More straightforward instances of post-performance print censorship relate to the *Acte to Restraine Abuses of Players* of 1606, which forbad the on-stage use of God's or Jesus' name. In practice, this legislation not only changed the way that dramatists wrote plays; it also meant that existing play texts were modified to remove any blasphemy, so that, for instance, 'by God' might be changed to 'by heaven'. Such changes can be detected because of disruption to the original metre. But often the metre was kept in making the change. For instance, from Ophelia's grave, Hamlet says to Laertes, 'S'wounds shew me what th'owt doe' in Q2 (1604: M4v). This direct reference to Christ's wounds would contravene the 1606 *Acte*. In the folio, Hamlet's line is changed to: 'Come show me what thou'lt do' (Sig. pp5v). The oath is replaced by a direct command, so the sense has not been entirely lost, but this change probably reflects revision in the light of the 1606 legislation.

Although several plays bear surviving marks of censorship, the vast majority of play texts offer nothing to suggest what might have been lost through the formal and informal mechanisms of state censorship. Sometimes such loss is subtle, difficult to discern, or even doubtful. In Thomas Middleton's *Second Maiden's Tragedy* (or *The Lady's Tragedy* in the Oxford Middleton), for instance, Sir George Buc's marks of censorship survive in the licensed manuscript held by the British Museum. Many of the cuts that he suggested seem to have little apparent purpose. For instance, Buc insists that 'I am poisoned' be deleted at the moment of the Tyrant's death. Buc was clearly anxious about this representation of tyrannicide. The phrase 'yor kinges poisond' is added to take its place (Briggs 2007: 624). Without the survival of the play's censored manuscript, there would be no sense that a censor touched this passage at all, as the changes largely seem arbitrary. The available, though slight, evidence might therefore suggest that all plays were similarly modified in small ways that are no longer detectable.

Without fuller evidence, however, the exact impact of censorship has been lost. Even for the dramatists themselves, the rules of the game might not have been very straightforward, as Janet Clare argues: 'For playwrights of our period it was, then, never quite clear what was prohibited and what would be permitted. The ill-defined terms of censorship encouraged some playwrights to take risks (which sometimes succeeded) and drove others into timidity or self-censorship' (1990: 213). The above examples point to the many ways in which censorship could impact upon the subsequent dissemination of a play in print. These known instances amount to a very small percentage of the plays surviving from the period. Most play texts show no obvious signs of censorship, but the lessons from censored play manuscripts suggest a mediating presence that might have, in small ways at least, impacted upon most instances of play-text transmission. Although Dutton (Dutton 1991) has successfully argued that the relationship between playwrights and the censors was one of mutual interdependence, as the Master of the Revels was paid in part according to how many plays he perused, it is nonetheless important to remember that surviving play texts are products of such censorship. Or as Richard Burt puts it, 'there is no point at which one can locate an uncensored text' (Burt 2007: 187).

PROMPTBOOKS AND LICENSED COPIES

Once a play text had been licensed, the theatre would have kept that manuscript as the only 'allowed' copy. Legally, it was the script to be used for any subsequent performances. This idealised text is of course subject to alteration owing to the ephemeral nature of performance, which sees words and actions change from day to day. Nonetheless, this ideal existed for many years in the editorial hope that any early printed version might directly reflect the allowed copy, which has usually been called the 'promptbook'. It was once established wisdom that no company would be keen to allow its promptbook out of its theatre, but escapes of versions of such texts are well documented, including for purposes of copying or printing. Humphrey Moseley complains of the lost *Wild Goose Chase* that 'a *Person of Quality* borrowed it from the *Actours* many yeares since, and (by the negligence of a Servant) it was never return'd' ('The Stationer to the Readers', in Beaumont and Fletcher 1647: A4). (Moseley later recovered the manuscript and printed the play in 1652.) The only legitimate owners of a copy of the play were the theatre company that purchased it or the authors who wrote it, but there were many ways in which texts could find their way to the printers. Who 'owned' a text was subject to repeated dispute, and texts could escape from the author or theatre in surprising ways. For instance, on 18 March 1600, Henslowe's *Diary* records that he 'Lent vnto [the c] Robarte shawe...to geue vnto the printer to staye the printinge of patient gressell the some of xxxx^s' (Henslowe 1961: 132). The *Diary* suggests that the play had been completed only two months before, as a costume for it was purchased on 26 January. There is no hint as to how the play escaped to the printer, though three hands, Thomas Dekker, Henry Chettle, and William Hawton, worked on it. As the printer had to be paid to 'staye the printinge', the clear implication is that he obtained a copy of the text through what was seen as legitimate means. The figure of forty shillings is a high payment that might reflect the cost the publisher paid for the theatrical manuscript, but that Henslowe was so willing to invest in blocking the printing shows that theatre companies saw value in retaining plays for their own uses. Hence copies published close to the date of first performance are unlikely to derive directly from promptbooks.

Copyright towards print publication was established when publishers took a manuscript to Stationers' Hall and paid a small fee to have the title entered into the *Stationers' Register*. Although not all titles from the period were so entered, and some were entered when the actual rights to a text seem spurious from a modern perspective, the system generally served to protect the interests of those who acquired legitimate copies of a play. Difficulties occasionally arose when two different publishers had acquired manuscripts of the same play. The printing of Ben Jonson's second folio (1640–1), for instance, was stopped, and the finished sheets were confiscated when John Benson and Andrew Crooke contested Thomas Walkley's rights to the material (Giddens 2003). Thomas Walkley had bought the rights to all of Jonson's unprinted works from Sir Kenelm Digby, Jonson's literary executor, for £40. Walkley neglected to enter the material in the *Stationers' Register*, however, which led to the legal battle with Benson and Crooke, who secured rights to Jonson's works in a series of *Stationers' Register* entries in 1639 and 1640. Before the legal dispute became problematic, Walkley's printer, John Dawson Jr, finished printing most of the volume, but these printed sheets (probably comprising almost all of the edition) were legally attached by John Benson, with the help of John Parker, another London stationer. Walkley was eventually able to have his sheets returned, after a significant interruption to printing, and Dawson continued printing the volume for publication in 1641. Such disputes were not uncommon, but perhaps the most interesting thing about them is the fact that different publishers had two apparently legitimate copies of the same material. This fact raises questions about the multiple types of manuscripts that might be obtained by a publisher, and what kinds of variant states of drafting or revision the manuscripts might disclose.

ACTORS' MODIFICATIONS: PARTS AND PLOTS

One legitimate source of a play manuscript would be the theatrical company that had the licensed right to perform it. This chapter has already investigated various ways in which a play might be written and reach the point of being licensed. Officially, a theatrical company would not be allowed to modify the play further from that point. However, there is strong evidence that further modification was common. In addition to the multitudinous ways outlined above that could impact upon the initial performances of a given dramatic text, modifications appeared within the performed life of a text. Plays were revived (and updated) as an important marketing tool. Many title pages from the period mention that a play is newly 'augmented'. The third quarto of Marston's *The Malcontent* (1604), for instance, says that the play was 'Augmented by *Marston*. | With the Additions played by the Kings | Majesties servants. | Written by *John Webster*.' In this case the title page misinforms the reader, as the author and augmenter are reversed, but this third imprint of the play was published in the same year as the first and second, attesting to public demand for an 'improved' text.

In part such modification at the point of performance would be expected, as actors might simply misremember their lines. The incidence of such changes making their way into a final printed text, however, would suggest something more permanent than an ephemeral performative moment. A theatrical company might find it necessary to annotate the manuscript with reminders about actors or stage business. For instance, the printed text of *Two Noble Kinsmen* (1634) includes notes that are suggestive of back-stage preparations: '2. Hearses ready' (C4v) and 'Chaire and stooles out' (G2v). See Figure 2.

These are clearly instructions for stage hands, not typical stage directions that could be appreciated by an audience as relating to the action, and therefore point to prompt copy behind the printed text. Equally, the quarto discloses directions that are for a very specific playhouse context:

Enter Messengers. Curtis. (I4^v)
Scaena 3. *Enter Theseus, Hipolita, Emilia, Perithous: and some*
Attendants, T. Tucke: Curtis.

$$(\text{L4}^v)$$

These references to specific actors, Tucke and Curtis, probably the King's Men actors Curtis Greville and Thomas Tuckfield, highlight that an annotator has specified actors for the otherwise vague roles of messengers and attendants. However, as Frederick O. Waller argues in 'Printer's Copy for *The Two Noble Kinsmen*' (1958), we cannot therefore assume that the play is not some form of annotated rough draft. Waller shows that the prompter's annotations actually come from around 1625 or 1626, around twelve years after the play was first performed. Such changes point to the continued uses

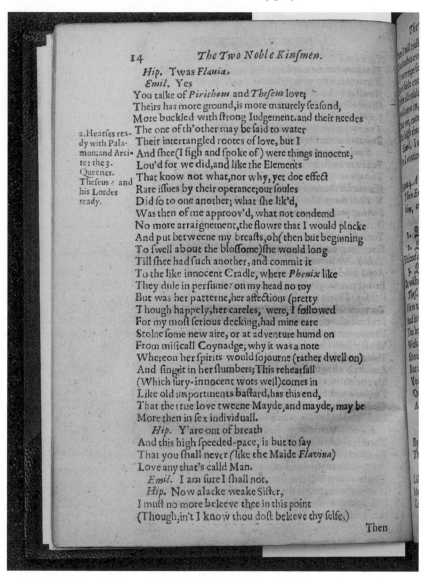

14   *The Two Noble Kinſmen.*

Hip. Twas *Flauia,*
    Emil. Yes
You talke of *Pirithous* and *Theſeus* love;
Theirs has more ground, is more maturely ſeaſon'd,
More buckled with ſtrong Iudgement, and their needes

2.Hearſes rea-dy with Pala-mon;and Arci-te: the 3. Queenes. Theſeus ﹕ and his Lordes ready.

The one of th'other may be ſaid to water
Their intertangled rootes of love, but I
And ſhee (I ſigh and ſpoke of) were things innocent,
Lou'd for we did, and like the Elements
That know not what, nor why, yet doe effect
Rare iſſues by their operance; our ſoules
Did ſo to one another; what ſhe lik'd,
Was then of me approov'd, what not condemd
No more arraignement, the flowre that I would plucke
And put betweene my breaſts, oh (then but beginning
To ſwell about the bloſſome) ſhe would long
Till ſhee had ſuch another, and commit it
To the like innocent Cradle, where *Phenix* like
They dide in perfume: on my head no toy
But was her patterne, her affections (pretty
Though happely, her careles, were, I followed
For my moſt ſerious decking, had mine eare
Stolne ſome new aire, or at adventure humd on
From miſicall Coynadge; why it was a note
Whereon her ſpirits would ſojourne (rather dwell on)
And ſingit in her ſlumbers; This rehearſall
(Which fury-innocent wots well) comes in
Like old importments baſtard, has this end,
That the true love tweene Mayde, and mayde, may be
More then in ſex individuall.
    Hip. Y'are out of breath
And this high ſpeeded-pace, is but to ſay
That you ſhall never (like the Maide *Flavina*)
Love any that's calld Man.
    Emil. I am ſure I ſhall not.
    Hip. Now alacke weake Siſter,
I muſt no more beleeve thee in this point
(Though, in't I know thou doſt beleeve thy ſelfe,)
                  Then

Fig. 2. Marginal stage direction in Fletcher and Shakespeare's *Two Noble Kinsmen* (1634), Meisei University Library, MR1057, C4v.

to which a playhouse manuscript might be subjected over several decades of its playing life.

A more immediate alteration to the text of the play came when actors had to learn their parts. In an age when both paper and scribal copying were expensive, lines were learned in the context of brief cues, not a copy of the entire play. A few such actors' parts survive, and they offer telling evidence of the ways that texts might be transmitted. Scrolls of parts were put together by scribes, who copied out only the words to be spoken and short cues from the licensed copy. Actors thus did not achieve a sense of the entire play in the first instance as a way of preparing for their roles. In fact, they would not necessarily know what other characters said about them until a brief rehearsal before initial performance, to which Henslowe's *Diary* sometimes alludes. The act of copying any text can introduce variants, but one of the interesting facets of the surviving actors' parts is a relative lack of punctuation (professional parts typically end with a dash), so that dramatic punctuation (and the delivery that might be implied by it) can especially be taken as *lost* information that could not survive in the printed play texts, which were probably never printed from a collection of actors' parts. Even the complete manuscript for *The Second Maiden's Tragedy* shows that short speeches might have no punctuation at all – not even a full stop or other terminal punctuation at the end of them.

Hamlet's injunction that the players should 'Speake the speech I pray you as I pronounc'd it to you' (G3v) discloses anxiety about the actors' delivery of lines. In this case the author of those lines, Hamlet, takes special care to rehearse with the actor, which might have happened in professional theatres when the author was also an actor, as with Shakespeare and early Jonson. Further lost information emerges in the material that actors, and particularly comic actors, were willing to ad-lib while performing the play. Hamlet touches upon this possibility in his admonition against comic actors:

let those that play your clownes speake no more then is set downe for them, for there be of them that wil themselues laugh, to set on some quantitie of barraine spectators to laugh to, though in the meane time, some necessary question of the play be then to be considered, that's villanous, and shewes a most pittifull ambition in the foole that vses it. (1604: G4)

It is clear that comic actors, particularly early in the Shakespearean period, were willing to embellish a play by speaking more than their parts required. Dramatists were not necessarily universally opposed to this practice. Letoy says in Brome's *The Antipodes* (1640), 'For I am none of those Poeticke furies, / That threats the Actors life, in a whole play, / That addes a sillable, or takes away, / If he can frible through, and move delight / In others, I am pleased' (D2v). Authors writing for the famous clowns of earlier in the Shakespearean period must have expected them to augment the text.

Such oral embellishment must usually be lost to history. Eric Rasmussen notes that it is unlikely that actors' added lines would ever appear in a promptbook (Rasmussen 1991: 126). However actors might as readily cut material as add to it, and there is little reason why changes that occurred over several productions might not leave some textual mark on a subsequent play text. Humphrey Moseley, perhaps the most important publisher of plays in the 1640s and 1650s, notes that the actors altered the texts of the Beaumont and Fletcher canon: 'When these *Comedies* and *Tragedies* were presented on the Stage, the *Actours* omitted some *Scenes* and Passages (with the *Authour's* consent) as occasion led them; and when private friends desir'd a Copy, they then (and justly too) transcribed what they *Acted*' (Beaumont and Fletcher 1647: A4). This comment suggests that transcribed copies from the theatre might readily differ from an authorial draft or the promptbook, but that this situation, for Moseley at least, was not ideal.

Such actor changes are especially relevant when one of the more popular theories for the transmission of poor-quality texts (usually 'bad' quartos) is considered. Memorial reconstruction has been used to explain the 'bad' quartos of Shakespeare's canon, which include Q1 *Romeo and Juliet* (1597), *Henry V* (1600), *The Merry Wives of Windsor* (1602), *Hamlet* (1603), and *Pericles* (1609), and sometimes other plays, both Shakespearean and non-Shakespearean. Bad quartos are characterised by being much shorter than other textual exemplars that survive for the same play (with the exception of *Pericles*, which has no alternative, as it did not appear in the 1623 folio). They also typically have texts that show clear signs of corruption.

The term 'bad quarto' was first used by A. W. Pollard in *Shakespeare Folios and Quartos* of 1909, but it has subsequently been subject to much challenge. An early theory to explain the existence of bad quartos had them written down at a distance from performance. As Harold Jenkins describes it: 'a group of actors, wishing to perform a play of which they had no book, would make a book from what could be remembered by one or more of their number who had acted in the play before' (Jenkins 1982: 20). This theory is known as memorial reconstruction. A further subset of memorial reconstruction might exist when someone in the audience took down a play in shorthand. Thomas Heywood complained about this practice in the prologue to *If You Know Not Me, You Know Nobody* (1605). Laurie Maguire's *Shakespearean Suspect Texts* (1996) has largely discounted the frequency of memorial reconstruction (especially that arising from stenography) as a basis for textual corruption. Maguire argues that evidence towards faulty memory is as likely to derive from other acts of transmission as it is from oral reporting of a previous performance. Nonetheless, she does acknowledge that memorial reconstruction seems to exist in a few known exemplars, and the most famous instance of it is the first quarto of *Hamlet*. As Harold Jenkins notes of the play: 'A comparison with the two "good" texts, Q2 and F, reveals in the various corruptions of Q1 – omissions, mislinings, paraphrases, verbal and morphological substitutions, misunderstandings, transpositions, anticipations and recollections – all the recognized signs of a play reconstructed from memory' (Jenkins 1982: 19). Few would probably agree today that this list describes traits unique to memorial reconstruction. The most solid evidence for it occurs when a part or parts are conspicuously accurate (as measured against other surviving exemplars), while the other parts are not. For *Hamlet* Q1 (1603), the parts of Marcellus, Lucianus, and Voltemand take on this characteristic accuracy (see Irace 1994). These parts might have been doubled by a minor hired actor (as opposed to a share holder in the King's Men) who subsequently left the company, carrying with him a sharp recollection for his own parts and a piecemeal memory of the rest of the play. Q1 *Hamlet* is just over half the length of Q2 (1604), so it is also possible that Marcellus played in an already-abbreviated version of the play. Nonetheless, Q1 has editorial value, as will be explored in Chapter 4, precisely because of this direct link to theatrical production. Such quartos sometimes offer fuller descriptions of stage business, and their length is more in keeping with the average length of plays in this period (Erne 2003).

Another play that survives as a bad quarto is *Pericles* (1609). Potential readers face much more difficulty with this play because no corrected subsequent versions survive. The first quarto possibly derives from a manuscript produced from memorial reconstruction. The play prints 'hid in Tent', an easy oral corruption for 'hid intent' (C1v). Earlier in the play 'wants' seems to be printed as 'once', a clearer indication of mishearing (B1v). Many lines are garbled so that they yield no direct sense. The quarto also frequently renders verse as prose and vice versa.

Both *Hamlet* and *Pericles* offer examples of bad quartos that might in part derive from actor transmission of their respective texts. Such transmission is now thought to be rare, but it offers an important possible explanation for corruption. When encountered, such texts are almost impossible to read without the assistance of the editorial tradition. Nonetheless, such extreme examples point to the dangers of original play texts as sources for critical understanding of the plays. In cases like *Hamlet*, where multiple texts survive, one's understanding of the play is imperilled by difficult negotiations of the early textual variants (Kidnie 2005). For *Pericles*, it is possible to reconstruct the text from the single surviving authoritative quarto, but that reconstruction is likely to be radically different from the experience of reading the play in modernised editions.

Very incomplete texts might simply be unfinished. As explored above under Henslowe's relations with Jonson, authors supplied plots, or 'plats' as they were called, to the theatrical company as part of the process of play commissioning. Two of Jonson's plays, *The Sad Shepherd* and *Mortimer*, survive only as fragments, because, in the case of *Mortimer* at least, 'Hee dy'd, and left it unfinished' (1640–1: Qq4v). *Mortimer*'s entire plot is printed, however, suggesting that Jonson composed plays late in his career as he had done earlier in association with Henslowe – by writing them out briefly in prose before constructing his scenes. Such theatrical plots are very rarely printed, but do highlight the variety of conditions in which a play text might 'survive'.

FURTHER MODIFICATIONS

Memorial reconstruction or an incomplete draft might account for those fortunately rare texts that have been designated 'bad'. More positive (and intentional) kinds of modification also existed in this period, even for a play that had been officially allowed by the Master of the Revels. Chief among these possible causes of modification is the need to reduce the resources required to perform a play when touring. Touring is an important, if contentious, source of play-text alteration that has long been used to explain the existence of bad quartos. This theory was first proposed by W. W. Greg in *Two Elizabethan Stage Abridgements* (1922). A touring company, by this thinking, would need to cut down especially on the number of actors, and therefore parts, required to stage a play, as the biggest production cost would be labour. But cutting the play down and copying out the manuscript, redistributing the parts, and relearning two differing versions of a play might not have been worthwhile for most companies, or certainly not sufficiently worthwhile to explain the variety of short plays that survive in the period. In addition, there is no evidence from the period that touring performances were in any way reduced ones. As Paul Werstine notes: 'Recent scholarship has done much to call into question Greg's narrative of "bad quartos" as provincial playing texts and, therefore, to call into question all that has issued from it in the last seventy years' (Werstine 1998: 55). Yet a further distinction, not between locations for performance, but between literary texts and plays, has emerged. Lukas Erne in *Shakespeare as Literary Dramatist* has argued that Shakespeare's lengthy texts could not have been performed on the Elizabethan and Jacobean stage, so that the author must have written them as literary documents intended for print circulation. For Erne, the 'bad' quartos are more likely to reflect original performance pieces, heavily trimmed by the theatre companies: 'the first quartos of *Romeo and Juliet*, *Henry V*, and *Hamlet* are related to what Shakespeare and his fellows performed in London' (Erne 2003: 217). This view is less contentious than his argument 'that some passages present in the long, literary texts are omitted or abridged in the short, theatrical texts because they are chiefly of value for readers and not for spectators' (225). Centuries of theatrical practice, including practice that has performed the lengthy texts expeditiously, would oppose that conclusion. Nonetheless, Erne's partial redemption of the 'bad' quartos as texts worthy of staging (and reading) is in keeping with a wider scholarly movement to legitimise their difference as relevant to an understanding of these works.

The above theories have shown that additions or modifications to a play are often introduced silently. We simply do not know the reasons why multiple texts survive, why one version might be more corrupt than another, or even from whence most printed plays might have their manuscript origins. In cases where multiple editions that have substantive differences survive, the theatrical company might have deliberately modified the text. These modifications might be occasioned by general updates, by changes to politics, by various performance venues or circumstances, or by touring. As revealed in Henslowe's *Diary*, these changes might or might not have been written by the original author of a play. Grace Ioppolo points out that, 'The text could return to the author at any or all stages of transmission: after the scribe had copied it; after a censor had licensed it; after the book-keeper had prepared the company book; after its rehearsal and performance; before one or more later revivals; and after it was printed' (Ioppolo 2006: 99). The difficulty with updates is that their origins are often left disguised, so that we cannot know for certain if a given text was updated or by whom.

Much evidence, however, survives to outline the nature of possible updates to dramatic texts, and the following section will describe some situations that could lead to revision. Some plays (like *The Spanish Tragedy*) were updated because they had been around for a long time. In those instances a company sought to refresh a play that was well known to London audiences. The theatrical life of a play could be very lengthy indeed. *Mucedorus* was performed in front of Queen Elizabeth, and then later in front of King James. On these occasions, presumably, special prologues or epilogues were written in honour of royal attendance. *Mucedorus* was also performed in Oxfordshire in 1654. The playing life of this popular play therefore spanned sixty years, and in that time the text went through several variations. These variations survive as additional passages that appear in the extensive publication history of the play, but the origins of these amplifications are obscure. Grace Ioppolo's explanation for such changes raises an important point: 'Dramatists not only revised when compelled to, as a result of censorship or of the desire to pass an old play off as a new one, but when they wanted to' (Ioppolo 2006: 94). The same explanation might certainly apply to theatre companies as well as dramatists.

A good example of known theatrical revision comes in John Marston's *The Malcontent*. Three issues of the play were published by William Aspley in 1604, and these issues disclose significant variation. Marston wrote the play around 1603 for the Children of the Chapel, a children's company playing at the Blackfriars Theatre. Soon thereafter Marston took the play to the Globe Theatre for the Chamberlain's or King's Men. This theatrical history is disclosed by Marston's elaborate metatheatrical induction, which appears only in the third imprint (Q3). Q3 discloses further additions, including a new character, Pasarello, probably to take advantage of the comic talents of Robert Armin. In total, 447 lines were added to Q3 (Hunter 1975: xlix). With the exception of Pasarello's part, most of the changes seem to serve little purpose: 'In some ways the dramaturgy gains (in complexity) and in others it loses (in directness); but there is no new emotion, no new interpretation of the scene involved. In this respect an augmentation of this kind may be described as typical of the Elizabethan theatre' (Hunter 1975: xlviii). Clearly, Marston felt some anxiety in transferring his play to a new company (for which, presumably, he had twice been paid). His Q3 induction offers one of the lengthiest available explanations for revision from this period. In it, one of the actors plays 'Christopher Sly', an audience member who takes a stool on the stage, a practice permitted in the Blackfriars, but not in the Globe. Sly quizzes the actors (Richard Burbage and Henry Condell, or 'Cundale') on their play as follows:

Sly: I would know how you came by this play?

Cun: Faith sir the booke was lost, and because twas pittie so good a play should be lost, we found it and play it.

Sly: I wonder you would play it, another company having interest in it?

Cun: Why not Maleuole in folio with vs, as Ieronimo in Decimo sexto with them. They taught vs a name for our play, wee call it *One for another*.

Sly: What are your additions?

Bur: Sooth not greatly needefull, only as your sallet to your great feast, to entertaine a little more time, and to abridge the not received custome of musicke in our Theater.

(A4)

Condell defends the theft of the 'lost' play by noting that the boys' companies had been willing to perform *The Spanish Tragedy* (an alternative title for 'Ieronimo') without having legitimate ownership of it. Interestingly, Sly, as a fictional representative of the audience, expects that the text will have been augmented in some way, to justify its performance elsewhere. Burbage's simple response that the play has been lengthened and had its music reduced, but not in a way that is 'greatly needefull' is largely justified by the surviving text of Q3, where the changes seem to be of little consequence, but certainly do lengthen the play. The inter-act music does not survive in any copy, but as the Globe did not have act breaks, that, of course, would have been lost. This exchange discloses that texts might be altered slightly for different performance venues and contexts, that audiences expected some alterations for revivals, and that such alterations might be minimal. The overall situation also reveals how casual a theatrical company might be with the text of a play. It is only the popularity of *The Malcontent* that allowed the exact changes from the first to the third quarto to survive. A less popular play might have appeared in a unique copy in one state or the other. The problem this raises for subsequent readings of early modern play texts is that a manuscript that reflects any stage of a text's revision history might appear at the printing press, in many cases years after those revisions took place. The circumstances of revision behind play texts therefore become lost and largely irrecoverable. Shakespeare's folio plays, for instance, published well after their first performances, may contain years of theatrical, authorial, or scribal tinkering, and therefore are at a distance from their original performance contexts. The two texts of *King Lear* reflect changes that are complex and seemingly 'authorial' (in the broadest sense). The same is true for other dramatists. Jonson heavily revised *Every Man In His Humour*, for instance. And of Thomas Middleton, Ioppolo notes that: 'Once the textual transmission and descent of the manuscripts of *A Game at Chess* are unravelled, it becomes clear that Middleton was revising the play as he wrote it, after he wrote it, as he recopied it, and after he recopied it' (Ioppolo 2006: 173). Middleton's revisions occur over the space of weeks, and therefore show that revision was not merely a product of a play's age, but that popular plays at least were 'living' documents that were never fully fixed in any one textual state. This fluidity is partially addressed by John Marston when he reports in his 'To the Reader' for *The Malcontent* (Q1) that 'onley one thing afflicts mee, to thinke that Scenes invented, meerely to be spoken, should be inforcively published to be read' (A4). The process of printing fixes words that were originally performed, and therefore subject to change, in the theatre.

Other, more heavy-handed, causes of revision are also evident from the theatrical practices of the period. These might be owing to more substantive shifts in politics, occasion, or venue. In these instances, changes were made in ways that go beyond a mere desire to update an older play text. A clear example of this kind of textual revision is discussed above in relation to the censorship of *Richard II*. A less clear instance occurs in a play that was almost certainly changed in subsequent performances, but whose text might or might not reflect that revision. The chorus of the folio version of Shakespeare's *Henry V* appeals directly to the 1599 audience:

Were now the Generall of our gracious Empresse,
As in good time he may, from Ireland comming,
Bringing Rebellion broached on his Sword;
How many would the peacefull Citie quit,
To welcome him?

(1623: sig. i6)

Scholars generally agree that the 'Generall' here must be the Earl of Essex, who travelled to Ireland to oppose the Earl of Tyrone's uprising in spring 1599. Against Queen Elizabeth's wishes, Essex agreed a peace and returned to London on 28 September. The chorus's lines of encouragement could not have been delivered after that date, especially as Essex faced increasing shame until his thwarted rebellion against the Queen in 1601, which led to him being beheaded on 25 February. If the Lord Chamberlain's (and later King's) Men removed these lines from the chorus following Essex's disgrace, it is surprising that they survive into the folio copy. More surprising still is the fact that they do not appear in the earlier quartos, including the quarto of 1600, which might be taken to be more proximate to the first performances of a year earlier. Andrew Gurr suggests that the play was initially performed without the chorus (Gurr 2000: 9–12). But the chorus makes no sense after 1599, and in fact it would probably have been politically dangerous to retain it from 1601. So the more likely conclusion is that in the case of *Henry V*, the first quarto reflects various kinds of corruption that could be subject to alternative explanations.

Part of the problem here is that texts can be strongly disassociated from their apparent contexts. An important lesson is that an earlier text is not necessarily closer to either the author's or the theatrical company's original or intended version of the play. A later printing might be both more authoritative and reflect an earlier state of the text. We know from certain exceptionally popular plays, like *A Game at Chess*, discussed above, that theatrical companies were prepared to make manuscript copies of their plays for those who requested them. These manuscripts might be of varying quality, depending upon their intended recipients, those who prepared them, and how much time and care might have been taken with them at a given moment. In the case of the King's Men, however, there was one exceptionally important scribe whose manuscripts not only survive in multiple copies, but who clearly prepared some of the texts behind Shakespeare's 1623 folio. Ralph Crane worked for the King's Men in the 1620s and is responsible for at least three of the surviving manuscripts of *A Game at Chess*. Although Crane had unique attributes in his transcription work, so unique, in fact, as to make his transcriptions identifiable, his practice serves as an important model for some of the ways that playhouse scripts were copied more widely before being made available to printers.

It seems very unlikely that authors' foul copies were welcomed by busy printers. In order to print effectively and efficiently, the underlying manuscript must be reasonably clear. Although surviving plays do demonstrate confusions that probably derive from a sloppy, illegible, or confusing manuscript copy, poor manuscripts cannot have been the acceptable norm. Therefore, fair copies of playhouse scripts, either prepared by professional scribes, the authors themselves, or others, offer an additional layer of mediation between the author's or theatrical company's text (which was itself potentially susceptible to several layers of revision) and the printing house. We know that scribes changed texts. Ioppolo argues strongly that scribes are just as willing to preserve as to interfere on the basis of surviving evidence, and that: 'Far too many Shakespearean or early modern drama textual scholars, then, including the editors of *William Shakespeare: A Textual Companion*, have seen scribes as "interfering", "careless", "sloppy" or "cavalier", in order to protect Shakespeare from his own textual cruxes, inconsistencies and occasional bouts of sub-standard writing' (Ioppolo 2006: 111). Certainly, scribes have been subjected to much blame (as have 'inept' compositors) that does not necessarily apply to them. Any human in the chain of textual production seems as likely as another to have made a mistake, and clearly even Shakespeare 'nodded'. But scribes today might be seen to have a function that did not fully apply to them in the early modern period. They were not the early modern equivalent of (fairly slow) photocopiers who aimed at perfect textual fidelity. Instead, they might better be described as the tidiers and enhancers of a text, who might take the role, too, of good copy-editors. Ioppolo's assessment of their habits is that:

Scribes did not act as editors or as authors, although they may have regularised mechanical or formatting features such as spelling, lineation, speech-prefixes, act-scene notations and stage directions. While they may have relocated stage directions, they would not usually rewrite dialogue or in any other way change plot, structure or any other content in the play. (Ioppolo 2006: 112)

Such heavy alteration might counter this view to suggest that scribes were, in fact, an early form of editor.

As Gary Taylor puts it: 'An attempt to reproduce exactly a pre-existing text is an act of transmission. Every such act of transmission has the potential to corrupt the information content of the original text/message' (Taylor 2007: 2.733). Scribes might very well 'rewrite dialogue' without intending to. The various Crane manuscripts of *A Game at Chess* disclose cuts and changes owing to transcription error. But in many cases, major variants seem systematic and intended, as Gary Taylor has shown, and probably derive from Middleton himself (Taylor 2007: 2.765–6). A scribe might be unlikely to make intentional changes to the verse and prose spoken by the actors – or the oral text. Yet T. H. Howard-Hill importantly warns against assuming that Crane's very polished transcriptions are entirely accurate: 'he was not reluctant to interfere with his text, consciously or unconsciously, when its meaning was obscure to him' (Howard-Hill 1972: 133). For the most part, such changes must be lost to history.

The general sense that a scribe would be reluctant to alter the text of a play almost certainly does not hold true for either the less substantive elements, including spelling, punctuation, and contractions, or the non-spoken elements, like stage directions. Because spelling, punctuation, and contractions (or expansions of contractions) that are characteristic of Crane survive, it is easy to determine that he was willing to make alterations that suited his personal approach to orthography. R. B. McKerrow has shown that 'in anything printed from a fair copy made by Crane the spellings will not be those of the author, and if this is true of the work of one professional scribe it may well be true of the work of others' (McKerrow 1927: 26). Therefore, the mediating presence of a scribe might often be a deliberate erasure of the spelling and punctuation written by the original authors and read by the actors. What is perhaps more surprising is Crane's willingness to change information about staging.

Crane's stage directions often seem like descriptions written for the benefit of readers. As Jeanne Addison Roberts has argued, these directions: 'not only prescribe action but they add descriptive adjectives which sound more like an account of what happened onstage than an author's advisory notes for production' (Roberts 1980: 214). The best-known instance of this kind of direction occurs in the banquet scene of *The Tempest*: '*Enter Ariell (like a Harpey) claps his wings vpon the Table, and with a quient deuice the Banquet vanishes*' (1623: sig. B1). Presumably the acting company would need to be aware of the kind of quaint device that the author had in mind, but this direction seems to describe the action after it has happened, and for a reader's imagination. As Roberts points out, 'Throughout the stage directions there are more adjectives, adverbs, and elaborations than one would expect from an author or certainly from a prompt book' (Roberts 1980: 214). Roberts helpfully compares one of Middleton's autograph stage directions in *A Game at Chess* held by Trinity College, Cambridge with Crane's transcription of the same direction in the Archdall manuscript:

Trinity: *Musique an Altar discovered | and Statues, with a Song*
Archdall: – *Musick | An Altar discov- | verd, richely adorned, |* and *divers Statues | standing on each-side.*

(Roberts's transcriptions 1980: 216)

Crane's style, when preparing a manuscript for reading (as opposed to for the playhouse), clearly involves adjectival insistence in an attempt to ingrain the scene within the reader's imagination. Equally important is the evidence that Crane was willing to change not only the incidentals of spelling and punctuation, but to alter the very fabric of the play's staging.

Crane is a somewhat unique case in that he seems to have been more willing to alter his copy deliberately while making transcriptions. We know more about Crane's habits than about those of any other scribe, and therefore it is difficult to judge exactly how far he deviates from any norm. However, the important factor here is that scribes did prepare manuscripts for publication. In the act of transcribing these manuscripts, some degree of alteration would be made, taking an additional step from the author or playhouse. This additional step makes determining the origins of accidentals, speech-prefixes, and stage directions almost impossible: 'the question of how much of *The Tempest*'s textual presentation can be attributed to Crane, to the compositors, and to Shakespeare's original can only be guessed at' (Orgel 1987: 60). Such guesswork has occupied the time of bibliographers and editors of early modern drama for decades, but the available evidence is unlikely ever to yield conclusive data about the origins of a given text.

Michael Hunter's *Editing Early Modern Texts* claims that 'The editor has a responsibility to try to reconstruct the aims of the author of a text, a task made more complex by the need to do justice both to its evolution in the author's hands and to its subsequent transmission to posterity' (Hunter 2007: 59). This statement adds little inflection to one made by W. W. Greg much earlier: 'The aim of a critical edition should be to present the text, so far as the available evidence permits, in the form in which we may suppose that it would have stood in a fair copy, made by the author himself, of the work as he finally intended it' (Greg 1954: xii). Such attempts to reconstruct authorial presence are difficult for most early modern dramatic texts, even if we might identify the author's original intention in them. As Jonathan Goldberg notes: 'Shakespearean practice authorizes the dispersal of authorial intention' (Goldberg 1986: 214). Yet publisher's copy deriving directly from a polished authorial manuscript was certainly promoted in the period. Humphrey Moseley, publisher of the Beaumont and Fletcher *Comedies and Tragedies* of 1647 claimed that 'here is not any thing *Spurious* or *impos'd*; I had the Originalls from such as received them from the *Authours* themselves; by Those, and none other, I publish this Edition' ('The Stationer to the Readers', A4). As Moseley makes clear, this situation was the ideal, at least for readers of plays in the 1640s. A different view survives from earlier in the period, where the theatrical experience is held in more esteem than the reading one.

This chapter has so far shown how theatrical companies commissioned and shaped plays, how those works were further revised through censorship, rehearsal, touring, and revision, and how authors might subsequently revise their own or other's plays. All of these various states of the text might find their way to the printing house, and these theories (from the straightforward to the entangled) of the possible origins of the early print witnesses impact heavily upon an understanding of the printed texts that survive. As the previous section has explored, the early life of a play text was a life in manuscript – all play texts existed in at least one manuscript in this period, and it is likely that they existed in at least two separate manuscript forms. We are lucky that so many manuscript exemplars survive, but their very survival points to ways in which these particular texts were *not* used. In other words, manuscripts in use are especially subject to decay (or to being destroyed, as, for instance, in the Globe Theatre fire of 1613). Manuscripts that resided relatively unread in private hands are most likely to survive, and of course those manuscripts are less likely to have had wide audiences or a close relationship with the theatre.

Since the early twentieth century there has been much scholarly effort to identify the kind of manuscript that served as the base text for a given early printed play. Increasingly, such attempts have been seen as fruitless, or at least open to question. There are cases, especially for texts by Marston, Jonson, or Shirley, where a direct line from author to publisher seems to have existed. More typically, however, the origins of a printer's manuscript are mysterious, and could derive from complex histories of revision, some of which do not necessarily reflect a given performance context. The printed texts that survive are likely to reflect a snapshot of a play's changing history: 'for most of Shakespeare's work only a single layer of this textual continuum is extant: time has "edited" the multiplicity of textual forms down to a single exemplar' (Wells and Taylor 1997: 3). These printed exemplars might, owing to the regularising forces of the press, look similar, but they are likely to have complex variance in their manuscript origins.

FROM MANUSCRIPT TO PRINT

The final part of this chapter will discuss theories of how plays came to be printed and the various possibilities that shape their production, including variations in format (for example, quartos, folios, et cetera); authorial input (for example, Shakespeare versus Jonson); and printer/publisher alterations. Although much can be said about the printing and publishing circumstances of specific early books, it is difficult to extrapolate generalisations about the period as a whole. The purpose of this section is not to describe in full the kinds of processes that printers undertook to generate the printed quires that would then be bound and read. The mechanics of publishing and printing in this period have been covered at great length by other scholars. The early chapters of Philip Gaskell's *A New Introduction to Bibliography*, for instance, discuss printing at much more length than I will here. I have selected the processes that seem to me to impact most upon a potential literary and bibliographical understanding of the dramatic texts in the early modern period.

Publishers

Plays started their journeys to print by being purchased or otherwise obtained by a publisher. Then that publisher, if he or she were also a printer, might print the play directly, or commission a printer or printers to do so.

Printing was a laborious process. William Stansby, for instance, required around three years of solid work to print Jonson's 1616 folio. Gary Taylor has suggested that the economic constraints of printing plays were unlikely to lead to much profit (Taylor 2006). It seems that publishing play texts was a fairly thankless task, unless a lucky publisher happened upon a success like *The Malcontent*, *Pericles*, or *Mucedorus*. Therefore, we can assume that publishers were choosey about the plays they decided to invest in. Peter W. M. Blayney notes that plays in general were not a particularly popular genre for publishers of the period (Blayney 2005). Of the 280 plays mentioned in Henslowe's *Diary*, only thirty survive in any form (Carson 1988: 80–84). Yet Lukas Erne has shown that dramatists, and especially Shakespeare, also enjoyed moments of exceptional popularity in print (Erne 2009). The survival of a play text in print possibly says something about its popularity in the playhouse, which would have been one of the few reliable measures of possible print sales. But publishers also worked to shape the dramatic canon through their specific publishing interests, as Zachary Lesser has argued (Lesser 2004). Authors, too, and especially Jonson and Beaumont and Fletcher, attempted to overturn a play's poor theatrical reception by promoting it to a different reading audience. Jonson frequently complained about the poor response his plays received in the theatre, and he blamed either the lack of understanding in the audience or the poor quality of the players who performed it. In *The New Inn* (1631), he does both. His 'Dedication to the Reader' proclaims that 'if thou canst but spell, and ioyne my sense; there is more hope of thee, then of a hundred fastidious *impertinents*, who were there present on the first day . . . To dislike all, but marke nothing' (sig. *2–*2v). The title page offers one of the most anti-theatrical statements in his canon: 'A COMOEDY. As it was neuer acted, but most negligently play'd, by some, the Kings Seruants'. Usually the theatrical origins of a play are deployed to attract a potential reader, but Jonson grew to have a distant relationship with the stage. Jonson clearly respected his potential print audience more than his theatrical one, and he took care with many of his plays to see them to the publisher in a good state. As Jonson, and not the King's Men, supplied (or rather sold) his manuscript to the publisher, Thomas Alcorn, the underlying copy is the author's polished draft, the text that New Bibliographers sought in their search for the copy-text 'ideal of an author's fair copy of his work in its final state' (McKerrow 1939: 17–18). The problem the New Bibliographers faced is that their ultimate aim was to apply this ideal to Shakespeare, whose printed plays strongly resist any disclosure of their manuscript origins. Certainly, the temporal distance between performance and publication for Shakespeare's folio, and the fact that he had been dead for several years prior to its publication, mean Shakespeare can never fit the easier, Jonsonian ideal of the omnipresent author.

Once the publisher received manuscript copy, he or she would need to negotiate with a printer or printers over the production of the text, or do it in-house for those publishers who also engaged in printing. The period is loose in its application of the terms 'printer' and 'publisher', as discussed further in the next chapter, but modern scholarship distinguishes between the person who mechanically reproduced the text in a printing shop (printer), and the person who financed the production of the text in the hopes of selling it for a profit (publisher). Theoretically, to secure his or her ownership of a play, the publisher would be required to enter its title into the *Stationers' Register*. Each entry incurred a small fee, but it asserted a near indisputable right to a text, howsoever it might have been obtained. Not all stationers chose to enter their plays. The first two quartos of *Romeo and Juliet* were not entered, for instance. Entry or non-entry cannot be taken as *prima facie* evidence of legitimate or illegitimate dealings by a publisher, but the *Register* is helpful at pinning down the date that a particular text might have been acquired, as the physical manuscript had to be taken to Stationers' Hall at the time of its entry into the register.

The publisher would agree a format for the play with the printer(s), and the price and delivery for the finished, printed sheets. Format was the initial technical consideration in play production, and early printed texts are still primarily identified according to whether they are quartos, octavos, and folios (and, more rarely, other formats). This consideration, when coupled with the selection of typeface, had a strong impact upon how much a play book might cost, how many pages it would be, and how it would be received by the reading public.

All of Shakespeare's plays were published as folios, quartos, or octavos, and the same holds true for most plays printed in this period. Quartos account for by far the most common format for separate Shakespeare editions. A quarto is a sheet of paper that has been divided into quarters, with four pages printed on each side (see Figure 3). When folded, a quarto sheet forms a quire of eight pages (see Figure 4). A quire for a quarto usually makes up one entire gathering, or a collection of pages that would be stitched through as part of the binding process and which had a unique set of signatures.

A folio is twice as large as a quarto and has only two pages printed on each side of the sheet (see Figure 5). When folded, a single folio sheet therefore yields four folio pages.

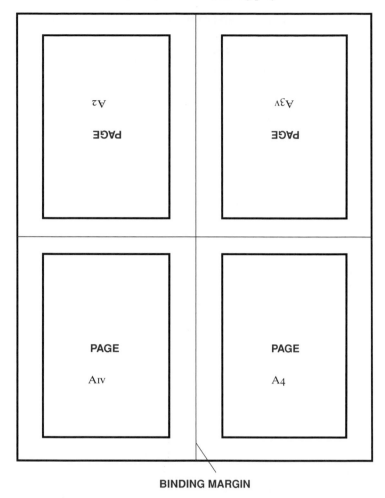

Fig. 3. One side of a quarto sheet.

An octavo has eight pages per sheet (see Figure 6), and therefore yields sixteen printed pages. Folios are generally the size of the average 'complete works' of Shakespeare produced today; whereas octavos are pocket-sized editions, slightly more narrow than a modern paperback novel.

Because the white space takes up a larger proportion of the sheet in octavos, less text per sheet might be printed on them (Weiss 2007: 208). On the other hand, on more expansive folio pages, the reader might

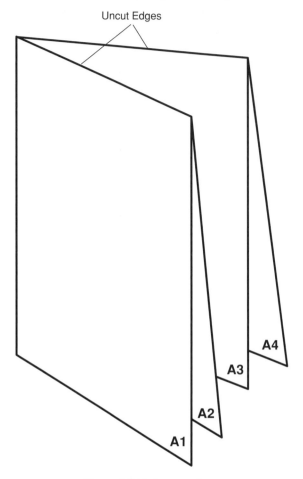

Fig. 4. A folded quarto sheet.

easily get lost on a densely printed page. As paper was an expensive commodity, and printed play books did not command a great price, probably around six pence for a quarto play, it follows that most publishers would seek to minimise production costs by printing the plays without wastage. There is also the question as to what format the play-buying public would expect to encounter a play text in. Both of these circumstances explain the popularity of quarto-sized individual plays. Folios provided a popular option for collections of plays following Jonson's 1616 *Workes*, the first large grouping of play texts from the public stage. Shakespeare's

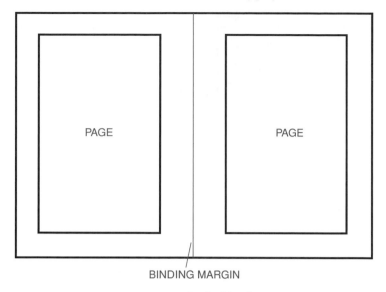

Fig. 5. One side of a folio sheet.

1623 folio builds upon Jonson's pioneering format, but in a less expensive, double-column and small-fount printing that manages to cram in many more words per page. The Beaumont and Fletcher folio of 1647 is similarly printed in small type, as Humphrey Moseley explains, 'because (as much as possible) we would lessen the Bulke of the Volume' (1647: g2). Subsequent groupings of plays could take folio or octavo format. Shirley's 1652–3 collection of *Six New Plays*, for instance, appeared in a very tightly printed octavo with binding margins that make the texts difficult to read.

Printers

Once the format and fount-size were chosen, the publisher would agree a price for the production of the text with a printer or printers. Two or more printers might work on a single text in order to get it published quickly. In these cases they would replicate the fount and style as far as possible, and print on a matching (or roughly matching) stock of paper, as supplied by the publisher. Often the only clue available to subsequent scholars about the presence of multiple printers is the stock of type (and particularly uniquely damaged type) and ornaments that was available to known printers. Multiple printers might split a text so that the labour was

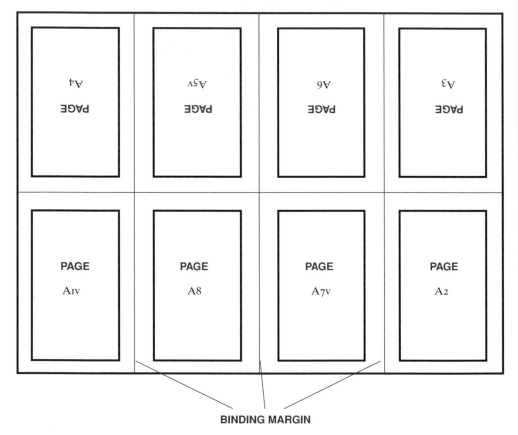

PAGE	PAGE	PAGE	PAGE
A4	A5v	A6	A3

PAGE	PAGE	PAGE	PAGE
A1v	A8	A7v	A2

BINDING MARGIN

Fig. 6. One side of an octavo sheet.

not equally divided. In fact one printer might print the beginning and end of a play, while another worked on the middle sections, or indeed any imaginable permutation of divided labour could be worked out in advance. In Shirley's *Six New Plays*, for instance, it is clear that two printers were at work. W. W. Greg's *A Bibliography of the Early Printed Drama* suggests that *The Brothers*, *The Imposture*, and *The Court Secret* were printed by William Wilson, and *The Sisters*, *The Doubtful Heir*, and *The Cardinal* were printed by Thomas Warren (Greg 1939–59: 1124). Individual plays might also be divided, as in the case of Q1 of Shakespeare's *Romeo and Juliet*. John Danter printed sheets A to D, and Edward Allde printed sheets E to K. Humphrey Moseley explains how such divided printing might expedite the production of a volume, in his 'Postscript' to the Beaumont and Fletcher folio: 'After the *Comedies* and *Tragedies* were wrought off, we were forced (for expedition) to send the *Gentlemens* Verses to severall Printers, which was the occasion of their different Character; but the *Worke* it selfe is one continued Letter' (1647: g2).

The process that permitted such exact prediction of where textual divisions might fall in a yet-to-be-printed volume is known as casting off. In casting off, the printing house would judge the length of a manuscript to determine both how many sheets would be needed, and what the divisions were between one forme and another. (A forme is one side of a sheet: four quarto pages or two folio pages.) Because formes do not have many consecutive pages, estimates would be further broken down by page. If a quarto forme includes a putative page one, for instance, that side of the sheet would also include pages four, five, and eight. The other forme on that sheet would have pages two, three, six, and seven. A folio forme would have pages one and four, or pages two and three, but usually folio formes are brought together in more complex gatherings, whereby two folios sheets are bundled to make eight pages ('folio in fours' as in the case of Jonson's second folio of 1640–41), or three folio sheets make up twelve pages ('folio in sixes', as in the case of Jonson's 1616 folio and Shakespeare's 1623 folio). Figure 7 shows how the pages would fit together in the case of Shakespeare's folio.

Because pages within formes are printed at the same time, formes make up an important unit for the understanding of texts, so Chapter 2 will address formes further, and how they impact upon reading early play texts. The process of negotiating signatures is also described in more detail in Chapter 2.

For very lengthy and complex projects, the printers did not always accurately judge the process of dividing up a play text. Even in more straightforward cases, like the first quarto of *Romeo and Juliet*, the variation of line lengths discloses different methods of casting off across the two printers. For Shirley's *Six New Plays*, which was also printed by two different printing houses, difficulty emerged in accommodating the prefatory material for *The Doubtful Heir* in sheet 'A', so that a blank page associated with quire A can appear before the title page (as it was meant to) or after A3 (as the page would naturally be folded). A more famous example concerns Shakespeare's first folio. The 'Catalogue' of plays at the beginning of the volume makes no mention of *Troilus and Cressida*. The play is placed in the volume between the tragedies and histories, however.

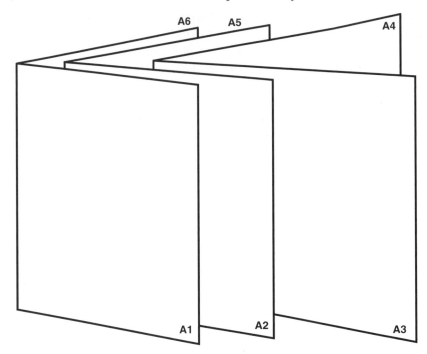

Fig. 7. Gathering of a folio in sixes.

A rights dispute appears to have interrupted the printing of *Troilus and Cressida*, as a cancelled sheet survives, following *Romeo and Juliet*, which prints the first two pages of the play. *Timon of Athens* replaced *Troilus*, apparently as a last-minute substitution, and as it is much shorter than *Troilus*, the signature run does not reflect a proper 'fit' for that play. Once the rights to *Troilus* were acquired, it too did not have a place in the run of signatures or pages, which explains why it is the only play in the folio not to be paginated, and why its signatures are ¶ sigla instead of letters. In the case of this large project, the insertion of a play does not seem to have caused much disruption, in part because it was within a multi-year process of printing a substantive book.

For individual plays, however, mistaken casting off could lead to the loss of part of the play, or to a disruption to the gathering of quarto or folio sheets. In Shirley's *The Bird in a Cage* (1633), for instance, signature C4 has part of its initial line shifted to C3v, which was reset in its final line because of crowding that almost certainly arose from a casting-off miscalculation. Methods for detecting such disruptions are outlined in Chapter 3. Setting by formes allowed the printer to save type and to start typesetting at any point of the book. Usually the first pages of the book, or the preliminaries (including the title page), would be the final pages to be printed. If these were to be given signature 'A', then the printer would typically start with signature 'B', choosing to set one side of a sheet first (i.e., starting with either the 'B1' side (the 'outer' forme) or 'B1v' side (the 'inner' forme) of the sheet). Equally, a printer setting by formes could have two or more different compositors working on the same text, to expedite the printing, or, as we have already seen, two or more printing houses might work on the same text. If the preliminaries did not require an entire sheet, or if the end of a quarto, for instance, required only four pages instead of eight, then those pages might be set by half-sheet imposition, whereby only half of one sheet of paper would be impressed. Similarly, a printer might set A1-A2 and Z1-Z2 on the same sheet, and then use this sheet to wrap around the other quires. These permutations, especially if an error in casting off was made, are significant, and W. W. Greg's *Bibliography of the Early Printed Drama* outlines them for any given printed play text. Although setting by formes required initial effort and potential error in the casting off of copy, it did permit maximum flexibility in the time-consuming business of typesetting and printing.

An additional option was available to printers who did not desire to cast off their copy. It was possible to start setting the type of the manuscript from beginning to end, by devoting a great deal of standing type, across at least two formes, to a print job. This process, known as setting type seriatim (as opposed to setting by formes) was used for difficult texts, especially. We did not know that plays were commonly set by forme (instead of seriatim) until the pioneering work of Charlton Hinman (1955) and George Walton Williams (1958). When reading earlier bibliographical work, therefore, there is some danger that the analysis is skewed by an assumption of seriatim printing. Peter Blayney notes that 'as more and more printing studies are published it becomes increasingly apparent . . . that setting by formes was the Jacobean norm' (Blayney 1982: 630). Most plays have not had their method of printing confirmed either way. One example of a seriatim-set play text is Shakespeare's *King Lear* quarto of 1608, and Blayney supposes that this most unusual strategy for typesetting this play emerged because 'the manuscript itself was a difficult one' (Blayney 1982: 184).

After casting off (or choosing to set seriatim), the manuscript would be given to a compositor or compositors for typesetting. A compositor would select individual pieces of type and place them in a composing stick – a slotted piece of wood or metal that held lines of type. Once a line was

full, it had to be justified to the right by the judicious use of spacing, or
sometimes by respelling words (for example, 'hee' or 'he' to make them
longer or shorter), and then laid into the appropriate place on the page.
The contents of the composing stick (with 'six or eight lines of type')
would next be placed on the galley, a 'tray holding a complete page of type'
(Greetham 1994: 118). The text of a page would be positioned in the forme,
or the frame that would hold the pages that would be impressed onto one
side of a sheet. This laborious work could induce accidental or deliberate
change to the nature of the text.

Accidental mistakes, such as character substitutions or upturned letters,
are often easy to detect. Yet deliberate changes present greater problems.
We can only guess at the degree to which a compositor might deliberately
alter the spelling of the underlying manuscript. McKerrow's detailed work
identified the following pattern:

> The evidence that I have been able to put before you is far from being as consistent
> and conclusive as might be desired, but I think that taking together all that is
> afforded by the work of Harington, Munday, Churchyard, Harvey and Greene,
> we may fairly say that up to about 1590 a certain number of compositors were
> strongly influenced by the text before them, especially if it was clear that the
> spelling of the author was systematic and careful, and might even follow such
> spelling consistently, but that even then many re-spelt what they were setting up
> according to their own ideas. After 1590 normalization became quite definitely the
> general rule. (McKerrow 2000: 39)

McKerrow also argues that spelling variation was frequently used to justify
lines of prose (McKerrow 2000: 30). It is possible that he overstates the
regularity of this practice, but it is certainly difficult to make convincing
statements about early modern dramatic spelling from the evidence of the
printed texts. Spelling differences within a single play text, in fact, are one
of the chief ways to distinguish between multiple compositors who might
have set it. But without the underlying manuscripts for comparison, first
printings of dramatic texts must be taken to have insecure spellings, at
least in terms of any derivation from authorial or theatrical manuscripts.
Second printings, such as the reset sections of Jonson's first folio that were
produced for special 'large paper' copies (as discussed further in Chapter 3),
demonstrate a high degree of compositor willingness to alter underlying
spellings.

Similar difficulty arises with punctuation. McKerrow offers evidence that
compositors sometimes ignored and sometimes replicated the punctuation
of their underlying copy:

Certainly in printing Harington's *Orlando Furioso* the printer paid little or no attention to the punctuation of the MS. On the other hand as has been pointed out by Mrs. Percy Simpson, there is abundant evidence that John Donne punctuated carefully, and his punctuation was in general carefully followed both by copyists and by printers. Donne, however, was of course a scholar, and it is quite likely that he would use exceptional care in a matter of this kind. (McKerrow 2000: 40–1)

The issue of how far an author might take part in correcting or monitoring the printing of his or her text is an important one, but the evidence seems to suggest that reliable statements about the origins of punctuation in individual play texts are also very difficult to make.

A compositor might deliberately alter the spelling and punctuation of his text, but even more significant alteration could occur if he misunderstood his copy, or simply made mistakes in setting it. Grace Ioppolo notes in a different context that, 'Given the lack of standardised spelling and punctuation and the frequent deviation in handwriting from standard letter forms and conventional usage, early modern readers, including theatre personnel and the censor, could have been left bewildered in reading a particular manuscript text' (Ioppolo 2006: 85). The same difficulty with a manuscript might affect compositors facing alterations, deletions, mistakes, multiple hands, or even damage to their copy. An interesting case of such difficulty being wrestled with by a compositor is revealed in James Shirley's *The Witty Fair One* (1633). On D4v, line 7, the text has three variant states that reflect compositor confusion. The first state reads 'bountifull   of pottage', with a large space left in the line, seemingly with the intention of filling it in later. Subsequent states read 'bountifull acemation of pottage' and 'bountifull ordination of pottage'.[2] Neither of these quantities of pottage seems like a convincing possibility, but whatever Shirley intended here has been lost to history, probably owing to a combination of an unusual word choice and a messy manuscript. The confusion between 'c' and 'r', 'e' and 'd', and 'm' and 'in' makes sense in the light of secretary letter forms commonly used in the handwriting of the period, where these letters strongly resemble one another. Less spectacular mistakes might result from a compositor setting the wrong piece of type, placing the correct type upside down (as in 'u' for 'n'), having a foul case (where type has been misplaced when redistributed), or skipping over sections of the text (eye skip, which results in repeated or omitted words or lines).

The possibility of mistakes was accounted for in early modern strategies towards correcting copy. Such corrections came in two stages, though those

---

[2] I am grateful to Dr Teresa Grant for bringing these variants to my attention.

stages have many additional points at which corrections might be made. The first stage of correction involved pulling a printed proof or 'foul' sheet from the forme. This sheet would be checked (we are not certain whether these checks were always done against the manuscript copy), and the sheet would be marked up to indicate corrections that the compositor would need to make. Copies of such marked-up proof sheets survive, but theoretically the chance of survival would be low, as there should be only one proof page in most printing jobs. This process of correction involved loosening the type and moving it around, so the correction itself might lead to further errors. Playwrights, like Ben Jonson, might also participate in this initial process of proof correction, but it is unlikely that Shakespeare ever did, or that others did so frequently. The Oxford editors note of Shakespeare: 'either he did not read proofs of the early editions of his plays, or he was an abysmal proof-reader' (Wells and Taylor 1997: 47). Dramatists and readers seemed to accept that an author's involvement with the text might cease when it reached the printing house. Expectations by individual authors and publishers clearly varied. Marston notes in his 'To the Reader' for the first quarto of *The Malcontent* (1604): 'my inforced absence must much reley vpon the Printers discretion: but I shall intreat, slight errors in orthography may bee as slightly o'repassed' (A4), implying that he wished to see his work through the press. On the other hand, the publisher of James Shirley's *Bird in a Cage* (1633) laconically states that, 'many other Errors, (though for the most part literall,) thou shalt meete, which thou canst not with safetie of thy owne, interpret a defect in the Authors Iudgment, since all bookes are subiect to these misfortunes' (K4). Despite the (acknowledged) existence of errors in the play texts of the period, proofing generally ensured that most were fairly well printed. But it is probably also true to say that printing houses were more concerned with mechanical than literary errors. In other words they would remove damaged type, turned over letters, et cetera, but sometimes ignored grievous errors of meaning. The compositor was responsible for replicating and somewhat regularising the text in front of him, but sometimes that text was misunderstood.

Once the proof corrections were made, the business of printing all of the necessary sheets of that particular forme would begin. During this printing process, if further errors were spotted (and they often were, from the evidence of play texts that survive in large numbers), then further corrections would be made. These corrections are generally known as stop-press corrections, as they are made in the context of imposition. There are three facts that are important to note in the context of stop-press correction:

(1) 'uncorrected' sheets would not be thrown away. Paper was too valuable to permit such waste, so a buyer might acquire a copy that was less correct than another (without any way of distinguishing between them).

(2) 'Uncorrected' and 'corrected' sheets could be mixed in no particular order, so that it is unlikely that any single volume contains only the most perfected states. For this reason, Charlton Hinman's 1968 facsimile of Shakespeare's first folio reproduced pages from multiple copies.

(3) The act of 'correction' might induce further error, or be a miscorrection, so it is not always possible to say with certainty which states are correct or uncorrected, or indeed to order such states chronologically.

These three facts combine to imply that a reader who wishes to learn what a printer intended as his best output would need to examine multiple copies and exercise judgement about the possibility of miscorrection. Chapter 3 will go into more detail about the available processes for collating or comparing texts. In practice, such collation discloses several variants for a given play text, if multiple exemplars of that text survive. But clearly, this was not an option available to the reading public in the early modern period, and so they must have been active readers who attempted to supply remedial readings for apparent defects. Similarly, contemporary readers who encounter texts from *Early English Books Online* (or indeed just about any facsimile except the Norton Shakespeare folio or Malone Society photo-facsimiles) should be aware that little effort has been devoted to finding the most perfect copies, in part because such copies would require excessive labour to discover, and in part because the bibliographical unit is the individual forme, and not the entire text.

Another category of error deserves brief mention. Accidentals – or inadvertent changes to a text – occurred when type was pulled out or shifted around during the extreme forces generated by the screw press. These accidentals can mean that letters disappear, or that they move from one line to another. Often, these movements can vary slightly from impression to impression in the course of the printing process.

Once all of the sheets were printed, they were dried, gathered together in quires, and folded in half. This process, too, might lead to errors in page order, or potentially to the loss of pages or addition of duplicates, causing another possible mode of corruption. Such corruption might be especially likely if the volume required unusual page formats, such as inserts or half-sheets, in addition to full and ordered quires. A further stage of production was binding. Readers in this period bought most books (and especially ephemeral works like plays) unbound, so paying a binder would be an additional expense (if indeed binding were desired). The low incidence of survival of early play quartos from this period might point to the fact that readers did not always bind these less expensive books, but might have opted frequently for the cheaper option of wrapping them in a paper or vellum cover, and such slight material would not be very sturdy compared to a leather binding. The fact that over 230 copies of Shakespeare's first folio have survived probably relates both to its bulk and to the fact that those who could afford its £1 asking price would also trouble to secure it with careful binding. The binder would be tasked to order the sheets (with the possibility of misordering them) and fold them (with the possibility of misfolding) before binding. A reader might have to cut the pages (for quarto or octavo) where they were folded, or the binder could cut them and gild or decorate the edges.

The above outline of the correction, sorting, and binding processes (and the errors that might emerge during them) points to sources of variation *within* a text. It should also be noted that multiple versions of a text might be printed by the same printer in the same year, and these versions might range from simply being new imprints (i.e., with differences on the title pages) to entirely new editions (with completely reset texts). Many plays were printed in this period with multiple title pages. Sometimes these disclose the interests of multiple publishers. For James Shirley's *The Duke's Mistress* (1638) for instance, the first imprint reads on its title page: 'Printed by JOHN NORTON, for ANDREW CROOKE'; the second: 'Printed by JOHN NORTON, for WILLIAM COOKE'; and the third includes the names of both publishers. It is likely that these different versions were intended for different points of sale, including the separate shops of both Cooke and Crooke. These imprints are given separate numbers in Pollard and Redgrave's revised *Short-Title Catalogue* (STC 22441, 22441a, and 22441b respectively), but only the title pages were reset, as the texts are otherwise undifferentiated. Similarly, different versions of Shirley's *The Opportunity* were printed in 1640, again for the partnership of Cooke and Crooke. Different imprints here specify different points of sale: 'to be sold at the Castle Gate in *Dublin*' (STC 22452) or 'to be sold at the Signe of the Greene Dragon in *Pauls* Church-yard' (STC 22451a). On the other hand, the same title page might be used for two different editions, as in the case of the 1609 first and second quartos of Shakespeare's *Pericles*.

The *Short-Title Catalogue* is not always an adequate indication of the differences between impressions and new editions. More substantive and complex alterations might also occur within a single print run. Marston's *The*

Malcontent went through three imprints in 1604. As all of these imprints concern the same printer and publisher, and all refer to the same point of sale 'in Paules / Churchyard', the differences are not owing to multiple points of sale. The first two imprints are largely similar, and George K. Hunter argues that they might reflect that the play was very popular. In 1586 the Star Chamber limited the number of copies that might be printed from one setting of type to 1250 to 1500. A play text that was likely to prove popular might demand two distinct print runs, although in this case the second edition reused much of the standing type from the first (Hunter 1975: xxvi–xxviii). Therefore the second quarto is partially a new edition and partially a new impression. The third imprint is actually an entirely new edition that reflects substantive changes by Marston, who, as shown earlier, made additions for the play's new home at the Globe.

The play texts of Marston and Shirley disclose that sometimes the distinctions between imprints are significant, and sometimes they are not. Generally, therefore, additional scholarship is needed *before* the act of reading an original or facsimile, in those cases where multiple imprints from the same year exist. This situation grows more complex when dealing with a play published by multiple publishers or across larger spans of time. Earlier sections of this chapter have highlighted some of the differences between noticeably 'bad' quartos and their expanded subsequent versions. But more often subsequent editions of the same play are likely to be based entirely on earlier printed editions. It was easier for printers to deal with printed texts than manuscripts (especially when casting off), so that for Shakespeare's folio, for instance, 'Eleven plays in the collection were printed from annotated copies of an earlier printed text' (Wells and Taylor 1997: 51). Printers relied upon an earlier printed text, even when they had an alternative manuscript. In this case, the printed text would be marked up for manuscript additions, or would be used alongside the manuscript to determine a new, composite text. This circumstance might apply even in the case of editions that are meant to correct bad quartos. There were frequent claims in the period by publishers about the superiority of their texts. Most famously, Heminges and Condell in their 'To the great Variety of Readers' in Shakespeare's folio dismiss the 'diuerse stolne, and surreptitious copies' of the earlier quartos (1623: A3). Yet the Oxford editors note that even the folio publisher must have relied upon them to some extent: 'The second editions of both *Romeo and Juliet* and *Hamlet* are printed for the most part from authoritative manuscripts, but both in certain respects clearly derive from an earlier edition' (Wells and Taylor 1997: 50–51). Shakespeare is by far the most bibliographically investigated dramatist from the early modern period, so it is relatively easy to find out information about which printed version might be more authoritative than another. But even for him difficulties arise, especially when two or more texts compete for scholarly attention. The Oxford editors decided to modernise both quarto and folio *King Lear* in 1986, providing a difficult choice for readers even of popular editions. Since then, the case for textual multiplicity has been made forcibly, so that the 2006 Arden edition of *Hamlet* prints all three early texts (Q1, Q2, and F) in two volumes. Such editions imply that reading two or more versions might be necessary if one is to 'know' the play, or that, on the other hand, there is no such thing as *the* play. The same must be true for other dramatists of this period whose work is available in multiple early editions.

This chapter has aimed to show how tortuous the movement from author's pen to printers' ink could be for play texts of the early modern period. Some authors, such as Jonson, Marston, and Shirley, established a direct relationship with their printers; while others, like Shakespeare, did not. Anything that might be imagined as happening in the commissioning, revising, transmitting, and printing of plays probably did happen at times. Patterns are therefore difficult to identify. These various sources of intention, alteration, and corruption are significant if we are to understand the surviving printed drama, as they heavily shape the material texts. The next chapter will consider these material texts in greater detail, by breaking them down into their component parts.

FURTHER READING

Blayney, Peter W. M. 1982. *The Texts of 'King Lear' and Their Origins*, vol. 1: *Nicholas Okes and the First Quarto*. Cambridge University Press

Carson, Neil 1988. *A Companion to Henslowe's Diary*. Cambridge University Press

Greetham, D. C. 1994. *Textual Scholarship: An Introduction*. New York and London: Garland

Ioppolo, Grace 2006. *Dramatists and their Manuscripts in the Age of Shakespeare, Jonson, Middleton and Heywood: Authorship, authority and the playhouse*. Oxford and New York: Routledge

Jackson, MacDonald P. 2003. *Defining Shakespeare: Pericles as Text Case*. Oxford University Press

Jowett, John 2007. *Shakespeare and Text*. Oxford University Press

Massai, Sonia 2007. *Shakespeare and the Rise of the Editor*. Cambridge University Press

Stern, Tiffany 2004. *Making Shakespeare: From Stage to Page*. London and New York: Routledge

Werstine, Paul 1999. 'Post-Theory Problems in Shakespeare Editing', *Yearbook of English Studies* 29: 103–117

2009. 'The Continuing Importance of New Bibliographical Method', *Shakespeare Survey* 62: 30–45

CHAPTER 2

The features of play texts

This chapter operates as the spine of this book, by explaining the physical features of early dramatic texts and their functions. Not all of these features appear in all play texts, and many of them have a history of marked change in the period from 1580 to 1642. Sufficient examples from across this period will be given to point to some of these changes. The features to be discussed include:

- title pages
- dedications
- illustrations
- dramatis personae
- arguments and scenes
- act and scene divisions
- stage directions
- speech prefixes
- verse and prose
- individual characters
- headlines and running titles
- marginalia
- signatures and page numbers
- catchwords
- other paratext: ornaments, colophons, advertisements, errata

Although it is sometimes possible to characterise these elements for the period as a whole, in each individual text they might perform a different function, so several examples will be offered in the discussion to follow.

TITLE PAGES

Title pages served several different and sometimes competing purposes in the early modern period. Readers would encounter a title page as the cover of a play text, because new books were sold before they were bound.

More importantly, because sheets of a book were stacked together and then simply folded in half, the book could not be 'read' as part of the browsing process. Only by separating the sheets into quires and folding them in order would the pages appear as they should. A reader at a bookstall interested in page three of a quarto would need to turn to the final 'page' in the stack of folded sheets, so that even the earliest pages of the book itself could not easily be browsed. The experience would be akin to folding a newspaper in half and attempting to read page two. Therefore, the title page was not only the first part of a book to be considered, it was also the only part of the book that might be easily consulted. Partially for this reason, title pages (and corresponding end papers at the back of the text) are often the most damaged part of a surviving exemplar, because unless the quires were carefully wrapped or bound throughout their lives, the title page was most exposed to the elements. But in the early modern period, title pages had the allure of new paper, and they were sometimes printed on higher-quality paper stock. They would almost invariably be the final part of a book to be printed, along with any other preliminary material and sometimes appeared on the same sheet as the final pages. When title pages are printed on the same sheet as the end papers, the resultant quire forms a kind of wrapper around the text of the play.

The title page for a 1590s play text followed a set formula that was rarely altered. The play's title would be followed by information about where the play was performed, and then information about the author might or might not be present, and then the publisher, with the city in which it was printed, the location of the publisher, and sometimes the name or initials of the printer, would be followed by the date of the imprint. (See examples in Figures 8 and 9.) Sometimes additional information, marketing statements, portraits, or engravings, might also be included. Each of these separate pieces of information should be considered in turn. As each also contributed to the marketing of the text, they should also be viewed (like all marketing material) with scepticism. As Gabriel Egan puts it, 'some title-pages just plain lie' (Egan 2006: 95). Fraudulent title pages also helped to avoid attention from authorities who might take offence at the printed material.

The titles of original play texts might differ radically both from the titles intended by the author/theatre and from those by which the plays are now known. In the 1590s, titles often were shaped by the publisher, who tended to emphasise the most significant characters of a play. Marlowe's 1594 *Edward II* offers an interesting example in this vein: 'The trouble-some | raigne and lamentable death of | Edward *the second, King of* |

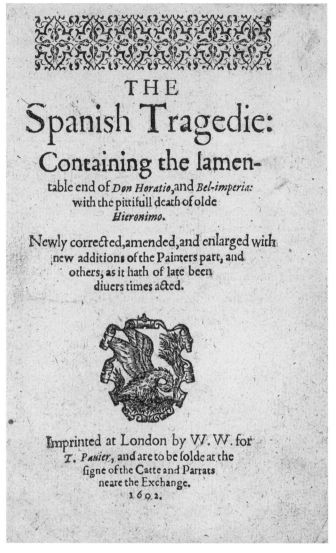

THE

Spanish Tragedie:

Containing the lamen-
table end of *Don Horatio*, and *Bel-imperia:*
with the pittifull death of olde
Hieronimo.

Newly corrected, amended, and enlarged with
new additions of the Painters part, and
others, as it hath of late been
diuers times acted.

Imprinted at London by W. W. for
T. Pauier, and are to be solde at the
signe of the Catte and Parrats
neare the Exchange.
1 6 0 2.

Fig. 8. Title page of *The Spanish Tragedy* (1602), Huntington Library copy, 62145.

England: with the tragicall | *fall of proud* Mortimer.' This title uses stock
phrases from previous play texts. For instance, the anonymous *Troublesome
Raigne of Iohn King of England*, a likely source for Shakespeare's *King John*,
had been published in 1591. The phrase 'troublesome reign' obviously has
strong associations with the history genre, but it here alludes to a specific

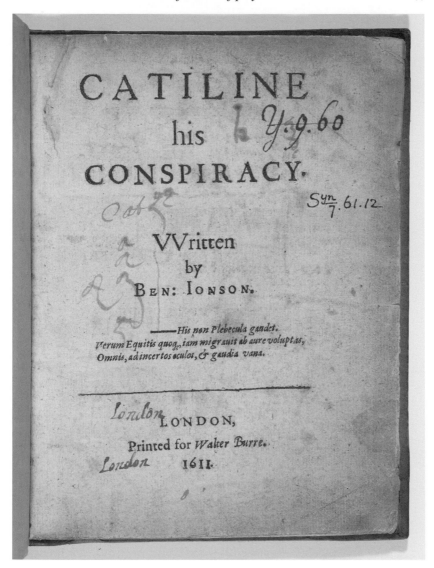

Fig. 9. Title page of *Catiline* (1611), Cambridge University Library copy, Syn.7.61.12.

play as well. Less obviously, the *Edward II* title also makes the play 'trag-icall', but again this term took up a stock position on title pages of this period for dramatic and non-dramatic texts. In fact, titles frequently mix the terms. Arthur Brooke's source text for Shakespeare's play, for instance, is *A tragicall historye of Romeus and Iuliet* (1562). Marlowe's title highlights

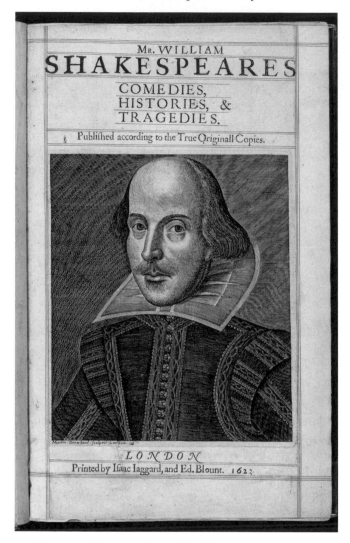

Fig. 10. Title page of Shakespeare's 1623 folio, Huntington Library copy, 56422.

how play texts from this period are chiefly concerned with generic designation.

Shakespeare's plays in the first folio are therefore not only divided by genre, but even the title of that collection (see Figure 10) reflects this overarching concern: 'Mr WILLIAM | SHAKESPEARES | COMEDIES, | HISTORIES, & | TRAGEDIES. | Published according to the True

Original Copies.' It seems that readers of play texts selected their purchases rather like some film-goers choose which films to view, based upon generic conventions. An additional similarity is the focus upon a central character, which is largely how we rename early modern histories and tragedies today: *Hamlet*, *King Lear*, or *Henry V*. What is perhaps more surprising in the case of *Edward II* is the inclusion of another character who, unlike Juliet, Cleopatra, or Cressida, is not romantically paired with the protagonist. Such doubling of character is remarkably common in play-text titles of this period, but that frequency has been elided in acts of 'modernisation'. For instance, the character of Pistol received sufficient notoriety to be an important part of the titles of the 'bad' and good quartos of *Henry V*, or, as they similarly phrase it, 'THE CRONICLE | History of Henry the fift, | With his battell fought at *Agin Court* in | *France*. Togither with *Auntient* | *Pistoll*.' Shakespeare's earlier histories receive more complex treatment. The short 1594 quarto of *Henry VI, part 2*, is originally called:

THE | First part of the Con= | tention betwixt the two famous Houses of Yorke | and Lancaster, with the death of the good Duke Humphrey: | And the banishment and death of the Duke of | *Suffolke*, and the Tragicall end of the proud Cardinall | of *Winchester*, with the notable Rebellion | of *Iacke Cade*: | *And the Duke of Yorkes first claime unto the* | *Crowne*.

This title is therefore both a partial cast list and a description of contents. Something similar applies to Shakespeare's comedies, although the propensity for his comedies to have elaborate titles is somewhat disguised by the fact that most of them were first printed in the folio, which trimmed the titles of all plays. *The Merry Wives of Windsor* (1602), which is again a 'bad' quarto, provides a good early example of a lengthy comic title:

A | Most pleasaunt and | excellent conceited Co- | medie, of *Syr Iohn Falstaffe*, and the | merrie Wiues of *Windsor*. | Entermixed with sundrie | variable and pleasing humors, of Syr *Hugh* | the Welch Knight, Iustice *Shallow*, and his | wise Cousin M. *Slender*. | With the swaggering vaine of Auncient | *Pistoll*, and Corporall *Nym*.

The adjectival insistence here is characteristic of the earlier title pages, although there are certainly exceptions, like John Lyly's *Endimion, The Man in the Moone* (1591).

Michael Hunter notes of title pages as a whole that, 'In the seventeenth century, a greater brevity in wording becomes the norm, often in conjunction with the use of pairs of rules to frame the title-page, together with rules separating its component parts' (Hunter 2007: 32). Titles for play texts also became shorter as the period progressed, and they reduced references to what today might be considered minor roles. Fletcher and Massinger's comedy, *Elder Brother A Comedy* (1637), for instance, is called just that. Other Massinger plays include *The Vnnatvrall Combat. A Tragedie* (1639) and *The Virgin Martir, A Tragedie* (1622). These short titles are characteristic of play texts in this slightly post-Shakespearean period, a move probably encouraged in part by Ben Jonson's influence. Jonson deliberately crafted minimalist title pages that therefore contained brief titles, like *Volpone Or The Foxe* (1607) or *Catiline* (1611), illustrated above. Jonson's 1616 folio, the first collected *Works* to include plays, certainly influenced the conception and design of Shakespeare's 1623 folio, which trimmed the earlier titles to much more simple forms, like *The second Part of Henry the Sixt, with the death of the Good Duke* H v M F R E Y and *The Merry Wiues of Windsor*, titles that remain current today.

Sometimes, the issue of titles is complicated by the use of half-titles, which appear on a subsequent page, usually just over the beginning of the text. Perhaps the most famous example of a clash between title and half-title appears in one of Shakespeare's non-dramatic texts, where the *Lucrece* of the title page becomes *The Rape of Lucrece* on the half-title. A less spectacular change happens to *Hamlet* (Q2), which is known as '*THE | Tragicall Historie of | HAMLET, | Prince of Denmarke*' on the title page, but becomes 'The Tragedie of | HAMLET | *Prince of Denmarke*' in the half-title. Thus it loses one of its distinguishing genres, a loss that is replicated on the headlines, an element of a play text that encourages concision.

A similar movement towards brevity relates to title page information about performance. Information about the original performing company (or companies) and theatre (or theatres) was considered an essential part of play-text title pages. Such details can be very specific, as in Lyly's *Endimion*: 'Playd before the Queenes Maiestie at Greenewich on Candlemas day at night, by the Chyldren of Paules.' A royal audience would provide a mark of esteem for a play text, and this information was frequently mentioned by publishers. *The Merry Wives of Windsor* (1602) was said to be 'Acted by the right Honorable my Lord Chamberlaines seruants. Both before her Maiestie, and else-where.' More typical are modest claims, like those for Robert Greene's *Frier Bacon, and Frier Bongay* (1594), of being, 'plaid by her Maiesties seruants' or of Marlowe's *D. Faustus* (1604), '*As it hath bene Acted by the Right Honorable the Earle of Nottingham his seruants.*' In other cases, plays are shown to have been performed in several different professional contexts. For instance, *Titus Andronicus* Q1 (1594) was said to be, 'Plaide by the Right Honourable the Earle of *Darbie*, Earle of *Pembrooke*, and Earle of *Sussex* their Seruants.' On the other hand, playing information could be vague, as in *The Spanish Tragedy* (1602) title page illustrated above, where the play is said to have, 'of late been diuers times acted'. The insistence that a play *was* performed also highlights a sense that play texts are for reading and not primarily to be used as scripts for future performance. If such information is missing or vague, it might point to the 'stolen and surreptitious' nature of the copy, as is the case with the first quarto of *Henry IV, Part 2* (1594), which does not mention a performance company or venue. Yet other 'bad' quartos, including *Henry V* (1600) and *Hamlet* (1603) do contain information about performance, and in the latter case, three performance venues are mentioned: 'the Cittie of London: as also in the two Vniuersities of Cambridge and Oxford'. Performance venues were therefore important for the marketing of a given text, but they might be deployed in differing ways by different publishers. Importantly, Gabriel Egan has shown that such information might serve as marketing *for* a theatre company, because 'Around 1600–10, the front matter of printed plays began to suggest a new way of thinking about the relationship between performance and the printed book. Instead of only harking back to past performances, title-pages began to refer to ongoing performances' (Egan 2006: 102). The information about performance functioned in complex ways that validated the text for sale and the company that performed it. It also supplies important context that is often otherwise lost, such as royal attendance at a performance, which theatre companies an author was writing for, or in some cases even which theatre company performed the play. In cases of anonymous plays, it can be the only source of information about the origins of a play.

In fact, it is axiomatic to assert that the theatrical company up until around 1600 held the author function in the minds of the play-buying public much more firmly than a play's author did. Richard Helgerson argues that just such a movement from a theatre of 'players' to a theatre of 'authors' took place in the period (Helgerson 1994: 199). This situation varies markedly from author to author, but it certainly holds true for Shakespeare and many of his contemporaries. Shakespeare's name famously does not appear on his printed plays until 1598, after several quarto texts now associated with him were already in print. These include *Romeo and Juliet*, *Richard III*, and *Richard II*. In 1598, however, Shakespeare was named on *Love's Labour's Lost* and subsequent quartos of *Richard III* and *Richard II*. For an author's name to appear on a title page, at least one of two conditions must apply: he (or his advocates) brought his text to the press and insisted upon his name appearing, or he was sufficiently well known that his name would help sell the printed play. The assumption in Shakespeare studies has been that the dramatist achieved the second of these conditions around 1598. It is possible that the first condition did not apply until the negotiations towards the folio began after Shakespeare's death. Many plays from the period retain their anonymity. By far the most popular play in the period, to judge by the number of printed editions, was *Mucedorus*, which was printed thirteen times before 1642. The publishers in this period felt little need to associate the play with a particular dramatist, even though it was subsequently (erroneously) ascribed to Shakespeare.

Jonson's career contrasts strongly with that of Shakespeare. Jonson simply published what he wished to (with the exception of *The Case Is Altered* and *Eastward Ho!*, plays probably printed without his consent), and his concern with his standing as an author must have meant that he carefully policed publication. It is notable, for instance, that Jonson's name appears fairly consistently on title pages (usually as BEN: JONSON or BEN. JONSON), unlike, for instance, the various ways in which Marlowe's name appeared, 'Chri. Marlow Gent.' in *Edward II* (1594) and 'Ch. Marl.' in *Doctor Faustus* (1604). Abbreviations and initials appear frequently on the title pages of play texts. Some of them seem deliberately calculated to evoke more famous authors, who probably did not write the plays. *Guy Earl of Warwick*, for instance, was first published in 1661, as written by 'B. J.', but the play is unlikely to be Jonson's. Similarly, Thomas Middleton's *The Puritan* (1607), claims to be written by 'W. S.', even though it was also *'Acted by the Children of Paules'*, when Shakespeare was writing for the King's Men.

On the other hand, spurious or incomplete authorship attributions are rife on play-text title pages in this period. Shakespeare's apocrypha grew over time with his reputation, and by the third folio (1663) had included the additional plays *Pericles, Locrine, The London Prodigal, The Puritan, Sir John Oldcastle, Thomas Lord Cromwell*, and *A Yorkshire Tragedy*, but with the partial exception of *Pericles*, these have been considered misattributions. Most of these plays had been published earlier under Shakespeare's name, or as by 'W. S.'. Mistakes or omissions might also occur. Many of Shakespeare's collaborative efforts, like *Titus Andronicus* and *Timon of Athens*, for instance, were named as only his, possibly because their collaborative nature was not known to those who had them published. Marston's *The Malcontent* (Q3) was mistakenly labelled as: 'Augmented by Marston. With the additions played by the King's Majesty's Servants. Written by John Webster.' For many of the period's quartos, authorship attribution is either deliberately misleading, mistaken, or incomplete, and therefore this part of a title page should always be regarded with suspicion.

A usually more accurate category of information, the imprint, appears at the bottom of title pages. The imprint includes information on the publisher or printer and the date of publication, and it might include places where the book could be purchased. As M. A. Shaaber notes, an imprint 'is no doubt primarily an advertisement, but it is also a declaration of responsibility' (Shaaber 1944: 120). Any offended authorities would be able to trace a book's source with this information. It would also be in the interests of the publisher to make his or her book readily available to the buying public, and therefore the location can be very specific. *Swetnam the Woman-hater* (1620), was 'Printed for *Richard Meighen*, and are to be sold at his Shops at Saint *Clements* Church, ouer-against *Essex* House, and at *Westminster* Hall.' For the purposes of marketing, generally the publishers took precedence over the printers, so a publisher's name will often appear alone. Sometimes, however, only the printer's name is supplied, as in the case of the anonymous *The Famous Victories of Henry the Fifth* (1598), 'Printed by Thomas Creede.' However, in this case Creede was almost certainly the publisher too. Increasingly, play texts of the period supplied both printer and publisher's names, although sometimes, confusingly, one or both might be supplied as initials, as in the case of *Hamlet* Q2 (1604), 'Printed by I. R. for N. L.' (James Roberts and Nicholas Ling), or imprints might point to more complex relationships, as with Jonson's *The Alchemist* (1612): 'Printed by *Thomas Snodham*, for *Walter Burre*, and are to be sold by *Iohn Stepneth*.'

In all of these cases, it is important to preserve the distinction between 'printer' and 'publisher', as outlined in Chapter 1. Unfortunately, these distinctions are not always kept in the early modern period. Shakespeare's folio is a case in point. Its imprint simply states that the volume was, 'Printed by Isaac Iaggard, and Ed. Blount.' In fact, Isaac Jaggard printed the volume. The publishers were a partnership of William Jaggard (Isaac's father), Edward Blount, William Aspley, and John Smethwick. Therefore, not only is the imprint incomplete, it also disguises the distinction between printers and publishers, possibly because Blount was the main publisher.

Similar confusion can arise over the dating of a title page. *Hamlet* Q2, for instance, was issued with the dates 1604 and 1605. As Greg argues: 'No doubt this was connected with the practice of post-dating books printed near the end of a year' (Greg 1939–59: xxxix). Further ambiguity might emerge as the legal calendar began on 25 March, while popularly, New Year's Day was 1 January: 'Consequently from 1 January to 24 March inclusive, while most printers would be dating their books as we should now do, a few of the more learned would be dating them a year earlier'

(Greg 1939–59: xciv). Similarly, printers might supply the following year's date if they were approaching the end of the year, so that the book would appear more up-to-date.

These examples of imprint variation highlight that title-page information might be deliberately or accidentally misleading, but it is fitting to close this discussion of imprints with the most famous instances of false title pages. The 'Pavier quartos' were a collection of ten Shakespeare quartos printed by William Jaggard in 1619. As W. W. Greg in 1908 (Greg 1908), and Allan H. Stevenson (Stevenson 1951–2) substantiated with watermark evidence in 1951–2, Thomas Pavier and William Jaggard did not hold the rights to these volumes, and one or both attempted to hide their illicit printing with deliberately misleading dates. These range from *Sir John Oldcastle* (1619), said to be 'Written by William Shakespeare' and '*printed for T. P.* | 1600', with appropriate initials and a false date, to the false date and publisher for *King Lear* (1619): 'Printed for *Nathaniel Butter*. 1608.' Butter did print *King Lear* in 1608, giving cause for potential confusion, but Jaggard's forged 1619 imprint does not specify a point of sale, unlike Butter's true 1608 one. (See another Pavier title page in Figure 11.) In this context, it should be noted that Pavier did own rights to some of Shakespeare's plays in 1619, and recently Sonia Massai has shown that Pavier and Jaggard's texts do not need to be read merely as fraudulent (Massai 2007). The situation does disclose that care should be taken over imprint information, especially for play texts that have not been as fully investigated as Shakespeare's.

In addition to title, theatre company, author, and printer, some play texts from this period included other information, usually to enhance the marketing of the text. Direct statements about competing volumes (from other publishers) are the most common form of additional information. (Although illustrations also usually occur on title pages, they will be covered in more detail later in the chapter, as they can be printed elsewhere in a play text.) Marketing statements can vary from the simple to the elaborate, and like all title-page information, they cannot be taken at face value. In a truthful statement, *Hamlet* Q2 alludes to the inferior quality of Q1, by noting that the newer text is, 'Newly imprinted and enlarged to almost as much againe as it was, according to the true and perfect Coppie'. Variations on the phrase 'true and perfect copy' are fairly common, with 'copy' referring to the nature of the underlying manuscript. Fletcher's *Elder Brother* is '*Printed according to the true Copie*' (1637), for instance. A more elaborate accusation is found by the publishers of the 1661 edition of Beaumont, Fletcher, and Massinger's *The Beggar's Bush*:

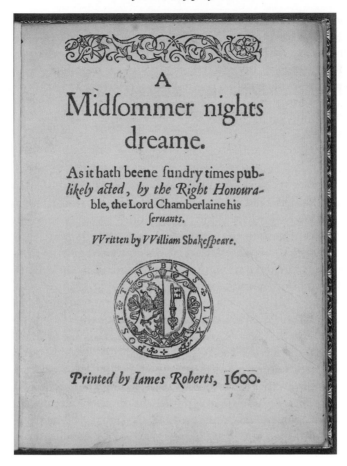

Fig. 11. The Pavier quarto of *A Midsummer Night's Dream* (1600) [1619],
Huntington Library copy, 69335.

You may speedily expect those other Playes, which *Kirkman*, and his Hawkers have
deceived the buyers withal, selling them at treble the value, that this and the rest
will be sold for, which are the onely Originall and corrected copies, as they were
first purchased by us at no mean rate, and since printed by us.

Humphrey Robinson and Anne Moseley, the publishers, here take issue
with Francis Kirkman, who in the same year had published another edition
of the play, which came out alongside several other 1661 editions of Fletcher
plays.

Title pages are one of the most difficult parts of an early modern play
text to read, because their assertions cannot be taken at face value. Every

category of information, from title to date, might include spurious details. W. W. Greg's *A Bibliography of the Early Printed Drama* (Greg 1939–59) will generally have caught misleading content, but his and others' examinations of the non-canonical plays can be cursory, which is understandable when the large number of surviving printed plays from this period is considered. But checking for further scholarship about title pages is a very important part of 'reading' them. Luckily, the other parts of play texts are not so potentially misleading.

DEDICATIONS

Dedications might contain misleading flattery, but that flattery can at least be detected with little effort. Dedications typically have three basic purposes: (1) promoting the material to readers or potential buyers; (2) seeking or substantiating patronage; (3) promoting friendship or collectives of authors. Such material is almost invariably written by the original author, the publisher, or other writers who are admirers of the author.

Shakespeare's early quartos lack dedications, and the absence of them has traditionally been the most important evidence towards assertions that he did not seek to have his plays published. Only one of Shakespeare's early quartos, the second quarto of *Troilus and Cressida* (1609), contains any kind of address to a reader or patron. Thirty-eight Shakespeare quartos had been published before the end of 1609, making his and his publishers' quantitative silence extraordinary in the light of other drama in the period. This statistic contrasts more markedly in the light of Shakespeare's treatment of his non-dramatic verse. *Lucrece* (1594) and *The Sonnets* (1609) have dedications to the Earl of Southampton and 'the only begetter' respectively. Although *Venus and Adonis* Q1 (1593) has no dedication, the second quarto (1594) is dedicated to the Earl of Southampton. A clear demarcation is therefore made between Shakespeare's play texts and his other works.

Even the *Troilus and Cressida* epistle seems mostly concerned to adjust an error made on the title page of the first quarto (1609), which had claimed that the play '*was acted by the Kings Maiesties seruants at the Globe*'. The second quarto corrected the title page and added an epistle from 'A neuer writer, to an euer reader' (¶2). The epistle attempts to sell this position by noting that the play was 'neuer clapper-clawd with the palmes of the vulger'. That this is written by someone who claims never to write suggests that it comes from the publisher. Whether or not the claims are true, the aim of the epistle is to enhance the saleability of the volume, so that the reader will see his or her 'testerne well bestowd' (¶2v). The almost accidental circumstances whereby the publisher, unaccustomed to writing to his readers, had to provide an epistle, provides the exception that proves the rule.

The paucity of dramatic dedications in Shakespeare's early play texts does not reflect the period's norms for such a prolific author. Following his death, his various friends and admirers remedied this situation by offering six dedicatory epistles, but even that number is low compared to earlier works by Jonson. *Sejanus* (1605), for instance, includes a dedication, 'To the Readers' (sig. ¶), and such addresses subsequently characterise his relationship to his audience. *Sejanus* also offers dedicatory poems from eight other poets, including George Chapman, Hugh Holland, and John Marston. Jonson's *The Alchemist* (1612) was Jonson's first printed play to seek aristocratic patronage, from Mary Lady Wroth. Nine sets of dedicatory verses are offered in Jonson's 1616 folio. Jonson, in turn, dedicated each of his major works in that volume to patrons or friends. Jonson's frequent use of such devices contrasts strongly with Shakespeare's silence.

Other dramatists in the period were much more ready than Shakespeare to address potential patrons or readers in the preliminaries of their play texts (see Parry 2002). But the frequency of such occurrences might tell us little about the dramatists that we did not already know – Jonson, for instance, is characterised by a heavy-handed relationship with his publishers and readers (Giddens 2010). Shakespeare has no relationship at all with his. Jonson's mode largely won out, and second-generation professional dramatists like Shirley frequently address potential or real patrons, even if they were not always effective in winning patronage (Parry 2002: 137).

It is important to consider such material on a case-by-case basis. The most famous dedication of the period combines the dramatists contrasted above. Jonson's dedication to 'MR. WILLIAM SHAKESEPARE: AND what he hath left vs' in the folio says as much about what Jonson expected in a dedication as it does about his views on Shakespeare. Importantly, Jonson notes that much dedicatory material is biased:

> *But these wayes*
>   *Were not the paths I meant unto thy praise:*
> *For seeliest Ignorance on these may light,*
>   *Which, when it sounds at best, but eccho's right;*
> *Or blinde Affection, which doth ne're aduance*
>   *The truth, but gropes, and urgeth all by chance;*
> *Or crafty Malice, might pretend this praise,*
>   *And thinke to ruine, where it seem'd to raise.*
> *These are, as some infamous Baud, or Whore,*
>   *Should praise a matron. What could hurt her more?*
>   (1623: A4)

This firmly Jonsonian approach to the politics of praise discloses a core problem with dedicatory material: it is biased for or against an author, or worse, it is written by those too ignorant to understand his works. Although Jonson develops several stock tropes as he goes on to praise Shakespeare, the phrases, '*He was not of an age, but for all time!*' and the '*Sweet Swan of* Auon' (A4v), have come to us as the best early criticism of Shakespeare. His disquiet with the genre reveals that even those who perfected it could regard its assertions with suspicion.

Rarely does such dedicatory material reach literary heights. More often it is doggerel verse written by poets now forgotten by history, or publishers' sales pitches. Sometimes, however, dedications give key insights into an author's attitude towards print versus playhouse audiences, as in Jonson's 'anti-theatrical prejudice', for instance, or Richard Brome's 'To the Readers – Or rather *to the Spectators*' in his *Five New Plays* (1659: A3). An author's attitude towards his contemporary dramatists, or, by its absence, an author's distance from the printed play text might equally be disclosed. Even publishers' pitches can provide (sometimes slightly erroneous) evidence about the printing history of a volume, as in Humphrey Moseley's 'The Stationer to the Readers': 'You have here a *New Booke*; I can speake it clearly; for of all this large Uolume of *Comedies* and *Tragedies*, not one, till now, was ever printed before' (Beaumont and Fletcher 1647: A4). Similarly, the fact that publishers were unlikely to comment on quarto play texts but did comment on major folio collections (including Shakespeare's and Beaumont and Fletcher's) reflects the very different values they might have placed on the two formats.

ILLUSTRATIONS

Illustrations are usually included amongst the preliminary material, and often occupy either part of the title page, or the page immediately next to the title page, to attract the would-be buyer. Such illustrations have been catalogued by R. A. Foakes in *Illustrations of the English Stage, 1580–1642* (Foakes 1985). The current chapter has so far reflected the notion that Shakespeare's early texts contain far less preliminary material than those of his contemporaries, and this maxim holds true for illustrations. But this circumstance should not lead one to conclude that illustrations in play quartos and folios are rare. In fact, there are marked distinctions in publishing illustrations, so that they are rare for Shakespeare and Jonson, and more common for slightly later authors such as Middleton.

Publishers often include illustrations that are purely decorative, and therefore have no direct relationship with the contents of the play texts. Such illustrations include printers' ornaments, devices, and initial-letter illustrations. These largely ornamental features can be reused in other books. They can therefore be useful in assisting with printer-identification, as discussed in Chapter 3.

More telling are the illustrations that were specially commissioned for a given play text. Famous early examples include those for Marlowe's *Dr Faustus* and Kyd's *The Spanish Tragedy*. What is perhaps the most striking fact about these illustrations is that they did not appear until several years after the plays were first published. Kyd's first appeared in 1615, twenty-three years after the play was published in 1592. For *Dr Faustus*, twelve years and three editions passed before it received its famous woodcut.

So the presence of bespoke illustrations might say something about the past and hoped-for popularity of a given play text, especially as such illustrations could be reused in future editions. *The Spanish Tragedy*'s woodcut accompanied the quartos of 1618, 1623 (see Figure 12), and 1633; *Dr Faustus*'s was used again in 1619, 1620, 1624, and 1631. In 1663 a new (and inferior-quality) woodcut was made, based upon the earlier design, which probably by then had been lost. In these instances, woodcuts are used to augment best-sellers (by play-text standards), as opposed to accompanying a new play. The distance of these illustrations from first performance suggests that they probably do not represent original staging. Towards the middle of the period 1580 to 1642, illustrations in play texts began to be more common, even in first editions. Thomas Heywood's *If You Know Not Me, You Know Nobody: or, The Troubles of Queen Elizabeth* was first published in 1605 with a woodcut of Elizabeth and went through several subsequent editions that retained the illustration. Samuel Rowley's *When You See Me, You Know Me* similarly has a representation of Henry VIII in its second edition of 1613, and in subsequent editions. But publishers were not always accurate in judging if a given illustration might be required again in a second edition. The anonymous *Swetnam, the Woman-hater, arrainged by women* (1620), for instance, devotes half of its title page to a woodcut of Swetnam at trial. As the play went to no further known subsequent editions, the investment in the woodcut might have been a poor one. A similarly sized illustration appears on the first quarto of Middleton's *The Roaring Girl* (1611), which also enjoyed no subsequent edition. Although Middleton's *A Fair Quarrel* (1617) was reprinted, its first edition also includes a bespoke woodcut. These examples highlight how publishers in the 1610s and 1620s were occasionally willing to invest in illustrations for first editions of

Fig. 12. Title page with wood-cut of *The Spanish Tragedy* (1623), Huntington Library
copy, 62142.

individual plays. Alan B. Farmer and Zachary Lesser's *Database of Early
English Playbooks* (Farmer and Lesser 2007–10) discloses that between 1580
and 1641, 108 play texts printed some form of illustration (other than
printer's ornaments). Of those, only eleven appeared before 1605, and only
forty appeared before 1620. Therefore, a marked rise in the illustration of
play texts took place towards the final third of this period. Yet it is difficult
to draw too many conclusions from this fact. Illustrations might highlight
an increased significance for play texts in the eyes of publishers. Clearly,
it cost extra to have an illustration produced, but the exact extent of that
cost is not known. A publisher might expect to keep a stock of a given play

text for several years, and perhaps illustrations helped to move that stock a little more quickly.

Such illustrations are suggestive in the history of the economics of publishing plays. They also disclose how plays might have been rendered as reconstructions of performance for a reader's imagination. But they probably do not provide an accurate picture of a real performance, and in fact many represent several separate moments from a play. Stephen Orgel notes of this composite style of illustration that 'The sources of this kind of representation are images that, however dramatic, have no connection with plays or theater' (Orgel 2006: 28). The illustration for *Dr Faustus*, for instance, depicts a stage devil of a kind that would be very difficult to re-enact, because it is smaller than even a child actor. It is also clear from the illustration for *The Spanish Tragedy*, which includes speech 'bubbles', that the craftsman responsible for a given illustration might not be familiar with the actual words of the play. Therefore, the connection between early modern visual representations and the play texts that contain them is not always strong.

Although play quartos were less likely to receive illustrations in their initial editions, collections of plays in folio or octavo usually did have a portrait of the author, or other illustration. The first of these collections, the 1616 folio of Jonson, includes an illustrated title page that frames the works with classical symbols, particularly in the representation of comedy and tragedy, and the Coliseum. (See Figure 13.) The engraved title page survives in three distinct states, suggesting that Stansby, Jonson's publisher, was willing to invest considerable attention to getting it right (see Riddell 1986). (In this context, it should be noted that Robert Vaughan's later engraved portrait of Jonson often appears in this and other of his folios, but it was added to them subsequently.) Following Jonson's pioneering collection, Shakespeare's folio includes the famous Droeshout portrait, again in several different states. The 1640s and 1650s were the great age for collections of plays, probably because the public theatres were closed by Parliament and therefore print was one of the few ways to experience drama. Subsequent collections by Beaumont and Fletcher (1647), Richard Brome (1653), and James Shirley (1652–3) all included illustrations. Humphrey Moseley was behind these collections, and all contain author portraits as their illustrations. In these texts, the frontispieces helped to justify the price of larger collections. The poem 'To the Stationer' in the Beaumont and Fletcher folio claims that '*The Frontis-piece will satisfie the wise* | *And good so well, they will not grudge the price*' (1647: a1). Moseley himself saw the

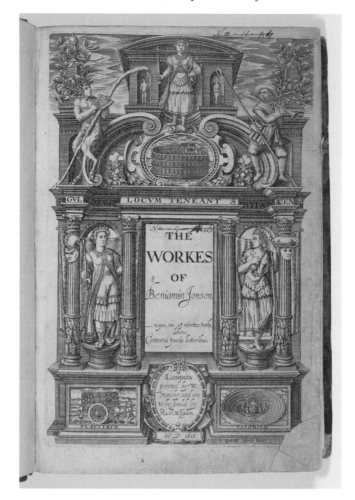

Fig. 13. Title page of Ben Jonson's folio *Workes* (1616), Cambridge University Library, Syn.4.61.19.

author portraits as essential to the shape of the volumes. His Beaumont and Fletcher contained only the portrait of Fletcher, and he noted that:

I was very ambitious to have got Mr. *Beaumonts* picture; but could not possibly, though I spared no enquirie in those *Noble Families* whence he was descended... This figure of Mr. *Fletcher* was cut by severall Originall Pieces, which his friends lent me, but withal they tell me, that his unimitable Soule did shine through his countenance in such *Ayre* and *Sprit*, that the Painters confessed it, was not easie to express him: As much as could be, you have here, and the *Graver* hath done his part ('The Stationer to the Readers', A4v).

That Moseley devotes so much attention to the portraiture of this volume is telling. By the 1640s, if not earlier, it was an essential part of the textual reproduction of a dramatic canon. This movement probably explains why Jonson's portrait was so often subsequently appended to his works.

From decorative title-page borders to newly commissioned scenic illustrations and author portraits, the history of early play-text illustration is perhaps most striking in its rarity. Shakespeare produced his works in a period in which drama illustration was rare, so it is unsurprising to find that there are no printed illustrations of his plays. (The Peacham Drawing, a manuscript sketch relating to *Titus Andronicus*, does survive in the collection of Longleat House.) Where illustrations do survive, they tell us more about the marketing of play texts than about how they might have been staged. That author portraits replaced composite representations of action also says much about how authority moved from the theatres to the dramatists in this period.

DRAMATIS PERSONAE

After the preliminary title page and dedicatory material, the next element a reader might expect to encounter is the dramatis personae, which might be called a list of characters or actors or 'persons' of the play. So far, this discussion of preliminary material, such as dedications or illustrations, has shown that the incidence of such material increased over the period. That pattern does not apply to lists of characters. Early plays tended to include cast lists, yet plays in the period 1590–1600 did so less frequently. Farmer and Lesser's *Database of Early English Playbooks* (Farmer and Lesser 2007–10) discloses that eighty-six play texts printed before 1590 included character lists. Only seventeen did in the 1590s. Intriguingly, none of Shakespeare's early quartos include cast lists. In keeping with the general rule that Shakespeare's texts are more stripped down than those of his contemporaries, the contents invariably jump from title page directly to the opening of the play.

In addition to distinctions between play texts that have or do not have character lists, there are wide varieties of practice in the format and contents of such lists, and some plays without them include lists of actors instead. Early character lists are often more informative than later ones. Not only do they include all of the characters (albeit small in number), but they also frequently offer information about the doubling of roles, essential to efficient amateur or professional performance. John Pickering's *Horestes* (1567), for instance, includes 'The players names' on the title page, a not-unusual location in this pre-Shakespearean period. But more interesting is the lower section of the title page, which gives 'The names deuided for vi. to playe', outlining how six experienced actors could take on the surprisingly heavy load of twenty-five parts. *Cambises* (1570) includes a tabular cast list that is broken down into parts for eight actors. Such division of parts implies that amateur performers would wish to re-enact these professional plays. Further, as they appear on the title pages, these casting charts suggest that the principal purpose of the plays is to be theatrical scripts, as opposed to reading texts.

The sense that play texts are for future performance soon gives way to a sense that they represent a past production, as the analysis of later title pages shows above. This reflection of a past and closed event becomes most apparent in texts that supply lists of the actors who performed in the 'original' theatrical context. Actor lists emerge with Jonson's *Hymenaei* (1606), Thomas Campion's *Masque at Lord Hay's Marriage* (1607), and Jonson's *Masque of Blackness* and *Masque of Beauty* (1608). Two facts are telling here: (1) actors' names are associated with the masque genre; (2) Jonson inaugurated the practice. Masques were written for specific occasions as court entertainments. They usually had amateur participants from the court as dancers, so they are specifically tied to a single event. Play texts did not print actors' names until Jonson's 1616 folio. Jonson's lists, which are placed at the end of the plays and in two instances name Shakespeare as an actor, offer a sense that the performance history of the play is in the past. Therefore, he textually closes off the possibility of future staging, in keeping with Jonson's overall sense of the primacy of print. It is nonetheless somewhat surprising that Jonson refers at all to staging history, as he had been at pains in earlier publications to erase the performance text. *Every Man Out of His Humour* (1600), for instance, is printed '*Containing more than hath been Publickely Spoken or Acted*'. Shakespeare's 1623 folio also includes a list of actors, which fits its place as a memorial volume to a dead dramatist put together by his former theatrical colleagues.

Despite Jonson's anti-theatrical prejudice, some of his early quartos also contain an innovative set of character descriptions. In *Every Man Out* (1600), after printing 'The names of the Actors', which is actually the names of the roles, he devotes four pages to what he calls the 'Character' of these parts (Aiii). These characters deserve fuller attention, as they provide background information that describes more than what might be immediately perceived by the original audiences. For instance, the character Fastidius Brisk is:

A Neat, spruce, affecting Courtier, one that weares clothes well, and in Fashion; *practiseth by his glasse how to salute; speakes good Remnants (not withstanding the* Base-violl *and* Tabacco:*) swears tersely, and with varietie, cares not what Ladies fauor he belies, or great mans familiaritie: a good propertie to perfume the boot of a Coach. He will borrow another mans Horse to praise, and backs him as his own. Or for a need on foot can post himselfe into credite with his Merchant, only with the Gingle of his spurre, and the Ierke of his Wand.* (Aiiiv)

This description provides some staging clues, with Brisk almost certainly being well dressed and spurred, for instance. Yet it also adopts a novelistic, narrative approach that would be difficult to mimic in a dramatic representation of the character. Jonson here mixes genres, with the 'character' or brief satirical sketch of a social type appearing alongside a standard dramatis personae. The approach nicely fits his new comedy of humours, a genre marked by character types afflicted with humoral imbalance. Jonson's intervention on cast lists as character descriptions continues further into his career, up until *The New Inn* of 1631.

More traditional lists of characters are found in the works of other dramatists, with the doubling charts, named actors, and character sketches as outlined above being more unusual interventions. Standard character lists appeared on title pages in early play texts, like *Queen Hester* (1561), which provides a simple list of 'The names of the players'. Slightly more elaborate lists might give some further information beyond their names. On the title page of *Jacob and Esau* (1568), brief descriptions are given, such as 'Isaac, an olde man, father to Jacob & Esau' or 'Zethar a neighbour'. Such relationship descriptors became a standard feature of cast lists, and the format survives today in modernised editions, including those that are based upon plays, like Shakespeare's, that initially have no list of characters. Another convention that can survive is the placement of female roles in a separate space at the bottom of the cast list. Although this convention was common, it was also frequently ignored. Doll Common is the third named character in Jonson's *The Alchemist*, for instance. Shirley's *Six New Plays* deploys a mixed mode, whereby *The Cardinal*, *The Sisters*, and *The Imposture* separate female parts from the male ones above them with a blank line. The other three plays in the volume mix male and female roles. (This is one of many distinctions that point to two printers at work on the volume.)

It is difficult to determine who might have had responsibility for preparing dramatis personae. Play texts heavily influenced by their authors, like those of Jonson, Marston, and Shirley, are more likely to include such lists. The plays of Shakespeare and Marlowe, on the other hand, do not often contain cast lists, although Marlowe's *Dido, Queen of Carthage* (1594), in a fairly old-fashioned way, does list the 'Actors' (i.e., characters) on the title page. Plays with lists of characters are potentially suggestive of authorial manuscript sources. However, that evidence is indicative only. Webster's *The White Devil* (1612), for instance, does not include dramatis personae, but it clearly discloses other evidence of the author's involvement in the play's publication.

Over time, it seems that dramatis personae became an expected part of a play text. Many exemplars from the period have the names of characters written in manuscript on the back of the title page. The Huntington Library copy of Shirley's *The Example*, for instance, includes a cast list, which was, unusually for Shirley, omitted in the printing of this play. Such additions might reflect changing expectations. What is clear is that cast lists were increasingly provided in the seventeenth century. According to Farmer and Lesser's *Database of Early English Playbooks* (Farmer and Lesser 2007–10), seventeen of the thirty-five plays printed in 1630 had them. Only three of twenty-two did in 1600, and that figure is skewed because it reflects three different imprints of Jonson's *Every Man Out of His Humour*. Such lists enable a reader to understand character in ways that are unnecessary on stage, where such relationships can be established through action, and point to an increased concern for the reader's experience of the theatre of the mind, instead of recording a past theatrical event.

Yet because such lists were part of adjusting the play text towards publication, a process subject to mistakes, they are often inaccurate or incomplete. Such inaccuracies are usually minor. For instance, Jonson's *The Sad Shepherd* (1641) leaves out various woodmen and servants. But the play also neglects the first character to appear, the speaker of the prologue, which seems like a more significant omission. So too, Shakespeare's folio of 1623 includes character lists for some of the plays, although it is difficult to say if this is an intervention by the publisher, Shakespeare's fellow actors, or a scribe, like Ralph Crane. Interestingly, these lists are placed at the ends of the plays, as the lists of actors were in Jonson's folio, so in part they seem to be motivated by concerns to mimic Jonson's important precedent. The practice is surprisingly mixed, however, with a handful of plays receiving brief lists, and *Henry IV, part 2* receiving a full folio page for its characters. Because they are of uncertain origin, it is difficult to determine how much authority can be associated with them. For instance, Caliban is described as '*a saluage and deformed slaue*' in *The Tempest* (1623: B4). More intriguingly, Falstaff and his party in *Henry IV, part 2* are called 'Irregular Humorists' (unsigned leaf before h1). It is probably best to view these characterisations as early *responses to* the plays, rather than as having any further authority.

Dramatis personae went through several transformations in this period. Originally used as fairly accurate aids to future performance, they became less common, and less accurate, through the middle of the period. Finally they become characteristic of a movement in play texts towards assisting readers with more effective frameworks of plot and character – much as they serve this function in student editions today.

ARGUMENTS AND SCENES

Arguments are effectively plot summaries or brief synopses of the action. Scenes are indications of location. Although they serve quite different functions, they are discussed together here because they often occupy a similar space within play texts.

Although plots or 'plats' were used by theatrical companies, as discussed in Chapter 1, they usually did not accompany play texts to print. Plays influenced by classical drama, however, were more likely to include synopses, perhaps because such plays were printed for their literary merit. Mary Herbert's *Antonius* (1592), Thomas Kyd's *Cornelia* (1594), and Samuel Daniel's *Cleopatra* (1594), are examples of dramatic translations that include arguments, or brief prose plot outlines. Marston's *Dutch Courtesan* (1605) is a public-theatre play that includes an argument for readers. In this case, however, it is more of a 'moral' than a plot summary: '*The difference betwixt the loue of a Curtezan, & a wife, is the full scope of the Play, which intermixed with the deceits of a wittie Citie Iester, fils up the Comedie*' (A2). Although more elaborate arguments for public-theatre plays were rare, Jonson specialised in them. The acrostic arguments for *Volpone* (1607) and *The Alchemist* (1612) demonstrate the care he was willing to give to such devices, but they, like Marston's, are fairly vague and do not give much of the plot away. However, a surprise ending is given away in Jonson's *New Inn* (1631), which devotes nine-and-a-half pages to the argument. Moreover, Jonson ends his 'Dedication, to the Reader' with 'Read | Ben. Ionson. | But, first | *The Argument*' (*3). This somewhat ambiguous set of instructions seems to insist that the reader consider the argument before the play. As *The New Inn* is perhaps second only to *Epicene* in terms of the shock of its surprise ending, such insistence seems to negate much of the effect of the play. As a recent editor notes, 'In light of the surprising twists in Act 5, readers unfamiliar with the plot of *The New Inn* are advised not to continue reading this introduction, but to read the play first' (Kidnie 2000a: xxv).

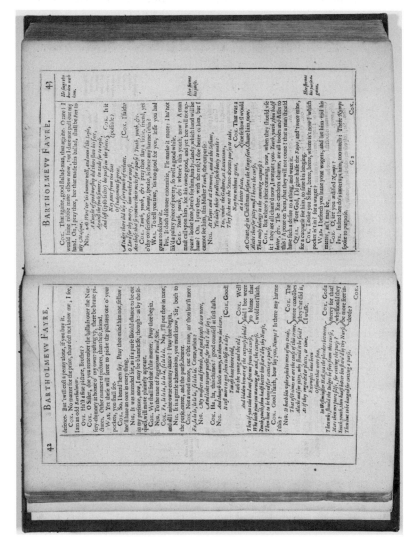

Fig. 14. An opening from Jonson's *Bartholomew Fair* (1631), Cambridge University Library, copy Syn.4.64.15.

Scenes, like arguments, are fairly rare in Shakespearean play texts, in part because, like arguments, they are not needed in dramatic performance. The public and private stages of the period relied on little or no scenery, so location is almost invariably conveyed in dialogue. For instance, the opening exchange between Barnardo and Francisco in *Hamlet* is shaped to convey the time and season:

Fran. You come most carefully vpon your houre.
Bar. 'Tis now strook twelue, get thee to bed *Francisco.*
Fran. For this releefe much thankes: 'Tis bitter cold . . .
(1623: nn4v)

Some play texts offer a brief additional notice of the overall location. The full titles of *Hamlet* and *Othello* convey the locations, of course, but other plays are less straightforward. Shakespeare's *The Tempest* (1623), for instance, offers the note: 'The Scene, an vn-inhabited Island' (B4). *Measure for Measure* has '*The Scene Vienna*' (1623: G6v). Jonson's *Sad Shepherd* notes that 'The Scene is *Sher-wood*' (1641: R2). Such locations are largely unnecessary, but they later were seen as helpful information for readers, so that editors frequently added the information scene-by-scene, either as part of the text or as a note. Such detail is now largely dropped in modernised editions, as the approach ignores the scenic imagination required by the original audiences and readers.

ACT AND SCENE DIVISIONS

Most play texts from the Shakespearean period do not print the kinds of preliminary materials outlined above, and instead start with the dramatic action. In many cases, that starting point is an opening stage direction, but often a play text starts with Act I, Scene I, or some derivative of that division. Shakespeare's folio, for instance, opens with *The Tempest*, and that play begins at '*Actus primus, Scena prima*'. Yet the five-act structures imposed by the folio do not necessarily reflect original staging divisions. Shakespeare's *Henry VI, part 2* (1594) includes no act or scene divisions. And such neglect does not apply only to 'bad' quartos. Marlowe's *Edward II* (1594) does not have them either. Scenic form in the public playhouses, where these plays were first staged, was fluid. There was no way of formally separating scenes, except for the fact that the stage might have been briefly emptied between them. Act divisions were introduced theatrically in the private, indoor playhouses, when brief non-playing time was required to ensure that the candles were trimmed. Therefore, one might expect that

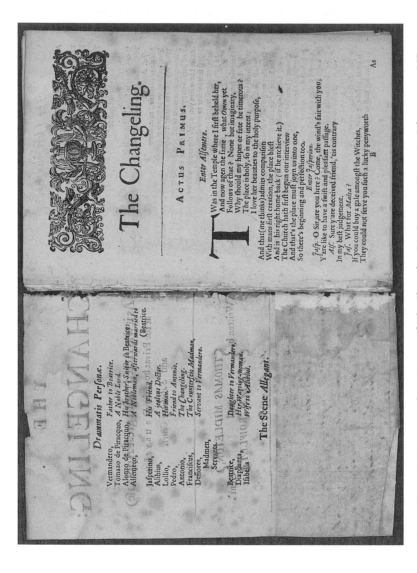

Fig. 15. Dramatis Personae and opening act of *The Changeling* (1653), Meisei University Library copy, MR1050.

only plays with private-playhouse origins would include act divisions. Yet from the beginning of the period, play texts included them frequently. W. W. Greg in 1928 examined 'the extent to which act-divisions are marked in the printed plays of the period' (Greg 1928: 152), and he found that 'under 50, actually about 46.5 per cent' of plays printed from 1590 to 1610 were so divided (156). But when he removed the children's plays from these tallies, he found 19 out of 102 plays with act divisions (157). As Greg concludes 'The data . . . point quite clearly to the fact that, as a general rule, the prompt-books of plays performed by children's companies at private theatres were divided into acts, and that the prompt-books of the plays performed by men's companies at public theatres were not' (158). Therefore it is unsurprising that Shakespeare's plays published before 1610 contain no act divisions, as those plays were probably written for public theatres. Gary Taylor's later research has shown that act divisions became increasingly important in the adult companies, so that they all had adopted them by around 1616 (Taylor 1993). (For a printed act division, see Figure 15.)

Greg notes that Jonson is an exception, as he studiously divides his plays of whatever theatrical auspices into acts (with the exception of the unauthorised *Case is Altered* (1609), which is only partially divided). Jonson's 1616 folio also divides all of its plays in this way, which perhaps explains why Shakespeare's 1623 folio generally attempts act divisions. Once again, those organising Shakespeare's volume might be mimicking Jonson's famous precedent. Yet the patterns of division in Shakespeare's folio arc highly confused. As Stanley Wells notes:

In the Folio, six plays are undivided; *Hamlet* is only partially divided; eleven plays are divided into acts only; the remaining eighteen are divided into acts and scenes. Some of the divided plays are ones which had been printed without divisions in quarto. (Wells 2005: 'act-and-scene divisions')

Although the folio is more consistent in attempting act divisions than dramatis personae, it remains enigmatic in its choices. *The Comedy of Errors*, for instance, is divided into: (1) *Actus primus, Scena prima*; (2) *Actus Secundus*; (3) *Actus Tertius. Scena Prima*; (4) *Actus Quartus. Scoena Prima*; and 5) *Actus Quintus. Scoena Prima*. In other words, it has act divisions, but no meaningful scene divisions. But the inclusion of scenes with four of the acts points to some confusion about how the play should be divided. The play that follows, *Much Ado about Nothing*, mentions a scene in the first act division, but from that point the folio gives up on formal scene divisions for the play. In all likelihood, the act divisions for most of the folio plays have no theatrical authority. Some might derive from scribal practice. Ioppolo notes of theatrical manuscripts of the period that: 'While many of Shakespeare's texts evidently printed from foul papers lack act and scene notations, it is not uncommon for dramatists of this period to use them sparingly or occasionally, often letting them drop as the play progresses' (Ioppolo 2006: 90). It is therefore possible that errors in act or scene divisions derive from early stages of composition, too. Wherever such divisions might derive within a theatrical manuscript, there certainly was no consistent approach to regularisation. The compositor of the opening of *Troilus and Cressida* set '*Actus Primus. Scoena Prima.*', but no other divisions follow. *Hamlet* stops at Act 2, Scene 2. Clearly, not much care was devoted to printing consistent divisions.

The folio provides a good model for understanding potential problems with act and scene divisions in the period. Although Greg correctly identifies some neatness in the practices of plays printed from 1590 to 1610, texts frequently disclose confusion. Scenes would flow into each other in public-playhouse dramatic structure, yet that structure is not always perfectly preserved in play texts. There is also some differentiation in what constituted a printed play-text scene in this period. For Shakespeare's folio, at least in the more structured plays, a new scene seems to start with the clearance of the stage. For Jonson's folio, however, a different scenic structure was applied. New scenes in that volume generally start when there is a significant entry, even if other characters remain on stage. Such variations in early printed act and scene divisions mean that they must be carefully negotiated. Modernised editions almost invariably disguise this looseness through regularisation.

STAGE DIRECTIONS

All of the above parts of a play text, where present, are effectively ephemeral to the play as conceived for the theatre. No one seeing the play on stage in the period would receive any of that information, except perhaps the title. But the play itself would open with the entry of one or more actors, therefore play texts must include just such an entry direction. This section will briefly look at stage directions as a component of the *mise-en-page*. Chapters 3 and 4 will consider them in more depth, especially in the light of potential understanding (and misunderstanding) of dramatic action.

Essentially, stage directions give occasion to difficulties similar to those caused with act and scene divisions. Directions were frequently omitted and sometimes misplaced. Theatrical manuscripts disclose that stage directions could be added after the play has been written in draft, and on these occasions there might not be much room in the manuscript for the insertions (Ioppolo 2006: 90). Such marginal or inter-linear additions might prove difficult for a printing-house compositor to read or locate, giving occasion to directions that are not placed correctly.

Printing houses, however, typically follow a fairly narrow range of options for the placement and typography of stage directions. (For a variety of brief stage directions, see Figure 16.) Directions are distinguished typographically with italics or, more rarely, small capitals. Entry directions are usually centred. The opening of the second quarto of *Hamlet* (1604) is typical:

Enter Barnardo, and Francisco, two Centinels.
(B1)

Other entry directions are similarly centred and in italics in the play. Exit directions are usually flush right in the period's play texts, and again *Hamlet* Q2 is typical:

Fran. Barnardo hath my place; giue you good night.   *Exit Fran.*
(B1)

Such directions would be located at the end of a line of dialogue, if space permitted.

The range of material that might be set in italic, including speech headings, character names, and exit directions, points to possible sources of compositor confusion, whereby it might be difficult to separate directions from other elements of the play. Later in this scene, for instance, the direction '*The cocke crowes*' is given (B3). In this case, the direction is placed in the margin, so it is clearly separated from dialogue, as that category of action might easily be confused with a character's lines. Marginal stage directions might be less likely to be confused with text, but they could give rise to ambiguity of placement. In *The Malcontent* Q1 (1604), for instance, an exit direction extends over two marginal lines, corresponding with two lines of dialogue:

Piet. Not: the best of rest, good night.   *Exit Pietro with*
Aur. Despight goe with thee.   *other Courtiers.*
(D3)

There is therefore a question as to whether the courtiers exit before Aurelia's jibe or are on stage to hear it. Modernised editions, which rarely print stage directions in the margins, make such stage time more linear. In *English Renaissance Drama: A Norton Anthology*, edited by David Bevington *et al.*

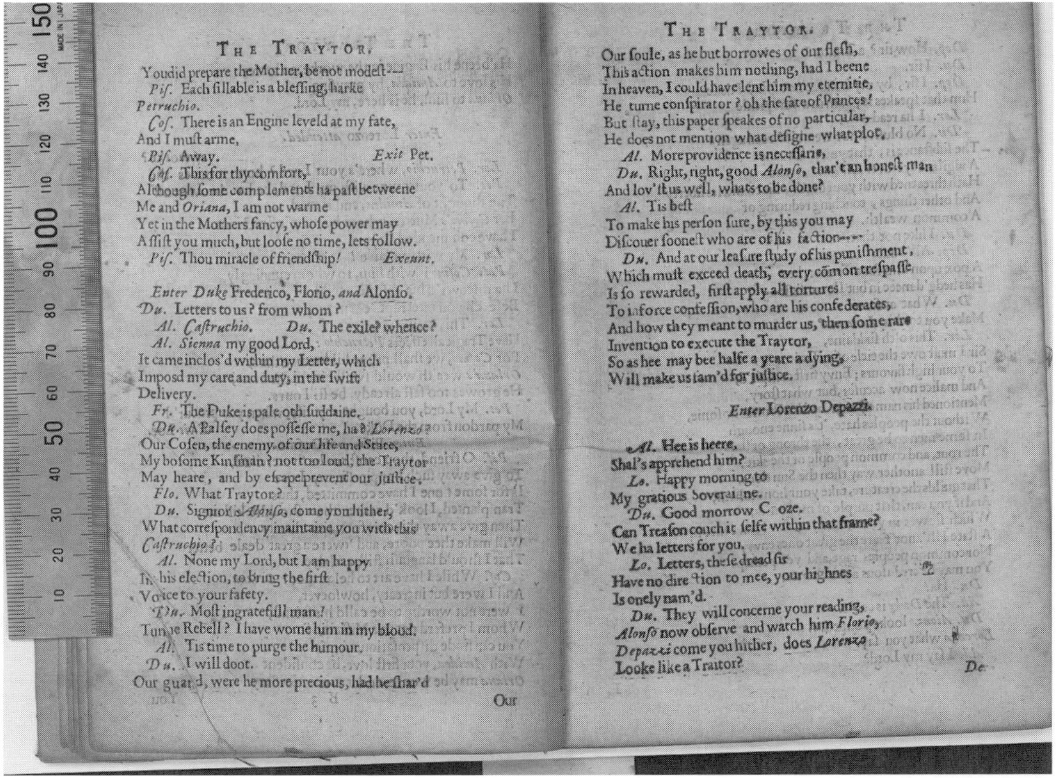

THE TRAYTOR.

You did prepare the Mother, be not modest---
Pis. Each syllable is a blessing, harke
Petruchio.
Cos. There is an Engine leveld at my fate,
And I must arme,
Pis. Away. *Exit* Pet.
Cos. This for thy comfort,
Although some complements ha past betweene
Me and *Oriana*, I am not warme
Yet in the Mothers fancy, whose power may
Assist you much, but loose no time, lets follow.
Pis. Thou miracle of friendship! *Exeunt.*

Enter Duke Frederico, Florio, *and* Alonso.
Du. Letters to us? from whom?
Al. Castruchio. *Du.* The exile? whence?
Al. Sienna my good Lord,
It came inclos'd within my Letter, which
Imposd my care and duty, in the swift
Delivery.
Fr. The Duke is pale oth suddaine.
Du. A Palsey does possesse me, ha? *Lorenzo*?
Our Cosen, the enemy of our life and State,
My bosome Kinsman? not too loud, the Traytor
May heare, and by escape prevent our justice.
Flo. What Traytor?
Du. Signior *Alonso*, come you hither,
What correspondency maintaine you with this
Castruchio?
Al. None my Lord, but I am happy
In his election, to bring the first
Voice to your safety.
Du. Most ingratefull man!
Turne Rebell? I have worne him in my blood.
Al. Tis time to purge the humour.
Du. I will doot.
Our guard, were he more precious, had he shar'd
Our

THE TRAYTOR.

Our soule, as he but borrowes of our flesh,
This action makes him nothing, had I beene
In heaven, I could have lent him my eternitie,
He turne conspirator? oh the fate of Princes!
But stay, this paper speakes of no particular,
He does not mention what designe what plot.
Al. More providence is necessarie,
Du. Right, right, good *Alonso*, that's an honest man
And lov'st us well, whats to be done?
Al. Tis best
To make his person sure, by this you may
Discover soonest who are of his faction---
Du. And at our leasure study of his punishment,
Which must exceed death, every common trespasse
Is so rewarded, first apply all tortures
To inforce confession, who are his confederates,
And how they meant to murder us, then some rare
Invention to execute the Traytor,
So as hee may bee halfe a yeare a dying,
Will make us fam'd for justice.

Enter Lorenzo Depazzi.

Al. Hee is heere,
Shal's apprehend him?
Lo. Happy morning to
My gratious Soveraigne.
Du. Good morrow Coze.
Can Treason couch it selfe within that frame?
We ha letters for you.
Lo. Letters, these dread Sir
Have no direction to mee, your highnes
Is onely nam'd.
Du. They will concerne your reading,
Alonso now observe and watch him *Florio*,
Depazzi come you hither, does *Lorenzo*
Looke like a Traitor?
De-

Fig. 16. Unmarked scene transition from James Shirley's *The Traitor* (1635), Meisei University Library copy, MR3091.

(Bevington *et al.* 2002), for instance, the editors place the exit before Aurelia's line. In the early play texts, exits and entrances can be imagined to take a span of time, instead of a moment before or after a given line of dialogue. Holger Schott Syme notes that: 'The modern page suggests a progressive relationship between speech and action alien to the stage, whereas the 1604 arrangement places dialogue and movement in juxtaposition, so that they occur simultaneously, as they would on stage' (Syme 1998: 152). Similarly, stage directions can work in proleptic ways that predict future action, as in *The Malcontent* Q1: '*enter Mendozo with his sworde drawne standing ready to murder Ferneze as he flies from the Dutches chamber*' (D2v). However, ambiguity of placement can also give occasion to irreconcilable difficulties. In the final act of *The Malcontent*, when Malevole pretends to die, the stage direction 'Starts vp and speakes' is given in the margin five lines after he has already started to speak (H2). Here the direction is both unnecessary and misplaced. A modernised edition could omit it to little detrimental effect, but the more common response to such situations would be to move a direction to a more appropriate location. Infrequently, play texts give precise indications of where a stage direction should be placed. For instance, *The Malcontent* uses asterisks on B1 and B2v to pinpoint the locations of marginal stage directions. These might derive from places in Marston's manuscript where he inserted the directions and used the asterisks as indications of marginal insertion.

The absence or ambiguity of stage directions in printed play texts might paradoxically relate to derivation from theatrical manuscripts. In this period, the only essential directions in a theatrical manuscript were those associated with entrances. Actors once on stage could be presumed to know what they were doing, and when to leave. Exit directions are also usually provided, but not always. As Antony Hammond notes, theatrical manuscripts of plays offered directions largely for the prompter's benefit: '. . . what an actor did on stage was his professional business, and was out of the prompter's control anyway' (Hammond 1992: 79). A modern editor of a typical play text will add stage directions, in part because contemporary readers need them much more than early modern actors did. Play texts prepared by authors for the page might have divergent approaches to stage directions, as they negotiate differences between the performance and printed text. For instance, Jonson pared down his directions in *Sejanus* (1605), so that rarely do they include anything but the names of entering characters. The opening direction, for instance, is: 'SABINVS. SILIVS. NATTA. LATIARIS. CORDVS. SATRIVS. ARRVNTIVS. EVDEMVS. HATERIVS. &c' (B1). Here the classicism of the spare style takes

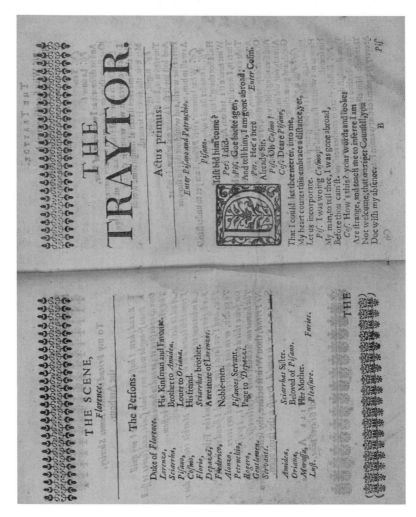

The left page:

THE SCENE,

Florence.

The Perfons.

Duke of *Florence.*
Lorenzo,   His Kinfman and Favorite.
Sciarrha,   Brother to *Amidea.*
Pifano,   Lover to *Oriana.*
Cofmo,   His friend.
Florio,   Sciarrha's brother.
Depazzi,   A creature of *Lorenzos.*
Frederico,
Alonzo,   Noble-men.
Petruchio,
Rogero,   Pifanoes Servant.
Gentlemen,   Page to *Depazzi.*
Servants.

Amidea,   Sciarrhas Sister.
Oriana,   Beloved of *Pifano.*
Moralfa,   Her Mother.
Luft.   Pleafure.   Furies.

THE

The right page:

THE
TRAYTOR.

Actus primus.

Enter Pifano and Petruchio.

Pifano.
Idst bid him come?
Pet. I did.
Pif. Goe backe agen,
And tell him, I am gone abroad.
Pet. Hee's here   *Enter Cofmo.*
Already Sir.
Pif. Oh Cofmo!
Cof. Deare Pifano,
That I could lee the center, unto me,
My heart counts this embrace a diftance, yet,
Let us incorporate.
Pif. I was wiſhing Cofmo,
My man, to tell thee, I was gone abroad,
Before thou cam'ſt.
Cof. How's this? your words and lookes
Are ſtrange, and teach me to inferre I am
Not welcome, that out-ript Counſell, yea
Doe with my abſence

B

Pif.

precedence over a fully informative set of directions. The '&c' so common in directions in this play text is an example of a 'permissive' direction that would not be very helpful in the playhouse. With some minor exceptions, other forms of direction, including exit directions and those indicating other action, have been stripped from his play. One of the retained directions functions to display the playwright's learning about Roman ritual:

the *Flamen* takes of the Honey, with his finger, and tasts; then ministers to all the rest: so of the Milke, in an earthen vessel, he deales about; which done he sprinkleth, vpon the Altar, Milke; then imposeth the Honey; and kindleth his Gummes, and after censing about the Altar, placeth his Censer thereon, into which they put seuerall branches of Poppy. (K4)

This direction includes three marginal notes that outline Jonson's classical sources. It is difficult to see how this elaborate direction might have been appreciated by the Globe audiences, however. Jonson clearly removes this play from its public-stage origins, but in stripping out relevant stage directions for literary reasons he paradoxically makes the play more difficult to read. His capital stage directions are more imposing, but less informative than their italic equivalents in other plays. Directions of both kinds may be seen as a kind of framework or skeleton that supports the text of the play, but in fact such directions in early modern play texts are highly selective. (For another of Jonson's elaborate engagements with complex stage action, see Figure 14.) At all points in a play some form of action is taking place. For most play texts, surviving directions merely mark what actions needed to be recorded for the play to be performed by professionals who worked together regularly. Mostly, these directions are positioned at the beginning of scenes to tell actors to enter – the action that followed was usually either up to them or implicit in the dialogue. (Figure 17 shows a variety of features discussed in the previous and following sections.)

SPEECH HEADINGS

Speech headings or prefixes are usually the final pre-dialogue features to be encountered in a play text. Sometime, the first lines of play texts have no speech headings, because it was conventional that the first speaker of a scene is the first character named in the entry direction. *The Alchemist*, for instance, opens with:

FACE. SVBTLE. DOL Common.
BEleeu't I will. SVB. Thy worst. I fart at thee.
DOL. Ha'you your wits? Why Gentlemen! for loue –
(1612: B1)

As Face is the first character named in the stage direction, he speaks the
opening half-line. In Marlowe's *Dr Faustus* (1604), however, there is a
repetition of entry direction and speech heading, an option equally available
to an early modern play script:

> *Enter Faustus in his Study.*
> **Faustus** Settle thy studies Faustus, and beginne
> To sound the deapth of that thou wilt professe.
>
> (A2v)

Here the speech heading is confusingly run into the text, as it is not
abbreviated nor in italics. *Dr Faustus* distinguishes speech headings by the
use of roman, as opposed to black-letter, fount. That fount distinction is
also applied to proper names within dialogue, however, thereby making
speech headings less distinct. Possible problems emerge in distinguishing
between speech headings and dialogue in the underlying manuscripts, and
these problems might be relayed to printed play texts. In the instance above,
it is clear that 'Faustus' is a speech heading because the verse that follows
is perfectly iambic pentameter. Other instances are more ambiguous. Such
ambiguity was avoided in earlier printed drama, like *Hycke Scorner* of 1550
or *Jacob and Esau* of 1568, where black-letter was used for both text and
speech headings, because the speech headings were either printed above
the text or printed in the margins. These devices survive occasionally in the
later drama, as in the early, centred speech headings of *Titus Andronicus*
Q1 (1594).

These exceptions aside, generally early modern play texts set speech
headings as italic abbreviations of three or four letters, followed by a full
stop, and in the same line as the first words spoken by a character. In
Hamlet Q2 (1604), for instance, Horatio is abbreviated to '*Hora.*' or '*Hor.*'
and Hamlet is '*Ham.*' Minor errors, like the '*Booth.*' for '*Both.*' at D4 are
fairly common in play texts of this period, but they cause few difficulties
for a reader. Sometimes speeches are more confusingly mis-assigned or
ambiguous, however. In Jonson's *The Sad Shepherd* (1641), for instance, the
brothers Scarlet and Scathlock are not well differentiated by the speech
heading '*Sca.*' (S3v, V1, V1v). Spelling mistakes might also creep into these
abbreviations. In *The Sad Shepherd*, Karolin is once abbreviated '*Car.*'
(V3), and Marian becomes '*Mor.*' (R4v). Full substitution of one character
for another might also occur. The abbreviation for Karolin ('*Kar.*'), for
instance, is clearly a mistake for Lionel at one point in the play (S3).
Such mistakes occur frequently in the play texts of the period, so that a
reader must remain alert to them. Similarly, some speech headings adopt
more complex forms. '*Ambo*' for 'both' is a common variant, as is '*All*' for

everyone on stage, but Jonson in *Poetaster* takes this convention further by naming several characters in one long speech heading:

HORA. TIBV. GALL. MECOE. VIRG. And thanks to CAESAR,
That thus hath exercis'd his patience.

(1616: Ff6)

This example again highlights potential difficulties caused when in-dialogue mentions of a character's name, in this case CAESAR, are set in the same fount as the speech headings.

More problematic is the frequency with which characters' names are changed over the course of a given play. R. B. McKerrow notes that, 'the designations of certain characters, not generally the protagonists but persons of secondary importance, vary from time to time' (McKerrow 1997: 1). He notes that in *The Comedy of Errors*, Egeon is both merchant ('*Mer.*', '*Mar.*') and later father ('*Fat.*', '*Fa.*'). The speech headings do not refer to the character by his proper name, but rather by his principal role at that point in the play. McKerrow provides an even more varied example from *Romeo and Juliet*, whereby Lady Capulet is '*Wife*', '*Old La.*', '*Capu. Wi.*', '*La.*', and '*Mo.*' (amongst other variations of these) at different points in the play (1997: 4). McKerrow goes on to suggest that such variation would be more likely to appear in an author's manuscript, highlighting what the author considers to be the principal function of the character at a given moment, but this assertion seems to have little grounding in theatre, scribal, or printing-house practices, which did not 'correct' such irregularities, and might have introduced at least some of them. As William B. Long argues:

Given the apparently very self-sufficient nature of the players on stage, the phe-nomenon of letting varying speech-heads stand in the playbooks should not be surprising. (Long 1997: 21)

Whatever the origins of this variance, it is one of the chief features that separates early modern play texts from modernised ones, which invariably regularise speech headings. Such errors disclose that speech headings were not carefully corrected and might therefore be subject to question when reading the originals or modernised versions.

Speech headings can be generally characterised as being abbreviated to save space, typographically distinct, usually in italics, and subject to change, error, and omission. Like stage directions, speech headings are made most clear when the actor concerned performs the required action, in this case speaking. They are another metatext to the play itself, an unspoken part of performance that is translated somewhat roughly to the printed page.

THE PLAY'S TEXT: VERSE AND PROSE

As the previous sections have shown, much supporting material is needed to shore up the text of a given play. Yet this material is distinct from the words as heard by the audience. Actors themselves learned only their lines and the short cues of their fellow actors. And there is some evidence that dramatists concentrated primarily on the spoken words of the play, and then added in the supporting information about speakers and staging. W. W. Greg notes of Hand D in the manuscript of *Sir Thomas More*: 'The writing is in some respects careless and impatient: speakers' names are omitted or mis-written' (Greg 1923: 45). Similarly, Jonson's composition practice seems to have included writing a play out as a prose narrative in the first instance. The content of a play might, therefore, be taken as being foremost in the minds of the authors, the actors, and the audiences. Plays are one form of literature in which the distinctions between the original encounter with the genre and subsequent readings of it are marked by a variance of hundreds of words – speech headings, cast lists, prefaces, and the like. The text itself cannot stand on its own, but must include ciphers that indicate who spoke it, and what they were doing while speaking. Therefore, a sense of an early modern play being a literary work was difficult to convey, and required the dedication of publishers (and authors like Jonson) to do so (Lesser and Stallybrass 2008).

The dialogue might open with an initial-letter illustration, or a large-fount capital, but generally little fanfare ushers in this most essential part of a play text. The conventions behind printing dialogue became well established by the Shakespearean period. Verse lines begin with capitals and prose continues justified to the right margin, much as the two are distinguished in modernised editions. Dialogue in prose or verse generally begins on the same line as the speech heading. It would be printed in roman fount as standard, except for the early exceptions printed in black-letter. Verse lines might need to be wrapped around to a new line when especially long. In Shakespeare's folio, a turnover could appear either above or below the line to which it belongs. In *The Comedy of Errors* (1623) an instance appears above (I1v) and below (H5v) the relevant line:

(stice,

E. Ant. Iustice most gracious Duke, oh grant me iu- (I1v).
Ant. Auoid then fiend, what tel'st thou me of sup-
Thou art, as you are all a sorceresse: (ping?

(H5v)

Shakespeare's folio is tightly printed in double columns, but the small fount makes such turnovers infrequent. They are almost invariably signalled with brackets as above, but occasionally they are turned over to start a new line, as in *A Midsummer Night's Dream* (1623):

Rob. When thou wak'st, with thine owne fooles eies
       peepe.   (me
Ob. Sound musick; come my Queen, take hands with
   And rocke the ground whereon these sleepers be.
                                  (O1)

Here 'peepe' is a little confusingly moved to the line below, its inclusion as verse is signalled with indentation instead of brackets. Such indented continuations also characterise Jonson's 1616 folio, but as that volume is more spaciously printed in single columns, they are rarely needed.

Clearly such turnovers are largely space-saving devices. They allow the line count from the casting off to be maintained even for slightly longer lines. Short lines cause another space dilemma for the printer. Often, short lines indicate that two or more characters are sharing a single verse 'line'. *Richard II* is entirely in verse, and includes the following exchange:

Aum. My Liege, one word.
Rich. He does me double wrong,
   That wounds me with the flatteries of his tongue.
                        (1623: c6)

Aumerle's half-line of four syllables matches Richard's initial half-line of six to form a regular iambic pentameter line. Most modernised editions would show this relationship more clearly, as follows:

AUMERLE My liege, one word.
RICHARD   He does me double wrong...

Such offsetting was 'exceedingly rare' in early play texts (Greg 1939–59: clx). But such half lines might also be run together into a single line with two or more speech headings. This approach is used in several of Jonson's play texts. For instance, *Sejanus* (1605) prints an exchange between Pomponius, Terentius, Cotta, and Trio as follows:

POM. Is not my Lord here? TER. Sir, he will be straight.
COT. What newes *Fulcinius Trio*? TRI. Good, good tidings.
                        (L3)

This forced set of iambic pentameter lines is run together, enhancing the sense of poetry, as opposed to dramatic dialogue. Jonson's strategy could break down when even more speaker-changes are required:

TIB. Whence are these Letters? HAT from the *Senate.* TIB So.
      Whence these? LA. From thence too. TI. Are they sitting now?
                                                                    (C2)

These lines barely fit into the rule width, so the compositor had to both cram them in and change the speech headings, and remove full stops from two of them.

   Prose presents fewer problems, as text is simply justified right. Justification would have increased the work of the compositors, however, as spaces would need to be inserted, or spellings changed, to condense or fill out the line. Hyphenating words at the ends of lines was an expedient way of keeping them to length. Lyly's elaborate prose in *Endymion* (1591) frequently received this treatment, as in:

      Tellus Vnhappie Tellus, whose desires are so des-
perate, that they are neither to be conceiued of any creature, nor to be cured by any arte.
                                                                    (C2)

This speech would have fitted onto three lines without hyphenation, but the hyphens offered the compositor a convenient way to justify the line. Such breaks might occur at alienating points in a word, as in 'creature' above (possibly pronounced with three syllables), or 'va- | liant' (E2v) or 'accu- | stomed' (E4). Usually, however, breaks are made between syllables as they would be today. Prose can also lead to difficulties in casting off, as line-widths would be more difficult to calculate in prose sections of play manuscripts. For instance, the very cramped final page of the folio *Much Ado about Nothing* (1623: L1) probably points to poor casting off, and that play has a high proportion of prose.

   A final issue to consider in the dialogue of play texts is the use of special typography. Usually this is limited to italics. *Hamlet* in the first folio (1623) makes use of italics for three different types of dialogue: letters, songs, and the play within the play (albeit only for three lines). Proper nouns, largely character or classical names, but including some places, are also italicised, as are foreign language words and phrases, like '*gratis*' in (Oo3v) and '*Cauiarie*' (Oo4). Jonson's 1616 folio had followed a similar strategy of setting out such material typographically. (See Figure 18.) Another difficult category

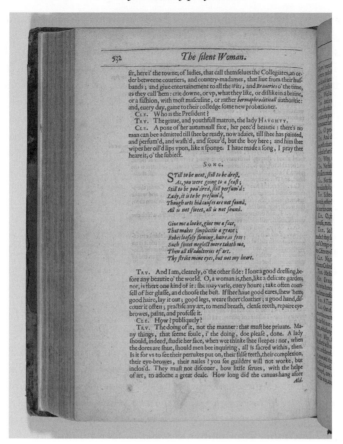

Fig. 18. A page from *Epicene, or The Silent Woman* from Jonson's 1616 folio, Cambridge University Library copy, Syn.4.61.19. Italics has been used to set off the song, and for key terms like 'Wits' and 'hermaphroditicall'; while small capitals are used for the song's heading and for the proper names.

of text that is neither text nor stage direction is a description of the content to follow. In *Hamlet*, his letter to Ophelia is labelled as '*The Letter*' (O03); the Song in Jonson's *Epicene* is 'SONG' (1616: Yy2v). The first quarto of *Hamlet* in addition sets off its sententiae, or proverbial maxims, although the folio text does not (Lesser and Stallybrass 2008). Marston's *Malcontent* follows Q1 *Hamlet*'s example and marks out sententiae frequently, as in Q1 (1604): '*When nothing helpes, cut of the rotten part*' (C3). Sometimes sententiae are also surrounded by double inverted commas to suggest that they are quotations.

These minor difficulties and occasionally alienating characteristics aside, the largest problem with verse and prose in early modern play texts comes in mistaking one for the other. Some plays, like *Pericles* (1609), have an exceptionally high level of such mistakes, so that almost as many lines are misidentified as set correctly. Errors occur with less frequency in most play texts, and half lines with semi-regular rhythms can often be read as verse or prose. This issue and others relating to reading the plays will be discussed at greater length in Chapter 3.

THE PLAY'S TEXT: INDIVIDUAL CHARACTERS

The page from Jonson's *Epicene* illustrated above reveals that a play text offers few difficulties on the level of individual characters. Confusions can emerge over long 's' and u/v or i/j substitution. 'VV' can be used to signify 'W' in the period. The first line of the *Epicene* page includes the word 'themselues', which contains both a long 's' (usually used in the middle of a word) and 'u' for 'v'. Other special characters include ligatures, or two or more characters joined on a single piece of type. For example, Jonson's *Every Man In His Humour* in the 1616 folio is called a '*Comœdie*' (A1), with an 'o-e' ligature. Jonson's 1631 *New Inn* calls it a 'COMOEDY', without a ligature, on the title page. Other unusual characters include 'swash' italics, i.e., letters with long tails, as discussed under headlines in Chapter 3. The more obscure abbreviations used in manuscripts of the period rarely make their way into print. Tildes over letters to signify omitted letters, for instance, are rare. The most common problems in the classroom arise over the long 's'; few other difficulties are likely to be encountered.

HEADLINES AND RUNNING TITLES

The final sections of this chapter will consider the kinds of metatexts that surround the play-text page. From the very top of the page, the first text that a reader will encounter is the headline, or running title. Headlines are the chief identifiers for a printed sheet, and therefore essential information in a period in which plays were sold unbound. Their significance for a reader of a bound copy is obviously somewhat less, and hence cheap books today often have no running titles. Headlines can be read from verso to recto, left to right, across an entire opening, or they might be repeated page by page. For *Hamlet* Q2 (1604), the running titles are '*The Tragedie of Hamlet*' on versos and '*Prince of Denmarke*' on rectos; obviously, the entire phrase is meant to be read together. The folio text of the play prints '*The*

Tragedie of Hamlet' on verso and recto pages, a style that is characteristic of the folio collections of plays from the period, but quartos also adopted it frequently. Headlines, as in Jonson's and Shakespeare's folios, might also be framed with decorative borders or lines. Quarto texts are usually undecorated. The fount of the headlines might be italic, roman, or full capitals. It might be set in the same size as the main text or much larger. There is far less consistency with running titles than there is with other elements of a play text, and therefore they provide telling bibliographical evidence, as further explored in Chapter 3. Unfortunately, headlines are also the most exposed part of a play text, and therefore they are frequently cut off by subsequent rebindings, which typically trim the pages to give a neater bound appearance.

MARGINALIA

Marginalia is not especially common in the play texts of this period, but it could be used in a wide variety of ways. Individual readers might annotate their copies with manuscript marginalia as they wished, but this section will be concerned with what William Slights calls 'printed marginalia' (Slights 2001). Marginalia generally takes the form of stage directions in early printed play texts. Such stage directions might or might not be distinct from the normal run of in-text directions. For instance, in Fletcher and Shakespeare's *Two Noble Kinsmen* (1634) the ten marginal stage directions offer instructions seemingly specific to the needs of a theatrical promptbook. For instance, the marginal direction '2. Hearses ready with Palamon: and Arcite: the 3. Queenes. Theseus: and his Lordes ready' (C3v), comes well before the hearses are needed, and in fact the direction is repeated and corrected at C4v. Other aides-memoires include 'This short florish of Cornets and Showtes within' (E4v) and 'Chaire and stooles out' (G2v). Additional marginal directions might also be reminders for backstage business, as they generally relate to music. The '*Florish*' direction at the very beginning, for instance, seems to herald the start of the play, as opposed to being music designed specifically to accompany the action. It is possible that these directions reflect marginal additions to the underlying manuscript, perhaps made by King's Men prompter Edward Knight, so that the compositor simply set the *mise-en-page* as he encountered it.

As marginal stage directions might be printed over several lines or oth-erwise be ambiguous, sometimes they are accompanied by a symbol in the text to show where the action should take place. Marston's *Malcontent*

Q1 (1604), for instance, uses asterisks for a handful of such directions. In only one instance, in the middle of a long speech by Malevole, is such pinpointing particularly helpful:

* To Pre-passo.   . . . here a *Paris* supports that *Hellen*, theres a Lady *Guineuer* beares vp that sir *Lancelot*. Dreames, dreames, visions, fantasies, *Chimeras*, imaginations, trickes, conceites, * Sir *Tristram Trimtram* come a lost Iacke a napes with a whim wham, heres a Knight of the land of *Catito* shall play at trap with any Page in Europe.

(B2-B2v)

Without the asterisk it would be difficult to know when Malevole stops railing in general and begins to direct his abuse at Prepasso. Most playwrights in this period supply no such 'To . . .' directions, but they occur frequently in this play.

Other forms of marginalia are rare. Early play texts like *The Trial of Treasure* (1567) or *Jacob and Esau* (1568) used the outer margins for speech headings. But on recto pages this practice meant a reader would need to scan to the right of the page before seeing who speaks a given set of lines. Such inconvenience was soon dropped as roman began to replace black-letter fount. The margins of printed books were also traditionally used as spaces for what we might today consider 'footnotes', or learned citations. Such citations were not, of course, generally associated with play texts, a genre that was cheap and popular. Ben Jonson, however, did attempt to place his play texts within traditions of learned literature. He notoriously provided scholarly annotations for *Sejanus* (1605), for instance, although he dropped these marginal annotations in the folio text (1616), and his attempt at offering citations was not taken up by other authors of public plays. Jonson continued to provide such annotations in his masques, however. He offered extensive annotations in his autograph manuscript of *The Masque of Queens* for Prince Henry, held in the British Library, and in many of his printed masques, in quarto and folio. As Jonson placed these texts in a different section in his 1616 folio (after the poems), he clearly thought they were different from his play texts.

Marginalia for play texts are usually limited to standard stage directions. Although exceptions might be made, so that marginal material found in the manuscript might be printed marginally, the costs of adding marginalia to a standard printed page must have mitigated against their frequent appearance in play texts. What an individual marginalium means needs to be considered on a case-by-case basis, but the overall likelihood is that it is simply a stage direction that either could not easily fit on the page, or was placed in the margins of the underlying manuscript.

Signatures supply the basic labels whereby early printers and bookbinders could order sheets and fold them correctly. Signatures appear at the bottom of some recto pages, and they are usually restricted to the first three rectos of a quarto gathering (a single sheet folded twice to make eight leaves), the first two or three rectos for folios (gathered in two or three sheets to make four or six leaves), or first three rectos for octavos (a single sheet folded three times to make sixteen leaves).

For most play texts, each gathering is given a unique siglum (usually running alphabetically from A–Z, then Aa–Zz – and Aaa–Zzz and so on for particularly lengthy books). I/J and U/V were considered the same letters in signatures, so there is no 'J' or 'U'. Each leaf of a given gathering is further identified with a number. The first leaf as printed will usually omit the number '1' (for example, 'B' instead of 'B1'), but the number should be included in any bibliographical description or citation of that leaf. For a folio in sixes (like Shakespeare's) these numbers would be 1 to 6. Therefore gathering 'B' in Shakespeare's folio has the following pages: B1, B1v, B2, B2v, B3, B3v, B4, B4v, B5, B5v, B6, and B6v. The 'v' signifies the verso, or reverse, of a given page, and versos are not labelled, so for citation purposes a reader must turn the page back to discover its identity. This problem is particularly acute for Shakespeare's folio, as only three pages (for example, B1, B2, and B3) of a given gathering have any label on them. But by counting backwards from any page it is possible to know its signature. Quartos have a higher proportion of labelled pages and are therefore easier to cite. Octavos, such as Shirley's *Six New Plays* (1653), present greater difficulty, as only three out of sixteen pages are identified. From a printer's and bookbinder's perspective, it is easy to see why the labels are so sparse. A bare minimum of three signatures for a folio in sixes is needed to identify the placement of each sheet. For quartos, with gatherings almost invariably made up of one sheet, clearly only one signature would need to be identified for the placement of the sheet within a group of sheets, but the additional numerical markers show how that sheet should be folded (and the same applies to an octavo sheet).

Further complications emerge when books were constructed in unusual gatherings or signature orders. Shakespeare's 1623 folio, for instance, opens with two 'A' gatherings, although the first is italic *A*. Gathering *A* contains the preliminaries, and is also made up of eight leaves, instead of the six used elsewhere in the volume. The folio as a whole restarts the signature series for each section, comedies, histories, or tragedies. Generally, books have fairly accurate signatures, as they were so important for constructing the bound volume, but the folio contains some mistakes (like mis-signing a3 in *King John* as 'Aa3', accommodating additional pages as extra 'gg' signatures in *2 Henry IV*), and even inserting an entire play out of sequence (*Troilus and Cressida*). Furthermore, books in this period could be constructed with partial or half-sheets, or use a single sheet for both the preliminaries and the final leaves of a play text. Non-alpha-numeric symbols (like the '¶' of *Troilus and Cressida*) were often used, too. The principles of describing signatures are outlined in greater detail in Chapter 3.

Despite the frequency of mistaken signatures in play texts, they remain the best way to cite specific pages. Page numbers are not usually present in play texts from the early modern period. When they are present, they appear at the top of the page, in the same line as the headline. Larger collections of plays, unlike individual quartos, usually include page numbers. Jonson's 1616 folio starts numbering pages from the first play and maintains a consecutive sequence until the final masque (at page 1015). Where Jonson led, the designers of Shakespeare's 1623 folio followed, except that they started the numbering over with each new section (with the largely unpaginated exception of *Troilus and Cressida*). There are several pagination errors in Shakespeare's folio, however, so that twenty pages are 'missing' between *Timon of Athens* and *Julius Caesar*, for instance, and *Hamlet* jumps from page 156 to page 257. In Shirley's *Six New Plays* (1652–3), page numbers are restarted for each play text. Overall, there was little incentive to offer accurate page numbers – errors in them often remain uncorrected in this period, and there is little consistency across texts, so they remain a poor choice for citation, even when present.

CATCHWORDS

Catchwords appear at the bottom right of play-text pages. They repeat the first words (or sometimes parts of words) to appear on subsequent pages. 'The practice was intended to help the compositor to get the pages in the right order for printing' (Gaskell 1972: 53), and like signatures, they are usually accurate. Inaccuracies might point to underlying difficulties behind the printing, as discussed in Chapter 3. Catchwords are generally considered of purely bibliographical interest, but they do also ensure smooth page turns for readers.

OTHER PARATEXT: COLOPHONS, ADVERTISEMENTS, ERRATA

A final word should be given to those parts of play texts that appear more rarely, but can offer valuable evidence about the text, its printing, or indeed about other play texts from the period.

Colophons appear at the end of a text, to provide information about its printing and publishing. They were infrequently included with play texts and they generally become more rare as the period progresses. Interestingly, Shakespeare's folio includes a colophon that offers more publication information than the title page: '*Printed at the Charges of W. Jaggard, Ed. Blount, I. Smithweeke, and W. Aspley,* 1623.' (bbb6). This colophon appears on the same page as the final words of *Cymbeline*. The colophon for the first quarto of *Henry VI, part 2* (1594) includes the exact same imprint information as the title page, including Thomas Creede's printer's ornament, and it appears that Creede might have reused the text from the title page (or vice versa) as space filler in this instance. For most play texts, the title page would be printed after the final pages of text, so such reuse of type might have been efficient, but colophons are a holdover from an earlier age of printing and are rarely present.

Publishers might instead take advantage of the space at the end of a play text or near the preliminaries to advertise for other business. In Shirley's *The Maid's Revenge* (1639), William Cooke included 'A Catalogue of such things as hath beene Published by *James Shirley* Gent.', in which he lists nineteen plays and masques. Cooke was one of Shirley's chief publishers, so he had a wider interest in promoting the dramatist. Similarly, Shirley's *Six New Plays* of 1652–3 includes 'A Catalogue of the Authors Poems already Printed', possibly at the instigation of Humphrey Moseley (F4-F4v). Helpfully, this catalogue informs readers that *The Coronation* had been '*Falsely ascribed to Jo. Fletcher*' (F4v). Moseley, a keen marketer of play texts, took advantage of space at the end of Middleton and Rowley's *The Changeling* (1653) to advertise his stock of '*PLAYES newly Printed*' and '*PLAYES in the Press*' by several dramatists, including Shirley (I3v). Such information evinces strategies towards marketing play texts, but it can also assist with authorship attribution and dating. The most impressive list in the period, which could not have been entirely motivated by a hope for further sales, is 'An exact and perfect Catologue of all *Playes* that are Printed' at the end of Goffe's *Careless Shepherdess* (1656). The list is fairly comprehensive, stretching to six tightly printed quarto pages, but it is not always accurate. *Edward I*, *Edward II*, *Edward III*, and *Edward IV* are assigned to Shakespeare, for instance.

A final category of paratextual information is the errata list. Errata were a common feature of printed books in this period, but they appear much more rarely in play texts. According to Farmer and Lesser's *Database of Early English Playbooks* (Farmer and Lesser 2007–10), only twenty-four plays produce errata lists between 1580 and 1642, and many of those are private entertainments or imitations of classical drama. The errata of public plays tend to be very simple, and by no means catch all errors. In John Day's *The Isle of Gulls* (1606), for instance, it reads simply 'In *B.* the last page, for Lord, read loue cannot be saued' (H4v). Commonly, errata take the form of general apologies for any errors found, as in Ford's *'Tis Pity She's a Whore* (1633): 'The generall Commendation deserued by the Actors, in their Presentment of this Tragedy, may easily excuse such few faults, as are escaped in the Printing: A common charity may allow him the ability of spelling, whom a secure confidence assures that hee cannot ignorantly erre in the Application of Sence' (K4). Although such lists are more substantive in scholarly tomes from the period, their general vagueness or absence should not be taken as evidence that play texts were not proofread. Play texts that survive in large numbers almost invariably show strong evidence of stop-press correction. Short play texts, in their very brevity, are unlikely to require extensive errata lists.

This chapter has considered several of the elements that make up early modern play texts. Many of these elements are unique to the genre, and therefore escape detailed discussion in more general introductions to bibliography. For elements that are common to other genres, such as title pages, errata, signatures, headlines, et cetera, supplemental information can be found in the standard bibliographical guides. This chapter has been concerned with how such elements appear specifically in play texts, however, and certainly the information on a title page, for instance, is uniquely inflected by the genre. Chapter 3 will turn to reading these unique texts as literary and dramatic works and as bibliographical texts.

FURTHER READING

Blayney, Peter W. M. 1982. *The Texts of 'King Lear' and Their Origins*, vol. 1: *Nicholas Okes and the First Quarto*. Cambridge University Press

Gaskell, Philip 1972. *A New Introduction to Bibliography*. Oxford University Press

Greetham, D. C. 1994. *Textual Scholarship: An Introduction*. New York and London: Garland

McKenzie, D. F. 1969. 'Printers of the Mind: Some Notes on Bibliographical Theories and Printing-House Practices', *Studies in Bibliography* 22: 1–75

CHAPTER 3

Reading the originals

This chapter will address how the experience of reading the original quartos and folios shapes an understanding of the plays. Ronald B. McKerrow's seminal study *An Introduction to Bibliography for Literary Students* (1927), began in an early form as 'Notes on Bibliographical Evidence for Literary Students and Editors of English Works of the Sixteenth and Seventeenth Centuries' (McKerrow 1911–13). This chapter will be shaped around such a dual focus on 'literary students' and 'editors', on the premise that bibliographical knowledge is needed for both pursuits. Therefore the chapter is split into an initial general discussion about reading the plays and a lengthy focus on bibliographical issues. The word 'literary' itself has become much more complicated than it was in McKerrow's time, and the distinction between a 'literary' and a 'bibliographical' approach is largely a false construction, but one that is maintained by some within the discipline of English studies. Nonetheless, literary scholarship has been given a new lease of life in the vigorous application of textual and literary theory by a new generation of scholars attuned to how these fields complement one another.

The extraordinary enlivening effect and variety of approaches that have emerged in the past two decades would be impossible to capture within a single chapter. This chapter will therefore focus upon: (1) the speeches (including who speaks them) and stage directions that make up the most important components of a literary reading; and (2) the material features of a text that particularly need to be investigated when producing a critical edition. Chapter 2 covered many of the visual elements of a play text in terms of their purpose and layout. This chapter engages more deeply with some of those elements by taking into account longer extracts from early modern play texts. It considers the impact of missing or brief stage directions, and how to negotiate misattributed speeches, uncorrected errors, and textual variants both within and across editions. In other words the features that are *not* apparent to the reader at first glance will be discussed. Of obvious relevance here will be the printing of stage directions, many of which were regularised or expanded by scribes or printing houses, while others were not supplied. Other features to be discussed are the rendering of verse as prose and vice versa, squeezing of lines because of space requirements, insertion of act and scene divisions, and some further distinctions between reading folios and quartos.

WHAT AND WHERE ARE 'ORIGINALS'?

Accessing the original play texts must first be considered. The selection of text is a loaded topic in bibliographical studies, and one that has vexed the discipline for over a century. Controversy surrounds the choice of copy text, or the control text from which a subsequent edition might be taken. But the complexities of that choice can apply equally to the selection of a play text to be read in the original. In this context it is important to note that most play texts offer very simple choices. Roughly half of Shakespeare's canon, for instance, was first published in his 1623 folio. So for readers of *The Tempest*, or *Macbeth*, or *Much Ado about Nothing*, for instance, the folio is the only text that can claim any authority. Things become more complicated for *Hamlet* and *King Lear*, however, and worse still for those (largely non-canonical) plays with multiple texts that have not yet been subject to careful scrutiny.

W. W. Greg's 'The Rationale of Copy-Text' of 1950–1 remains the most important essay of copy-text theory, but, as he himself noted, the term 'copytext' was invented by R. B. McKerrow and was 'a conception already familiar' (Greg 1950–1: 19). For Greg, it was axiomatic '. . . to choose whatever extant text may be supposed to represent most nearly what the author wrote and to follow it with the least possible alteration' (Greg 1950–1: 21). But Greg went on to refine this theory by dividing alternative readings into 'substantive' and 'accidental' ones:

The true theory is, I contend, that the copy-text should govern (generally) in the matter of accidentals, but that the choice between substantive readings belongs to the general theory of textual criticism and lies altogether beyond the narrow principle of the copy-text. Thus it may happen that in a critical edition the text rightly chosen as copy may not by any means be the one that supplies most substantive readings in cases of variation. (Greg 1950–1: 26)

Greg here promotes a kind of eclectic text whereby differences are chosen on a case-by-case basis. It is important to note that Greg's arguments are directed towards the production of critical editions. Such eclecticism went on to define much of the editing of Shakespeare in the second half of the twentieth century, where an edition of say, *Hamlet*, might include substantive readings from Q1, Q2, and F. The corollary for a modern reader of an early modern *Hamlet* would be the need to sit with all three early editions and compare them to determine a single 'authoritative' text – an unenviable task, perhaps.

Jerome J. McGann, in *A Critique of Modern Textual Criticism* (McGann 1983), problematises the basis of Greg's initial choice of copy text. McGann argues that it is difficult to know which text might hold 'what the author wrote' in the first place. In other words, selecting the text that might be the basis of even the accidentals can be tricky. Greg's desire to choose the text most associated with final authorial intention was part of a wider desire held by most editors and bibliographers of the time. His refinement of the 'best text' model, whereby only one text supplies all readings, is still influential, as textual choice has remained an important ideal in Shakespeare studies.

That ideal was inflected heavily by Gary Taylor and Michael Warren's groundbreaking *The Division of the Kingdoms* (Taylor and Warren 1983), which contained essays arguing that both the quarto and folio versions of *King Lear* were Shakespeare's drafts, and most importantly of all, that Shakespeare revised his own work. Such thinking was put into editorial practice in the Oxford Shakespeare of 1986, edited by Stanley Wells, Gary Taylor, *et al*. The Oxford editors developed very certain-sounding origins for Shakespeare's early printed texts. For instance, the folio copy for *Hamlet*, 'whether at one or more removes, reflects a theatrical manuscript of 1600–3' (Wells and Taylor 1997: 400). Further, they suggest that, 'Shakespeare prepared a fair copy of the foul papers, that in making that fair copy he revised the text in a number of ways, and that F derives, at one or possibly more removes, from that fair copy' (Wells and Taylor 1997: 401). But alongside these confident (and thoroughly considered) claims came the radical idea that a theatrical text was to be chosen above an authorial draft: 'The Oxford editors prefer, when there is a choice, copy based on the prompt-book to copy based on the author's own draft' (Greenblatt *et al*. 1997: 75). *Hamlet* in the Oxford Shakespeare is therefore based upon the folio text not solely because Shakespeare prepared it, but largely because it 'reflects a theatrical manuscript'. Most editions before the Oxford Shakespeare preferred to conflate Q2 with F because a conflation was purportedly closer to Shakespeare's draft. The Oxford editors upheld the conclusions of Gary Taylor, Michael Warren, and others that Shakespeare revised his own work (Taylor and Warren 1983), and therefore multiple texts might have equal authority. However, as Jonathan Goldberg wryly notes of this practice with respect to *King Lear*: 'The kingdom has been divided, but Shakespeare reigns supreme, author now of two sovereign texts' (Goldberg

1986: 214). Although they did not print two versions of *Hamlet*, they did print separate quarto and folio texts of *King Lear*, a radical step for a single-volume Shakespeare. The clear implication is that for plays with multiple authoritative texts, readers must be familiar with each of them.

Coinciding with this movement was the emerging idea that all surviving texts might be considered 'authoritative'. Chapter 1 explored debate over what had been termed 'bad' quartos, and the subsequent rehabilitation of such texts in the 1980s and 1990s. Such rehabilitation had an effect on scholarly editing, and in 1991 Paul Bertram and Bernice W. Kliman edited *The Three-Text Hamlet*, a ground-breaking parallel-text edition of all three versions of the play (Bertram and Kliman 1991). Increasingly, critics note that the 'bad' quarto of *Hamlet* has scholarly value, especially as a possible relic of original performance. Therefore, not only should Q2 and F be considered as 'good' play texts, but Q1 might also be worthy of literary and theatrical attention. The results of this thinking for mainstream modernised editions include the Arden Third Series 2006 edition of *Hamlet*, edited by Ann Thompson and Neil Taylor, which spans two volumes and includes modernised editions of all three texts (though Q2 is privileged by its place in Volume 1, which contains most of the introductory material, commentary, and textual apparatus).

In a movement corresponding to the rejection of a single copy text, comes the rejection of texts that have been edited at all (no matter what early exemplars they might be based upon). G. Thomas Tanselle highlights an increasing 'disaffection with critical editing as a supposedly authoritarian imposition of stasis on inherently unstable material' (Tanselle 1994: 4). David Scott Kastan argues that 'Editing can only obscure or distort some of the evidence provided by . . . early texts, erasing marks of the texts' historicity' (Kastan 2001: 123). The only possible response to such disaffection is to read one or more of the original play texts.

Because of challenges to ideals of *the* copy text, the choice about which of these artefacts to read, when choice is available, is somewhat less complicated than it might have been forty years ago. All early (and indeed later) exemplars can now be subjected to literary readings. As Jonathan Goldberg argues:

As textual properties, Shakespearean texts are produced by a multitude of determinations that exceed a criticism bent on controlling the text or assigning it determinate meanings or structures. Although all we have to go on are the texts, we must go on knowing that they do not make the Shakespearean text *proper*. No one can own the text. No one can clean it up. (Goldberg 1986: 216)

This textual freedom has not been fully embraced in a widespread scholarly uptake in reading the originals, a process rarely practised and even then largely confined to some of Shakespeare's more famous plays. In fact for some plays, scholars are not fully apprised of the differences between early or later quartos for the simple fact that no one has yet published detailed comparative investigations of them. (This status includes, for instance, some of Shirley's plays.) Goldberg's position is made tenable only by the bibliographical work that he partially seeks to deconstruct, but his overall sense of textual freedom, given the constraints of early modern dramatic textual production, is a sound one. Therefore the choice of early play text can be seen as fairly open, but that choice should be informed by some awareness of investigations of differences between texts, where such research has been done.

To determine what texts might be available, the *English Short Title Catalogue* (ESTC 2010) should be consulted (http://estc.bl.uk). The ESTC builds upon the printed *Short Title Catalogue* that had already gone through three careful print editions, the first compiled by A. W. Pollard and G. R. Redgrave and published in 1926. The ESTC documents most known printed books (including play texts) from the Shakespearean period. It also highlights some of the holding libraries where surviving exemplars are kept and gives physical descriptions of the texts. When searching the ESTC, care must be taken to use the original spellings of words, so that, for instance, a search for Shirley's *Traitor* will yield no results, because it was spelled *Traytor* in the 1635 play text. Further caution is needed because the ESTC is not a hundred per cent complete (May 2001), nor is it entirely accurate. Stephen Tabor notes that around 80,000 of the ESTC records have at least one error (Tabor 2007: 372), partially because of the way that the material was compiled, but also because the ESTC can be continually updated (sometimes mistakenly). Although information, such as title-page transcriptions, found in the ESTC should be checked against originals, it is generally sufficiently accurate to identify how many different editions of a given play were produced. It might in addition identify false duplicates, because the STC gave separate entries for each imprint, so that, for instance, the second quarto of *Hamlet* appears as STC22276 with the 1604 title-page date and STC22276a with the 1605 date. (ESTC material retains its original five-digit designation from the STC – sometimes plus decimal place or letter – and should be so cited.)

Once the text has been selected, it must be consulted either in facsimile or in a real exemplar. The locations of some exemplars will be offered by the ESTC, but the accuracy or extent of such listings will vary from play to play. Shirley's *Hyde Park* (1637) is listed as held by twenty-three libraries in Britain and North America, for instance – an unusually high number, but nearly double that many copies are known to exist. The ESTC also does not always list copies outside of Britain and North America, including the very extensive holdings of Meisei University in Tokyo. (None of the Meisei copies of Shakespeare's folio are listed, for instance, but they have the second largest collection in the world, after the Folger Shakespeare Library.) Compiling an accurate finding list of every known surviving exemplar is very time-consuming, and involves writing directly to many potential (sometimes unlikely seeming) holding libraries. Even identifying the nearest copy, however, does not guarantee access to it, as institutions or private collectors will have their own policies about consulting materials.

Far more expedient is consultation of a facsimile, and indeed even the most open institutions, like the British Library, now frequently enquire if a reader might be better served by consulting *Early English Books Online* (EEBO) instead of an original text. EEBO builds upon the University Microfilm International (UMI) collections of STC microfilmed content by digitising it both as PDF page images and as searchable SGML texts. Before the advent of EEBO in 1999, scholars had to use the UMI microfilms (generally held in university libraries) or travel to national repositories to see surviving originals of non-canonical play texts. EEBO is available electronically and has revolutionised the availability of Shakespearean play texts. Such access comes at a price, however. Access requires subscription, usually by universities or other agencies (as with the UMI microfilms). EEBO, like the ESTC, is also somewhat incomplete and subject to error. Punctuation can be difficult to decipher, and show-through means that parts of the text often are illegible. Depending upon the copies chosen, pages may be lost or cropped. Shirley's *Lady of Pleasure* (1637), for instance, has signature B3 [mis-signed 'B2'] obliterated with the messages 'CROPPED PAGES' and 'FOXING'. Presumably that means that the microfilm operator chose not to attempt reproduction of the lines owing to 'foxing', or the browning of old paper. Such missing or damaged pages are not uncommon. More difficult are pages that have been altered in ways that do not show up on the microfilms. EEBO's reproduction of Shirley's *The Royal Master* (1638, STC22454), for instance, is taken from the Cambridge University Library copy. An early reader of that exemplar meticulously changed over 500 commas to semi-colons. In the PDF file of the microfilm, the changes look like legitimately printed differences. The slight variation in ink colour in the manuscript alterations can be spotted only in the original. PDF scans of microfilm are not high resolution, and EEBO files, as well as being subject to such inadvert manipulation, are not easy to read. EEBO does have the advantage, however, of being updatable, so further improvements might come with time.

A further option for canonical texts is to consult a photo-facsimile, although this resource is also subject to error and manipulation (Tanselle 1989). Arthur Brown notes that even the most careful photograph can be distorted when he warns:

against the slight curve in the surface to be photographed, which may easily distort letters and spaces, particularly those near the margins; against badly inked letters and punctuation marks which assume a different form in the reproduction; against letters which have not inked at all, printing 'blind' in the original but disappearing altogether in the reproduction; against any haphazard ink mark or fly spot in the original to which a reproduction may give a new lease of life. (A. Brown 1960: 70)

The most famous photo-facsimile is the Norton facsimile of Shakespeare's first folio, first published in 1968 and edited by Charlton Hinman. Hinman used the most-corrected sheets of several copies from the Folger Shakespeare Library, so the volume is a composite, ideal Shakespeare, as opposed to being a facsimile of a single exemplar. But it is a high-quality reproduction with through line-numbers (starting afresh for each play), an intervention that makes it easy to cite specific points in the folio. Several other publishers and libraries have produced high-quality photo-facsimiles of Shakespeare and other contemporary dramatists. Many of these are freely available on the internet. For more obscure plays, the Malone Society's steady flow of high-quality reproductions of single exemplars is unsurpassed, and has slowly introduced through line numbers to Shakespeare's quartos and many of the texts of his contemporaries.

All versions of a text from the hand-press period come with attendant dangers. The potential for stop-press variants from one exemplar to the next potentially alters specific passages. Individual copies might also be subject to deliberate or accidental alteration by the pens of subsequent readers. For this reason, editors and bibliographers consult multiple original copies of a single text to find its most corrected (or unadulterated) states. That seems like an unrealistic proposition for literary scholars. EEBO copies offer a good combination of accessibility and reliability as reading texts, and they are likely to be the texts that scholars 'know' for some time into the future. EEBO has opened up a potentially wider canon of early modern drama for literary analysis, and has multiplied many times the number of scholars at all levels who have been able to encounter these play texts in a facsimile of their original forms.

So far this book has been concerned with the difficulties attending any consultation of an original play text. It will be equally clear to scholars of early modern literature that most publications in the field do not cite the originals, except in cases of those plays that have no modern editions. Similarly, such unedited texts are very rarely subject to critical scrutiny, in part owing to the preference for easy-to-read editions. When combining the difficulty of access and the dangers that come with reading the originals, it is easy to see why the scholarly community prefers a thoroughly researched modernised edition. However, the rise of EEBO, and in particular its use in the undergraduate classroom, should lead to familiarity with, and use of, original texts for critical books and articles.

READING THE ORIGINALS

As it would be impossible to contain all of the approaches to 'reading' a play text within a single book chapter, this section will outline some of the techniques available to scholars to help with encountering the originals. The canon of Renaissance drama stands at more than 700 plays, and this book has so far mentioned only a very small proportion of them. This section will primarily consider Shakespeare, the most canonical of authors, including some of his less familiar texts, *Titus Andronicus*, *Timon of Athens*, *Pericles*, and his more famous ones, *The Tempest*, and *Hamlet*. The aim is to outline some of the principal concerns that a reader will face when encountering original play texts. Ultimately, such concerns will vary on a case-by-case basis, and this overview will not cover all contingencies. The best way to learn how to read Shakespearean play texts will always be to read as many as possible. The examples below offer suggestions as to how such initial readings might be conducted.

Titus Andronicus was published in 1594, in a quarto discovered in 1905, and not available for wider scholarly consultation until the Folger Shakespeare Library opened in 1932 (McKerrow 1938: 86). As one might expect from its relatively early date, the quarto is largely unadorned – it offers no author's name or dedications. Immediately after the title comes the opening stage direction:

Enter the Tribunes *and* Senatours *aloft: And then enter* Saturninus *and his followers at one dore, and* Bassianus *and his followers, with Drums and Trumpets.* (A3)

With only two characters named here, and a potentially variable number of tribunes, senators, and followers, the vagueness of this stage direction would seem to suggest a minimum of eight players on stage. Although only two separate points of entry are mentioned '*aloft*' and '*at one dore*', the implication here is that Bassianus would enter '[*at the other*]', which would be a typical phrase from the period and indeed appears in the folio (1623, cc4). Otherwise, this stage direction, except for the spelling, would probably stand as it is in an edited text and present few problems to a reader. The opening lines of the play are similarly straightforward, yet worth considering at length:

> *Saturninus.*
> NOble *Patricians*, Patrons of my Right,
> Defend the iustice of my cause with armes.
> And Countrimen my louing followers,
> Plead my successiue Title with your swords:
> I am his first borne sonne, that was the last
> That ware the Imperiall Diademe of Rome,
> Then let my Fathers honours liue in me,
> Nor wrong mine age with this indignitie,
> *Bassianus.*
> Romaines, friends, followers, fauourers of my Right,
> If euer *Bassianus Caesars* sonne,
> VVere gratious in the eyes of Royall Rome,
> Keepe then this passage to the Capitoll,
> And suffer not dishonour to approch,
> The Imperiall seate to vertue, consecrate
> To iustice, continence, and Nobillitie:
> But let desert in pure election shine,
> And Romaines fight for freedome in your choice.
> *Marcus Andronicus with the Crowne.*
> Princes that striue by factions and by friends,
> Ambitiously for Rule and Emperie,
> Know that the people of Rome for whom we stand
> A speciall Partie, haue by common voice,
> In election for the Romaine Empery
> Chosen *Andronicus*, surnamed *Pius* . . .
>
> (A3–A3v)

Interestingly, the speech headings are centred, so that Saturninus' and Bassianus' verbal struggle is situated in an earlier tradition of printing drama, reflecting, too, the rhetorical nature of their set speeches. They are not in dialogue, but conducting political debate. Their verse is set with a mixture of capitalisation and italics that is fairly typical of the period. Proper names are italicised, for instance, and key nouns, like 'Title', 'Diademe', 'Capitoll', and 'Partie', are capitalised, emphasising the factional nature of the contention. It is important to recognise that neither italics nor capitalisation can be taken as having any authority other than the compositor's – he may or may not have reflected these features from the underlying manuscript. The entry/speech heading for Marcus probably was in the original manuscript. It seems very likely that he enters at this point (and not in the opening direction), as '*with the Crowne*' is suggestive of an entry. Yet the word 'enter' is missing. Also, does Marcus enter aloft, or does he use a stage-level door? If so, is it a middle door? Equally, as he seems to reflect the voice of the Senate, he could be part of the original entry party. The folio stifles these questions of timing and place by offering the direction '*Enter Marcus Andronicus aloft with the Crown*' (sig. cc4). It is interesting that the folio offers more extensive stage directions in this section than the quarto. A possible implication, taking this brief selection as evidence, might be that the folio text gives a more complete account of the original staging.

Further interest arises in the passage's punctuation. Although it generally runs close to modern practice, Saturninus' speech ends with a comma. Such speech-ending commas are not uncommon in the drama of the period, and they may have a number of valences, but here it might be indicative of Bassianus interrupting Saturninus' speech. The absence of punctuation at the end of the speech also sometimes suggests interruption, as in Marston's *Malcontent* Q1:

Celso. . . . till you of all
Mal. Of all was quite berefte.
> (1604: B3v)

In the manuscript for *The Second Maiden's Tragedy*, many such short speeches have no punctuation at all. Actors' parts had little punctuation, so presumably it was not seen as essential within the workings of early modern theatre. The folio *Titus* somewhat forecloses the possibility of interruption by ending the speech with a full stop. There is no way that we might know Shakespeare's (or George Peele's) intentions towards this scene, or if either mark of punctuation in any way preserves that of the manuscript, which might itself have been altered over time or in transcription. But differences in punctuation do highlight multiple possibilities that a critic might wish to pursue.

In this scene, the folio solves further riddles that emerge in the quarto. The quarto has a false start in Marcus' praise of Titus, who has:

        at this day,
To the Monument of that *Andronicy*
Done sacrifice of expiation,
And slaine the Noblest prisoner of the *Gothes*.
> (A3v)

This sacrifice is repeated elsewhere in the quarto scene; the folio removes this duplication by cutting the earlier lines. Further confusion about the actors' movements is clarified in the folio. It includes the direction '*A long Flourish till they come downe*' (cc5), as Bassianus and Saturninus had earlier gone '*vp into the Senat house*' (cc4). The quarto has a direction for them to go up, but no direction for them to come down. The use of vertical space in this scene is complex, so the folio's added direction is helpful.

The first quarto is manifestly different in content to the folio. A literary reading could make use of these differences by choosing the folio as a 'correct' text, which would suppose that a critic must read multiple surviving copies to be fully informed of possible corruption and variation. Equally, a critic might accept the quarto readings and ignore those of the folio. In that case, Marcus is not fully informed about his brother's sacrificial activities, perhaps. Saturninus might remain aloft for more of the scene, emphasising his new elevated status. Another lesson emerges in comparing these two texts: errors that we will never be able to correct (or even recognise) probably remain. An editor might be able to solve all of the *Titus* quarto cruxes without any reference to the folio, but that guesswork – which most modernising editors would hazard in these cases – is also an act of criticism, criticism that shapes the reception of the text for a much wider audience. Similarly, some difficulties remain even when consulting both quarto and folio. For instance, in the quarto Titus slays Mutius after a brief exchange, where Mutius blocks his path, but in the folio the killing of an unnamed 'sonne' happens without reason. In neither text is Titus' act justified, but in the folio it seems more callous, and interestingly Bate and Rasmussen's RSC Shakespeare (Bate and Rasmussen 2007) includes Mutius' lines from the quarto, even though their copy text is the folio. Such conflation commonly continues even in modernised 'best text' editions, where it can be disguised by complex, or even incomplete, textual apparatuses. Readers of the originals can conduct these acts of critical distinction themselves, possibly in ways that reshape thinking about a given play.

Timon of Athens and *Pericles*, like *Titus Andronicus*, circulate in the far reaches of Shakespeare's canon. Yet unlike *Titus*, these plays survive in single authoritative early editions. *Timon*'s place in the folio might be a fortunate one, as its inclusion seems to have emerged as a stop-gap to fill the space left by the rights dispute over *Troilus and Cressida*. If that is the case, then we are lucky to have any copy of this play, but its limitations might lead it to be called a 'bad folio' text. Similarly, *Pericles* is alone amongst Shakespeare's texts in surviving as a 'bad' quarto only. This play, like *Two Noble Kinsmen*, was excluded from the folio, probably in part because it is a jointly authored work. (That explanation is not entirely satisfactory, however, as *Titus* and *Timon* are probably also jointly authored.)

Both texts give occasion to difficulties, but for different reasons. *Timon*, jointly authored by Shakespeare and Middleton, has confusing stage directions. The opening stage direction, for instance, presents problems similar to those encountered in *Titus*: '*Enter Poet, Painter, Ieweller, Marchant, and Mercer, at seuerall doores*' (gg1v). There appear to be five characters, each entering at '*seuerall*', or separate, doors. In fact a further reading of the scene discloses that the poet and painter enter together at one door, and the jeweller and merchant enter at another. Further, the merchant *is* a mercer (or dealer in silk), as opposed to one of two distinct characters. Although it is probably apparent that only two doors are needed after ten lines or so, when the painter and poet talk about the jeweller and merchant, confusion about the possibility of the mercer might last much further into the play, or indeed remain a point of confusion. A similar difficulty surrounds the start of the masque:

Sound Tucket. Enter the Maskers of Amazons, with
    Lutes in their hands, dauncing and playing.
Tim. What meanes that Trumpe? How now?
                    Enter Seruant.
Ser. Please you my Lord, there are certaine Ladies
    Most desirous of admittance.
Tim. Ladies? what are their wils?
Ser. There comes with them a fore-runner my Lord,
    Which beares that office, to signifie their pleasures.
Tim. I pray let them be admitted.
        Enter Cupid with the Maske of Ladies.

                                        (gg3)

As John Jowett has discussed at length, this scene presents several difficulties. Chief amongst them is the double entry of the masquing ladies. Jowett notes: 'Somehow the vagaries of inscription have produced a text that, taken at face value, is radically at odds with the very stage action it prescribes' (Jowett 2006a: 75). It appears obvious in the passage above that the ladies do not enter until the second direction. But a key remaining question is, do they enter '*with Lutes . . . dauncing and playing*'? Jowett notes that, 'it would be so much more straightforward in practical terms simply to avoid specifying that the ladies play lutes' and then goes on to demonstrate how such an act violates gendered and staging decorum in the period (Jowett 2006a: 80ff). An interesting possibility might be that Middleton chose the lutes at first and then changed his mind, for the very reasons of decorum that Jowett outlines. The process that resolves (or attempts to resolve) these difficulties is one of reading forward to understand what had happened, and then reassessing the staging in the light of that new knowledge. This 'forwards-looking' and 'backwards-looking' reading characterises encounters with ambiguities or errors in early play texts, especially when those problems concern who exactly is on stage, and when they enter and exit. This style of reading presents two problems: (1) firstly, it is non-linear; (2) secondly, it is open to constant, and interpretation-driving choices. Here, the act of choosing or not choosing the lutes is loaded with meaning.

A different problem emerges with the 'bad' 1609 quarto of *Pericles*, which unlike *Timon* contains fairly sound stage directions. Only occasionally does the play have ambiguities of entry or exit directions. During the tilt scene, for instance, when King Simonides says: 'We will with-draw into the Gallerie', it is not clear who withdraws – and the King speaks the next line, apparently on stage, after a stage direction notes: '*Great shoutes, and all cry, the mean Knight*' (C4v). Far more problematic are the lines of the play itself. The text confuses verse for prose and vice versa, and makes up pseudo-verse out of what might have been blank verse lines. For instance, the quarto prints Pericles' first lines thus:

Peri. I haue (*Antiochus*) and with a soule emboldned
     With the glory of her prayse, thinke death no hazard,
     In this enterprise.
                                                                    (A2v)

In a modernised edition, such as the Penguin text, these lines might be rearranged into rough blank verse:

PERICLES
I have, Antiochus, and, with a soul
Emboldened with the glory of her praise,
Think death no hazard in this enterprise.
          (Giddens 2008: I.1.3–5)

Conversely, there are seemingly prose lines in the play printed as verse, like the Third Fisherman saying:

3. But Maister, if I had been the Sexton,
     I would haue been that day in the belfrie.
                         (C2)

With twenty syllables, this might at first have struck the compositor as two lines of pentameter, but the rough rhythm is probably prose, which in the drama of the period often has sections with pronounced rhythm. Such decisions require careful thought and there are hundreds of them in this quarto. The problems presented by corrupt verse and prose are not usually so prevalent in the early texts, but correction is occasionally needed and requires a sharp eye. Even a play entirely in verse, like *Richard II*, might have confusing lines, as on b6v of the folio:

King. Coosin, throw downe your gage,
  Do you begin.

These two lines form one line of iambic pentameter. Although verse lineation does not appear to have been as changeable for compositors as spelling or punctuation, space pressures, or a corrupt or confusing manuscript might lead to alterations such as this one. These alterations make reading the originals potentially slow – depending on the accuracy of the chosen play text and the reader's desire to respect versification.

Titus Andronicus, *Timon of Athens*, and *Pericles* are collaborative plays not known as Shakespeare's best. (They are, of course, substantially more famous than many non-Shakespearean plays.) *The Tempest* and *Hamlet*, on the other hand, have been subject to significantly more critical interest.

The Tempest is the opening play of the 1623 folio, and it is well printed, seemingly from a tidy underlying manuscript (perhaps revised by Ralph Crane). Bate and Rasmussen's very brief assessment of the folio play in the RSC Shakespeare labels the play as having a: 'Generally good quality of printing' (Bate and Rasmussen 2007: 5). The editors of the Arden third series go further, to note that, '*The Tempest* is generally acknowledged to be the cleanest of Shakespeare's early printed texts' (Vaughan and Vaughan 1999: 125). Therefore, it presents a more straightforward original play text than those discussed above. The complex partial lines of Miranda and Prospero's verse in Scene 2, for instance, are clearly set out so that the line divisions and rhythms can be perceived at a glance:

> [Miranda]
> Had I byn any God of power, I would
> Haue suncke the Sea within the Earth, or ere
> It should the good Ship so haue swallow'd, and
> The fraughting Soule within her.
> *Pros.* Be collected,
>   No more amazement: Tell your pitteous heart
>   there's no harme done.
> *Mira.* O woe, the day.
> *Pros.* No harme.
>
>   (A1v)

The final three lines of this passage become one line of iambic pentameter. Similarly, Prospero's initial 'Be collected' finishes Miranda's seven-syllable line (and adds a feminine ending). Although *The Tempest* is not perfect, the high quality of its original text means that it presents few challenges to a modern reader, beyond some archaic spellings and punctuation. Therefore, the scholarly use of modernised editions of the play might be more subject to question than it would be for, say, *Pericles*.

The same is clearly not true for *Hamlet*, with its three competing and substantively different editions. A largely non-consequential moment from Act 1, Scene 4 highlights some of the more straightforward issues of comparison. Printed below are the first lines of the scene from all three of the early texts:

Hamlet, first quarto (1603)

> *Enter* Hamlet, Horatio, *and* Marcellus.
> *Ham.* The ayre bites shrewd; it is an eager and
>   An nipping winde, what houre i'st?
> *Hor.* I think it lacks of twelue,   *Sound Trumpets.*
> *Mar.* No, t'is strucke.
> *Hor.* Indeed I heard it not, what doth this mean my lord?
> *Ham.* O the king doth wake to night, & takes his rowse.
>   (C2v–C3)

Hamlet, second quarto (1604)

> *Enter Hamlet, Horatio and Marcellus.*
> *Ham.* The ayre bites shroudly, it is very colde.
> *Hora.* It is nipping, and an eager ayre.
> *Ham.* What houre now?
> *Hora.* I thinke it lackes of twelfe.
> *Mar.* No, it is strooke.
> *Hora.* Indeede; I heard it not, it then drawes neere the season,
>   Wherein the spirit held his wont to walke   *A florish of trumpets*
>   What does this meane my Lord?   *And 2. peeces goes of.*
> *Ham.* The King doth wake to night and takes his rowse.
>   (D1)

Hamlet, first folio (1623)

> *Enter Hamlet, Horatio, Marcellus.*
> *Ham.* The Ayre bites shrewdly: is it very cold?
> *Hor.* It is a nipping and an eager ayre.
> *Ham.* What hower now?
> *Hor.* I think it lacks of twelue.
> *Mar.* No, it is strooke.
> *Hor.* Indeed I heard it not: then it drawes neere the season,
>   Wherein the Spirit held his wont to walke.
>   What does this meane my Lord?
> *Ham.* The King doth wake to night, and takes his rouse.
>   (NN6v–OO1)

Most would agree that the gist of the moment is maintained across the three editions. It could be argued that the two main points of this brief passage are to establish that it is very late at night and that the King is revelling. Both points are sustained in all three. The same characters are ushered onto the stage. In details of language, however, there are radical differences. The second quarto's 'The ayre bites shroudly' would be considered the more difficult or obscure reading, and might be preferred because it offers more complex valences than 'shrewd' or 'shrewdly'. However, the folio's use of the first quarto form might imply that some form of 'shrewd' is the more authoritative. The folio's Hamlet, however, is insensate, and asks, 'is it very cold?', while he can detect the temperature in the other versions. At the level of spelling and punctuation, the texts demonstrate why both issues are generally discounted when reading early play texts. So too, the texts show how stage directions might be taken as optional extras. The second quarto gives the fullest staging information about the noise that Horatio does not understand. If the folio survived alone, editors and readers would be vexed by Horatio's question, 'What does this meane my Lord?' Such vexing omissions are unfortunately common, and most modernised editions add or alter many stage directions for this reason.

The differences in these interactions between Hamlet, Horatio, and Marcellus might point to the differing manuscripts that lie behind the printed texts. The first quarto shortens the exchange between Hamlet and Horatio about the weather and the time – basic information that the audience needs to imagine on the bare summer stage of the Globe. Exactly who says what is fairly insignificant at this point. All that is required for an effective and understandable performance text is contained in this section of Q1, even though it differs substantially, and perhaps moves more quickly than, the texts of Q2 or F. In fact, Lukas Erne (Erne 2003) has argued that Q1 might be an original playing text, unadorned in comparison to its more literary alternatives in Q2 and F. Ann Thompson and Neil Taylor reinforce this view by calling Q1 'the only one of the three [texts] that could plausibly have been acted in its entirety' (Thompson and Taylor 2006: 1.8). Stephen Orgel goes further by noting that Q1 is '. . . almost unique among Shakespeare texts in being the right length for the canonical two hours' traffic of his stage' (Orgel 2006: 22). It is certainly debatable that Shakespeare's lengthier texts could not have been acted in full. But Q1 is substantially shorter than either Q2 or F, and so it seems to befit modern theatrical sensibilities at least. As Thompson and Taylor note in the most comprehensive stage history of the quarto: 'Q1, if staged with speed, energy and talent, not only may provide us with evidence about the nature of a performing text in Shakespeare's theatre, but may even, as theatre, be "not bad, but excellent"' (Thompson and Taylor 2006: 2.37).

For those with a theatrical interest in *Hamlet,* it seems that any one of the three texts might be worthy of consideration. Of course, the three texts of *Hamlet* have manifest differences that are not indicated in the brief excerpts analysed above, including missing passages and reconfigured scenes. Nonetheless, the 'story' of *Hamlet* is largely preserved: a basic plot summary of all three plays would run much the same, which accounts for why the first quarto's performance history has been a generally successful one.

Some difficulties with reading early play texts cannot easily be represented by a single passage from a single text. Speech headings present special difficulties because they can change over the course of a play. Chapter 2 explored how speech headings might be inaccurate or variable. Characters who speak in a scene are often absent from entry directions, for instance. Equally problematic are so-called 'ghost' characters, who are said to enter, but who have no lines. Clearly the drama of the period, as the opening of *Titus Andronicus,* with its senators and tribunes, demonstrates, could tolerate non-speaking characters. But editors have generally been keen to get rid of characters who say few or no lines. Martin Wiggins has shown how editors of Webster's *The White Devil* have tended to remove six characters, including 'Carlo and Pedro, the conspirators at the court of Padua; and the four "ghost characters" – Little Jaques the Moor, Christophero, Guid-Antonio, and Farnese – who are named in stage directions but have no lines to say' (Wiggins 1997: 448). Although the excisions of *The White Devil* are extreme, minor non-speaking characters appear in several play texts of the period. Violenta of *All's Well That Ends Well* and Innogen in *Much Ado about Nothing* have not survived as characters in many editions. However, their potential presence on stage could alter the effect of a scene, and therefore removing them is a critical judgement. Less famous play texts, particularly those without cast lists, will be potentially more confusing when they contain such absent presences. More difficult still is absent text. Plays in this period typically contained much music, but the text of songs (not to mention the tune) is frequently missing. When the songs from Middleton's *The Witch* were reused in *Macbeth,* only the cues were included. A reader of the folio *Macbeth* would therefore also need to consult Middleton's play for the full text. Printed plays might also have text omitted or altered because of censorship. Marston's Q1 *Malcontent* prints '( )' instead of 'pox' as a kind of self-censorship (G3). It is impossible to know if the word would have been spoken onstage or not. Such changes might require more than reading slightly ahead to determine what is happening. They require either a detailed knowledge of the entire play text, or in cases like *Macbeth* or perhaps even *Pericles*, a knowledge of other texts entirely.

Whenever play texts are read in the original, some form of the problems discussed above will occur, as there is no perfect early printed play. Greg's notion of the substantive and accidental with respect to copy text might be helpful here (Greg 1951–2). The texts with multiple editions, *Titus Andronicus* and *Hamlet*, are full of minor variations of spelling, punctuation, word choice, versification, speaker, and stage direction. Only the first two items of this list would count as accidentals. Changing text at the level of the word might conceivably be less consequential. But alterations of verse, speaker or stage direction potentially impact heavily upon a sense of language, character and plot. The passages selected above do not offer too many difficulties. But cruxes in play texts in this period can include radical difficulties that are yet to be settled satisfactorily. *Pericles* has some garbled passages that continue to perplex, for instance, like Cleon's lines about famine in Tarsus:

Our toungs and sorrowes to sound deepe:
Our woes into the aire, our eyes to weepe.
Till toungs fetch breath that may proclaime
Them louder, that if heauen slumber, while
Their creatures want, they may awake
Their helpers, to comfort them.

(B3v)

The pronoun confusion and the mixing of the senses of speech and sight here lead to textual corruption that could only have conjectural solutions.

To the question of 'how to read a Shakespearean play text?', then, the answers largely depend upon what the reading is *for*. The selection of text is probably the most crucial part of this process. In the case of *Hamlet* and other plays with two or more early play texts and one of them designated as 'bad', a reader interested in the theatrical attributes of the play, for instance, might well choose the early quarto. If theories of textual auspices affect the selection of text, then such choice would also impact upon a study seeking knowledge of 'Shakespeare' or any other author in the period. (The attendant dangers of finding authorial input in a play text have been outlined in the previous two chapters.) However, it is clear that an almost unimpeded construct of textual selection has shaped recent critical editing, so that any edition might be based upon any early text, or offer a conflation of two or more texts. It is still the case, however, that selecting a 'bad' quarto for a critical reading requires some form of explanation, in ways that selecting, say, the Oxford edition of *Romeo and Juliet* would not.

Editors of critical editions usually make highly informed choices, but those choices limit readings, all the same. Such limitations are part of the process of interpretation for any advanced scholar, but this section has been exercised to show that such decisions are difficult work and subject to potential pitfalls.

BIBLIOGRAPHICAL INVESTIGATIONS OF THE ORIGINALS

Increasingly, literary scholars are asked to consider original play texts not as objects for critical interpretation, but as copy texts for their own editorial work. One of the biggest shifts in the field towards the end of the twentieth century has been a widening of the types of scholars asked to put together critical editions. Many first-time editors have taken part in the latest projects involving Shakespeare and his contemporaries. For the most part, these projects demand both the critical skills required of introductions, performance essays, and commentary, and the bibliographical skills demanded of editing, textual notes, and textual essays. (Some editions have been collaborative, mixing critical and editorial expertise across two or more scholars.) R. A. Foakes has even noted that, 'One of the curious aspects of the explosion of writing about textual criticism and about editing in recent years is that many of those publishing advice or admonitions to editors have never edited a work themselves' (Foakes 1997: 425). It is worth pointing out in this context that W. W. Greg did not edit very frequently, either, but his work is essential reading for both novice and experienced editors.

Even those who have no intentions towards editing will need to know reasonably advanced bibliography in order to understand the kinds of introductory discussions that frame current scholarly editions. The second generation Arden text of *Hamlet*, edited by Harold Jenkins in 1982, for instance, devotes most of the lengthy introduction to the textual situation (Jenkins 1982). Many critical editions shape much of their discussion around textual issues, although it is interesting that great variation exists within single series. The Arden third series *Pericles*, edited by Suzanne Gossett, devotes forty-four pages to a discussion of the text, for instance; whereas the same series' *Timon of Athens*, edited by Anthony B. Dawson and Gretchen E. Minton, has a mere six pages (Dawson and Minton 2008).

This difference is partially explained by the very complex text of *Pericles*, but as explored above, *Timon* also presents textual difficulties.

There are currently few helpful guides to editing available, and this section will spell out some of the textual issues that might face anyone concerned with generating a critical edition, either for publication or as an aid to a full engagement with a play text. Because the works of James Shirley have not been subjected to modern editorial treatment, and because, as Lukas Erne has shown, Shirley was the fourth most popular dramatist in print in the period up to 1642 (Erne 2009: 18), the sections below will make frequent reference to his canon.

Bibliographical investigation can take a very wide variety of forms, from investigations of ligatures (i.e., multiple characters on a single piece of type), damaged type, and spellings, to paper, ornaments, and binding. Instead of attempting to consider every type of analysis, the following section will be concerned with those aspects of a play text that are most likely to yield telling results. For instance, headline investigation is one of the most expedient ways to determine how a volume was printed, but headlines alone do not indicate if multiple presses were at work, or the order of printing the sheets. Although not all of the following considerations need to be pursued, generally more than one type of bibliographical evidence is needed in order to understand the larger picture of how a play text was printed.

It should be noted that bibliographers must 'read' plays in very different ways to literary scholars. For bibliographers, the basic unit of change and analysis tends to be the forme, or one side of the printed sheet. Stop-press corrections, for instance, impact upon the level of the forme, and corrections might be found on B1, but not on B1v, which was subject to a different moment of printing and correction. Although changes and variance can take place on the level of the page, and even smaller levels, as is demonstrated by the fact that two separate compositors worked on some of the same pages of Shakespeare's folio, focusing too closely on individual pages can be deceptive in terms of tracing larger patterns of variation. Most of the examples below will concern formes. The 'inner' forme of a quarto is A1v-A2-A3v-A4, and is usually printed first; the 'outer' forme is A1-A2v-A3-A4v, and is usually printed second, to 'perfect' or finish the sheet.

This section will consider the following approaches to the bibliographical understanding of an early printed play text:
• preliminary research
• visiting holding libraries

- determining format
- title-page variation
- checking the copy for completeness
- printers' ornaments
- catchwords
- headlines
- distinctive type
- type shortage
- rule width
- line counts
- paper
- compositor identification: spacing, spelling, and punctuation
- stop-press correction
- reader annotations

Although this list is lengthy, many of these areas can be investigated in minutes. Others require considerably longer.

Preliminary research

Very few dramatic texts escaped fairly detailed scrutiny by the New Bibliographers, Greg, Pollard, and others working in the first half of the twentieth century, who aimed to understand with near-scientific precision the production of printed texts. Although that work is often incomplete, and occasionally inaccurate on particular points, it provides an important place to start. W. W. Greg's *A Bibliography of The English Printed Drama* (Greg 1939–59) and *The English Short Title Catalogue* (ESTC) (ESTC 2010) remain the most important resources in the field. These offer a formal description of the formes, indications of *Stationers' Register* entries and other contemporary references to the work, and often some brief indications of compositor or printer division or other interesting features. Greg provides the best resource for formal collations and any difficulties that might surround a play text.

Visiting holding libraries

As a first step towards visiting holding libraries, a facsimile of the text, either as digital photographs, a photo-facsimile, photocopy or EEBO printout, should be obtained as a working copy. The first real copy seen should be a local exemplar, and ideally, archival travel should move from closest to most distant exemplars. An awareness of any unique features across the copies is likely to increase over time. Therefore it might be necessary to return to copies in order to check subsequent findings. When visiting an archive, be sure to carry a ruler with measurements in millimetres.

Determining format

In almost all instances the format (quarto, octavo, folio) of a play text will have been accurately identified by previous scholars (Greg 1939–59; ESTC). However, some individual play texts present difficulties. Shirley's *Gentleman of Venice* and *Politician* (1655), for instance, were printed from the same settings of type as both quarto and octavo (with signatures partially altered). Although the signatures generally correspond to the format (i.e., four signatures per gathering for a quarto, or eight signatures per gathering for an octavo), there are occasions such as 'quartos in eights', where two quarto sheets make up a single gathering with eight signatures. And folios are usually gathered in fours or sixes. However, it is unlikely that a folio would be misidentified, both because of its noticeably larger size and because we can be confident that all surviving dramatic folios are well documented. Chain lines offer additional assistance for format identification. For quartos, they are parallel to the text; for octavos, they are perpendicular. Watermarks for octavos are in the upper binding margins of up to four leaves; watermarks for quartos are in the middle of the binding margin for up to two leaves. Greg often records if the format departs from expectations, for instance if the initial pages are set as part of the final pages. But it is important to look out for single leaves or half sheets that have been added to the normal run of gatherings. Disbound copies can be especially helpful in determining whether pages are contiguous (together on the same sheet of paper), or have been printed separately using half-sheet imposition, where only half of a sheet is printed at a time. Another test to determine if pages are contiguous (for copies that are tightly bound) is to see, in quarto, if chain lines run into each other in the binding margin. For more details on determining format, and some of the more unusual formats, see Gaskell's *A New Introduction to Bibliography* (Gaskell 1972).

Title-page variation

For the *English Short Title Catalogue*, a variation in title page is usually considered an entirely separate imprint. However, subsequent pages might not differ from imprint to imprint, and title-page variation can simply reflect shared rights in a text, or an alternative point of sale (for example,

Dublin and London in the case of some of Shirley's quartos). It is worth paying special attention to any variations in the title page, however, and these include variations of spacing, so consider not just the individual letters, but also where they are on the page with respect to one another. Often, a printer reused parts of the setting of a title page (as in the case of Shirley's *Six New Plays*). It can also be worth comparing a printer's output in a given year, to determine, for instance, if plays or other books might have been printed alongside each other (as in Shirley's 1637 quartos, *Hyde Park*, *The Young Admiral*, and *The Lady of Pleasure*).

Checking the copy for completeness

One of the most important things to do with any copy, and that includes those in EEBO, is to check it for completeness. A. W. Pollard outlines the basics of bibliography as follows: 'The object of the examination and collation of a book is twofold: (i) to discover whether it is perfect; (ii) to ascertain in what relation it stands to other copies of the same work' (Pollard 1907: 193). The first part of the task, then, is to check that all of the gatherings and leaves are present. Greg's *A Bibliography of the Printed Drama* (Greg 1939–59) will help determine what should be there, but missing pages or stubs might be apparent. And Greg's formula is not infallible. Fredson Bowers, *Principles of Bibliographic Description* (Bowers 1949) describes more fully the 'Greg-Bowers formulary' of how early printed books should be set out in a technical collation formula, or as Philip Gaskell defines it, a 'shorthand note of all the gatherings, individual leaves, and cancels as they occur in the ideal copy' (Gaskell 1972: 328). The formulary can range from the extremely simple to the complex. Jonson's *The Alchemist* (1612), for instance, collates as follows:

$$4°: \text{A-M}^4[\$3 \text{ signed } (-A1, -D3, -I3, -K3)]$$

The '4°' before colon designates the format as quarto. '2°' and '8°' would be folio and octavo respectively. After the colon come the signatures, which for *The Alchemist* run from A to M without interruption. The square brackets contain information about how the signatures are labelled. '$3 signed' means that usually the first three signatures (for example, A1, A2, A3) of a gathering are signed, while the fourth is not. The information that follows shows which signatures break this general rule and are not signed. For any fourth signatures that were signed, a plus sign would be needed to designate them (for example, +I4). *The Alchemist* has a simple bibliographical construction, and this brief formula is effective at communicating which pages should be present, and how they should be labelled. The foliation and pagination (if present) should be checked in any exemplar to ensure that they are correct. Inaccuracies were usually, but not always, caught by Greg, and both signatures and page numbers could have been subject to stop-press correction or damage.

A slightly more complex collation formula applies to Shirley's *The Coronation*:

$$4°: \ A^2 \ B\text{-}I^4 \ K^2 \ [\$3 \ \text{signed} \ (\text{-}A1)]$$

Although it is a quarto, like *The Alchemist*, Shirley's play prints signatures A and K as half sheets (of two leaves), as signified by the superscript twos in the collation formula. It would be possible for these half sheets to have been printed on one sheet, that would then be folded and wrapped around sheets B-I, but as it happens, both A and K were set by half-sheet imposition (as determined by the investigation of chainlines as discussed below). Collation formulae for larger volumes grow correspondingly more complex. The third volume of Ben Jonson's 1640–1 folio, which contains material that had not been published in his 1616 folio, collates as follows:

$2°$: B-Q^4 R^2 S-X^4 Y^2 Z-2O^4 2P^2 2Q^4, ^{2}A-P^4 Q^2 R-V^4, ^{3}A-K^4 L^2 M-R^4 [\$2 signed (+B3, +^{3}C3, -C1, -R2, -Y2, -Z1, -2P2, -2Q2, -^{2}A1, -^{2}I1, -^{2}R1, -^{2}Q1, -^{3}A1, -^{3}M1), mis-signing 2B2 as 'B2'] 290 leaves, paged 1–292, ^{2}3–122 [123–132] 133–155, ^{3}1–132, misnumbering 93 as 87, 285 as 283, ^{2}50 as 52, ^{2}80–89 as 70–79, ^{2}151 as 143, and ^{2}154 as 146

CONTENTS: B1: *Christmas his Masque*; C1: *Masque in the House of Lord Haye*; C4v: *Vision of Delight*; D3v: *Pleasure Reconciled to Virtue*; E3v: *For the Honour of Wales*; F4: *News from the New World Discovered in the Moon*; G4: *Masque of the Metamorphosed Gypsies*; M1: *Masque of Augurs*; N2v: *Time Vindicated*; P1: *Neptune's Triumph*; Q3v: *Pan's Anniversary*; S1: *Masque of Owls*; S3: *Fortunate Isles*; V2v: *Love's Triumph through Callipolis*; X2: *Chloridia*; Z1: *Under-woods*; 2N4v: *King's Entertainment at Welbeck*; 2P1: *Love's Welcome at Bolsover*; 2Q2: *Mortimer his Fall*; ^{2}A1: *Magnetic Lady*; ^{2}I1: *Tale of a Tub*; ^{2}R1: *The Sad Shepherd*; ^{3}A1: *Horace, his Art of Poetry*; ^{3}D4: *The English Grammar*; ^{3}M1: *Timber; or, Discoveries*.

This collation is based upon, but slightly corrects, the formula found in Greg's *Bibliography* (Greg 1939–59: 1079–82). As the book is longer than a play text quarto, the signatures must extend to Aa, Bb, et cetera. However, this book is also made up in sections that repeat the same signatures, just as Shakespeare's folio does, albeit less consistently, for the three sections of comedies, histories, and tragedies. Repeated signatures are signified by the superscript numbers before the letters, so that the second set of signatures from A is shown as '^{2}A-P^4', while the third set is '^{3}A-K^4'. (The superscripts do not appear in the play text's signatures.) Sections are separated by commas, which appear just before those new, repeated signature runs. Page numbers are included after the statement of signatures, and the superscripts before the numbers again reflect separate sections. Finally, a section on contents should be given for volumes with complex sub-divisions. The third volume of Jonson's folio is found bound with its contents in various orders. Although the collation formula above applies to all 'ideal' copies, any individual exemplar might order the sections differently, or indeed have missing sections or components. Checking for completeness against the collation formula is therefore particularly important when dealing with complex collections of plays. It should be noted that the formulae for bibliographical description can vary slightly in different handbooks. Greg's final volume to his *A Bibliography of the English Printed Drama* notes that, 'Professor Bowers and I do not always see eye to eye' (Greg 1939–59: iv, note). There are, however, more similarities than differences, and any deviations generally remain readable, especially as most play texts have fairly straightforward gatherings.

Because many play texts are incomplete, sometimes missing only a leaf, it is important to check if a chosen archival copy has all of the pages outlined in Greg, including any blank pages that might survive in rare perfect copies. These pages can offer vital clues about the printing of a given book, but of course the pages with print on them are the most important, and all of these should be accounted for. Also look for stubs in the margins that might indicate the removal of pages (perhaps with pages from another exemplar pasted in subsequently). Incomplete copies can still be investigated, but omission or damaged/trimmed leaves should be recorded. The folding of a gathering should also be checked, as it can vary from exemplar to exemplar. In Shirley's octavo *The Doubtful Heir*, a blank associated with quire A can appear before the title page or after A3. Such variations should be noted, as they can disclose confusion about the make-up of the volume and information about how it was printed – in the case of Shirley's play, A1-A4 were set by half-sheet imposition. See below under chainlines for the determination of conjugate sheets.

Printers' ornaments

Ornaments can help identify printers, when they are not specified on the title page, or confirm the identity of doubtful printers, when a volume is suspected, like the Pavier quartos, of having a false imprint. Printers might hold similar ornaments, and ornaments could be lent out or shared amongst a group of printers, so this work requires a detailed knowledge and a keen eye. As Peter Blayney points out: 'printers were in the habit of borrowing, more or less frequently and for a variety of reasons, each others' ornaments' (Blayney 1982: 36). But an ornament could be associated with a given printer, an obvious example being the Oxford University coat of arms ornament that appears in the University Press printing of William Gager's *Ulysses Redux Tragoedia Nova* of 1592. McKerrow's *Printers' and Publishers' Devices* (McKerrow 1913) and McKerrow and Ferguson's *Title-page Borders* (McKerrow and Ferguson 1932) are the standard guides for identifying the types of ornaments from the period. If the identity of a printer or printers is in doubt, compare ornaments across the other books of possible printers from around the same year of publication. Slight damage to ornaments can also be a useful guide to printing chronology, if the damage emerges as part of a print run or across a series of printed books.

Catchwords

Another way to ensure that a copy is complete is to check that all of the catchwords at the bottom right of both recto and verso pages marry with the words on subsequent pages. Again, variations are usually recorded in Greg. Gaps or even differences of spelling can be significant. Such breaks might point to some disruption to printing, which could include inattention by a compositor, missing texts or pages, a change of compositor, or even a division in the production of the texts across two printing shops. Catchword disruption, however, is not very conclusive evidence of its own; instead, it highlights a possible area of further enquiry. Subsequent tests below will help determine with more security any possible causes of a mismatch. It should be noted that some texts seem to have many catchword errors. The folio text of Shakespeare's *The Tempest* has several catchword errors or disagreements. The catchword of B2v, for instance, is 'Didst'; whereas 'Did' is the first word of B3:'Most cruelly [Didst (c. w.)] / Did thou *Alonso*, vse me, and my daughter'. In this instance, the catchword might correct the text.

Most catchword errors give occasion to few bibliographical conclusions, and are probably simple mistakes. In four out of five of the mismatches in *The Tempest*, the same compositor set both catchword and the next page, according to the compositor breakdown offered in Wells and Taylor's *Textual Companion* (Wells and Taylor 1997: 148–9). Further, no discernible pattern affects the printing order of the mismatched pages, with three out of five of the subsequent pages set before their catchwords, following the printing order offered by the *Textual Companion*. Although the play was set unusually from the outer pages (i.e., 1 and 6) towards the inner pages (i.e., 3 and 4), against the normal working pattern for the folio of setting from the inner pages outwards, the catchword evidence does not seem to be affected by this reversal. Therefore, the catchwords of this play do not tell us much about its printing, but they do offer a possible correction to the compositor mistake of 'Did' for 'Didst'. For any play text it is useful to determine how many catchwords are erroneous and to seek explanations for such errors. The results are not always significant, but the data can be attained quickly.

Headlines

Headline analysis offers one of the most powerful and expedient tools for the bibliographer. Fredson Bowers pioneered the process of running-title analysis and what kinds of conclusions might be reached from it (Bowers 1938), although such conclusions have been challenged by D. F. McKenzie (1969), so that headline evidence should be combined with other forms of evidence to reach firm conclusions. Headlines, or running titles, were usually reused (i.e., left in the skeleton forme) when subsequent pages were set. Therefore, in a play text that was set in one uninterrupted process, a pattern of headline reuse would typically emerge. For a play text set using two skeleton formes, as was often the case, a minimum of two sets of headlines (for a total of eight individual headlines for a quarto) would be used. If a play text were set from a single skeleton, then a minimum of four headlines would be required. Such headlines or running titles frequently have unique features – borders, spelling, spacing, orthography, or characteristic type – that can be used to identify them. Note that running titles might also be changed in the course of printing. Identify unique running titles, including those that might have been changed. Label them A, B, C, et cetera, and then chart their distribution in the volume. If the distribution of running titles is consistent with formes, then the type was almost certainly set by formes, instead of seriatim. Changes in the headlines might indicate the order in which the pages or formes were set, or point to disruptions to printing.

Some early dramatic texts, such as Shirley's *Triumph of Peace*, have no headlines, but most do, making headline analysis widely applicable. There are several techniques that can be applied to identify headlines that match. The overall length of the headlines, or spaces between words or characters, can be measured. Ideally, there will be alternative spellings or distinctive

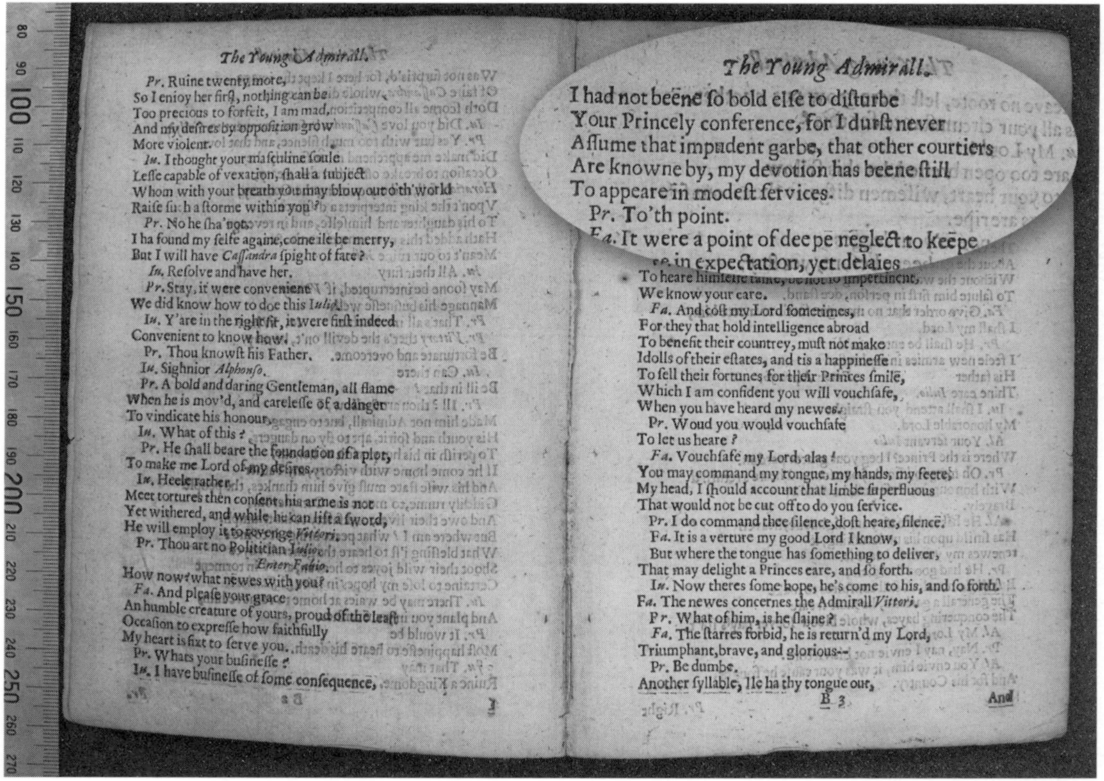

Fig. 19. Headline, B3.

type that make the process fairly straightforward. For instance, in Shirley's *The Young Admiral* (1637), the headlines are easy to differentiate, as in Figures 19, 20, and 21.

In these examples, the first letter of 'Admirall' takes on characteristically different forms, from the standard italic A, to the swash-A, to the swash-A with a curly tail in Dιv. Although all three titles are spelled the same, the type is clearly different. It is possible to compare headlines using photographic and mirror-imaging techniques, as outlined by Randall McLeod (1979), but eye-balling real copies or high-quality images is usually sufficient. Such a survey might yield a table of headline distribution, like this one for Shirley's *Young Admiral* (see Table 1).

This quarto, like most play texts, has no headlines in its preliminary material, so this type of evidence will say little about the printing of the first quires. This chart discloses several pieces of key information about the other printed formes of the quarto, however. Two skeleton formes were used throughout the printing process, one made up of Headlines A–D, the other made up of Headlines E–H. These headlines were consistent throughout the process of composing the play, which suggests smooth composition. Changes in the pattern of headline usage would point to possible areas for further investigation, but the change here is very slight, with the headlines associated with H1r and H3r being swapped around at I3r and I1r. Because this swap was maintained for signature K, it can fairly confidently be said that signatures I and K were printed as a distinct grouping, either after or before signatures B–H. (The normal pattern would be after, but as McKenzie points out: 'If copy is cast off for a quarto text, there is no compelling reason why any sheet should not be printed in any order – say, H, F, A, C, D, B, E, G. One might expect and assume a straightforward progression through the book, but there is no compelling reason for it' (McKenzie 1969: 41).) More complicated headline distribution charts with more severe changes, like that required for the third volume of Jonson's second folio, help determine printing order and disruption for complex printing jobs that extended over months or years (see Giddens 2003).

Folio play collections often also have rules that frame the headlines, and these rules can also be subject to identification. Headlines can be altered or damaged over the course of a print run, and as a general rule the more they change, the more information, especially about printing order, they convey. Difficulties with headline analysis can emerge when play texts have been heavily trimmed (often headlines are affected), or poorly or heavily inked. Further, headlines do not in any way confirm the number of compositors or presses, or shape the process of stop-press correction,

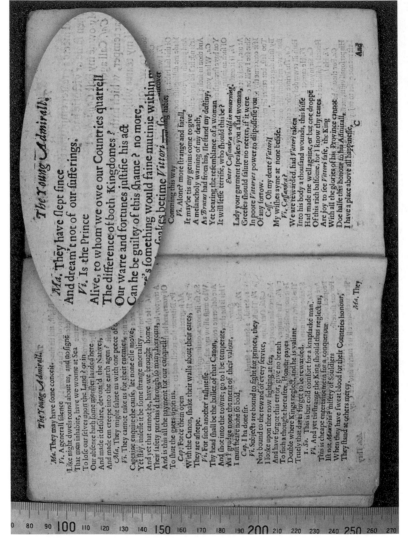

Fig. 20. Headline, C1.

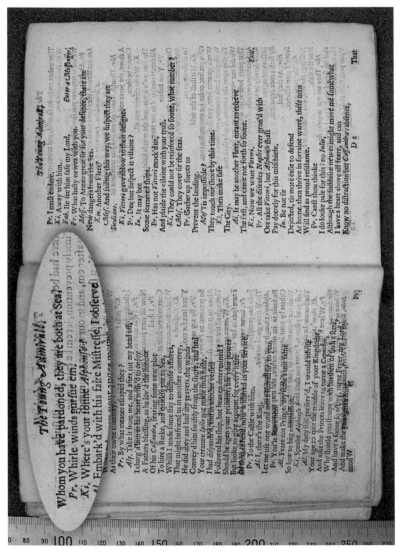

Fig. 21. Headline, D1v.

Table 1. *Headline analysis of James Shirley's* Young Admiral *(1637)*

Headlines	Sigs								
A		C_1	D_1	E_1	F_1	G_1	H_1	I_3	K_3
B	B_{2v}	C_{2v}	D_{2v}	E_{2v}	F_{2v}	G_{2v}	H_{2v}	I_{2v}	K_{2v}
C	B_3	C_3	D_3	E_3	F_3	G_3	H_3	I_1	K_1
D	B_{4v}	C_{4v}	D_{4v}	E_{4v}	F_{4v}	G_{4v}	H_{4v}	I_{4v}	
E	B_{1v}	C_{1v}	D_{1v}	E_{1v}	F_{1v}	G_{1v}	H_{1v}	I_{1v}	K_{1v}
F	B_2	C_2	D_2	E_2	F_2	G_2	H_2	I_2	K_2
G	B_{3v}	C_{3v}	D_{3v}	E_{3v}	F_{3v}	G_{3v}	H_{3v}	I_{3v}	K_{3v}
H	B_4	C_4	D_4	E_4	F_4	G_4	H_4	$I_{4}?$	

as McKenzie demonstrates (McKenzie 1969: 24ff). But generally, headline analysis can be conducted quickly, and therefore it makes a good diagnostic technique before other bibliographical tests are applied.

Distinctive type

Contrasting strongly with headline analysis in terms of a scholar's time commitment is the search for recurring, damaged, or distinctive type. Antony Hammond calls it, 'perhaps the most time-consuming and potentially frustrating bibliographical labor yet conceived, and should not be undertaken lightly in hope of easy and certain results' (Hammond 1986: 170). For this reason, very little type recurrence analysis has been conducted outside of the non-canonical play texts of the period, and even some of those have not been investigated using this technique.

Distinctive type, or type 'which differ[s] at all noticeably from the normal appearance of that character' (Blayney 1982: 93), can usually be identified only under magnification. Types that appear noticeably damaged to the naked eye 'are likely to be noticed by the compositor or proof-reader, and discarded rather than distributed' back into the case (Hammond 1986: 160). The process of magnifying each piece of type, either with an optical instrument or by enlarging high-resolution photographs, is clearly very time-consuming. But the process is made more laborious for two reasons: (1) characters will often fracture at the same point, so that, for instance, 'Letters which have a vertical joining a curve are most prone to damage at the join. . . . Letters with ascenders and descenders will sooner or later get bent' (Hammond 1986: 160); and (2) letters that appear damaged might be the products of poor or heavy inking. Therefore, damaged type is difficult to determine. It must be uniquely damaged, so that there is no risk of false recurrences, and multiple copies of the text must be examined to determine if the damage is repeatable across multiple impressions.

Type recurrence can be useful in answering several questions about an early play text. For instance, if the same piece of type appears in B1 and B1v of a quarto, then that sheet at least was set by forme, instead of seriatim. In that instance, the type from one side of the forme would be redistributed and used to set the other. Seriatim printing demands one set of type per gathering, and no type should reappear except possibly on the eighth and final page of a quarto gathering (which could await setting until type from the inner forme, pages two, three, six, and seven, was redistributed). Therefore, the sustained reappearance of type on both inner and outer formes of a sheet would indicate composition by forme. Distinctive type also helps to disclose the order in which formes were set. If a piece of type appears on two pages, one page was set either before or after the other. Repeated instances of recurring type therefore establish complex chronologies. Patterns of recurring type can also show if more than one case of type was used, and help identify the different cases. However, as Peter Blayney has shown, such identification can be muddled by the mixing of cases (Blayney 1982: 128). Recurring damaged type is therefore one of the most powerfully indicative types of bibliographical evidence, but acquiring that evidence comes at the expense of a great deal of time.

Type shortage

A less exhausting investigation of type concerns its shortage, when one letter is required to an unusual degree, runs out, and then has to be replaced by a substitution or near-matching piece of type or types. Peter Blayney points out that even texts that were accurately cast off can suffer type shortage: 'The approximate quantity of type needed to set a given number of pages can be estimated in advance, but the individual requirements of the separate sorts cannot' (Blayney 1982: 131). Plays made particular demands in typesetting, as the frequency of speech headings strained the supply of capital italic letters. Peter Blayney has investigated the type shortages caused by the frequent need for italic *E* in *King Lear*'s first quarto, a character used frequently in the repeated headings for Edgar and Edward (Blayney 1982: 129ff). Substituted characters included the swash italic '*E*' or the roman 'E'. Other common examples include substituting short-s for those instances that would normally have a long-s, or 'J' for 'I', or 'VV' for 'W'. The compositors for Shirley's *The Traitor* (1635) experienced an unusual demand on the letter 'I' towards the end of the play. Gathering H

Table 2. *Occurrence of 'I' and 'J' (for 'I') in* The Traitor *(1635)*

	Outer				Inner			
	G1	**G2v**	**G3**	**G4v**	**G1v**	**G2**	**G3v**	**G4**
I/*I*	6	17	15	13	6	0	15	6
J	0	0	0	0	0	7	0	2
	H1	**H2v**	**H3**	**H4v**	**H1v**	**H2**	**H3v**	**H4**
I/*I*	26/1	8	6	15	10	12	9	0
J	0	0	5	0	16	3	0	17
	I1	**I2v**	**I3**	**I4v**	**I1v**	**I2**	**I3v**	**I4**
I/*I*	12	13	12	6	10	12	8	10
J	2	0	1	4	0	0	0	0
	K1	**K2v**	**K3**	**K4v**	**K1v**	**K2**	**K3v**	**K4**
I/*I*	14	6	11	11	13	5	12	9
J	0	0	0	0	0	9	0	0

is the most heavily affected, although the problem emerges in gathering G and continues from that point throughout the play, as shown in Table 2, above.

Gathering G required seventy-eight total instances of roman 'I'. Gathering H required eighty-six; gathering I, eighty-three; and gathering K, eighty-one. These figures are close enough to each other to be suggestive of a regular pattern of redistribution of type. The frequency of substitution of 'J' for 'I' strongly points to setting by formes, as it is concentrated in one forme of each gathering, but not both. Further, the forme demanding the most 'I's was H outer, and the forme suffering most from shortage is H inner, suggesting that this sheet was composed using the same stock of type. The bare overall pattern outlined above is suggestive of the outer side of the forme being set before the inner for sheets G, H, and K, but sheet I reverses the pattern, so other additional evidence would be required to establish the sequence of composing for even this brief section. The setting order of pages within the forme also cannot be argued with certainty, because 'It is not uncommon to find a compositor reacting to an *imminent* shortage by making sporadic substitutions before the box is entirely empty' (Blayney 1982: 129). Indeed, the shortages have highly variable impact *within* the formes, suggesting either that the starting point for composition within a forme was variable, or that the redistribution of type from formes that had been printed came at different times. Varying efficiency of redistribution is the more likely answer, which raises a question about whether one or two cases of type were used for this job. The total amount of type used for the job, however, is easy to determine; it runs to around eight quarto pages.

Interestingly, signature 3v for each gathering suffers no type shortages. Possibly it was the first page of the forme to be set, before type ran short, or the last page to be set, after type had been redistributed. There are usually several possible solutions for replacing unavailable type. The upper-case roman 'I' might be replaced by italic '*I*', for instance, as happens in just one instance in *The Traitor*, at H1. If distinct substitution patterns emerge, that might be evidence of separate compositors at work, although that does not apply to *The Traitor* sample. These and other hypotheses are best answered by combining type-shortage evidence with other types of data.

Type shortage does not, of course, impact upon every play text from the period. However, it is easy to spot at first reading and, if present, offers a quick source of bibliographical information. Type shortage can offer clear and efficient evidence towards setting by formes, as it does above for *The Traitor*. It can also be combined with other evidence to highlight printing order and patterns of the redistribution of type.

Rule width

When setting a page of type, compositors used a 'stick' to determine the width of a line of prose. Such sticks might be adjustable or fixed and cut from wood, but once the width had been determined by a compositor, he would use the stick to ensure that type was justified on the page. Sometimes, pages disclose varying widths, and these point to different sticks, or different stick adjustments, being used. Such variance can help separate stages of composition (or, indeed, compositors). Be aware that paper shrinkage, owing to the storage history of a given volume, can make the width of the rule vary from exemplar to exemplar. Deviation can be as much as two millimetres. Therefore, measurements should be taken from a single exemplar, or from an average taken over several copies.

D. F. McKenzie has questioned the proficiency of rule-width evidence by noting that, 'Not only do the widths of type-pages set by the same compositor vary, but different compositors are often found setting to an identical measure, and interruptions are routine' (McKenzie 1969: 23). Line widths are therefore not foolproof as a means of differentiating compositors. However, they may nonetheless be taken as indicative evidence. Accurate casting off would require a pre-determined line width, so there was some need for consistency. When that consistency varies, it might suggest separate compositors, a gap in printing, or a conscious decision to widen or narrow the stick to adjust for inaccurate casting off. Such evidence is best coupled with other bibliographical information. For instance,

Jonson's second folio, Volume 3, has a rule that is consistently 124 millimetres, until a point late in the printing of the volume (^{3}R), where it jumps to 128 millimetres. This change corresponds to changes in headlines, line count, and the frequency of stop-press correction. Therefore, the change in rule width can be indicative of a disruption to printing when used alongside other bibliographical evidence (Giddens 2003).

Line counts

The number of lines used to fill a page (discounting the running title and catchword) can provide similarly indicative evidence. Alterations in line count can disclose places where space became pressured in the typesetting, where casting off was done poorly, or where there were separate stages of composition. Jill Levenson has investigated the line counts of pages in *Romeo and Juliet* Q1 (1597) to note that gatherings A–D have thirty-two lines per page, while gatherings E–K have thirty-six (Levenson 2000: 109). This change of line count is coupled with a change of fount size, with the latter pages being more densely printed, with a smaller fount. Further, the headlines change at this point as well. The change in line count is therefore part of a wider body of evidence that highlights a significant disruption or division to printing. In fact, the play was printed separately by John Danter (named on the title page) and Edward Allde (not named). Variations in line count can also point to either different methods of casting off or to the discovery of poor casting-off calculations, with an attempt to correct them during the print run.

Paper

The physical paper of a book can provide helpful bibliographical information about the printing of a play text. G. Thomas Tanselle notes that:

One of the peculiarities in the historical development of descriptive bibliography has been the small attention paid to paper. Since paper and inked type-impressions are the two principal physical ingredients of a book and since paper is the one which gives a book its most obvious physical characteristics (shape, size, weight, bulk), it would seem natural for a description of paper to occupy a prominent position in any description of a book. Yet the majority of descriptive bibliographies of the past make no mention of paper, except the indirect references afforded by an indication of format or leaf measurement. (Tanselle 1971: 27)

There are many ways to investigate paper. Tanselle has helpfully outlined a full range of possibilities, including testing for strength, absorbency, and smoothness (Tanselle 1971: 55). This section will consider the basic elements of watermarks, chainlines, dimensions, and type impressions.

Paper is usually identified by its watermarks, or the designs left in paper by wire moulds. (The chief use of watermarks is to identify the format of a book, as discussed above.) For this form of analysis, however, only real copies or photographs of the watermarks may be examined. Watermarks can also be difficult to determine. Paper that has been heavily printed or is darkened with age can make identifying watermarks impossible. Further, watermarks in quartos and octavos are frequently obscured in the binding (in the middle of the binding edge, or in the upper binding corner), and paper from the period might be unwatermarked. Professional studies of watermarks might rely on beta radiography or incandescent light and film to make watermarks more clearly visible (Spector 1987; Gants 1998). Watermarks usually take on characteristic shapes (pots, flowers, or initials). Groupings of paper with the same watermarks in an exemplar or in a wider body of books from a printer may therefore be tabulated much as headlines or other features are, except that watermarks affect sheets, instead of individual pages or formes. To assist in identification, works such as Charles M. Briquet, *Les Filigranes* (1907) and Edward Heawood's *Watermarks, Mainly of the 17th and 18th Centuries* (Heawood 1950) point to many of the available designs from the period.

As discussed in Chapter 1, the publisher was responsible for paying for or supplying the stock of paper for a given print job. However, that paper might be mixed in origin and quality: 'many quartos contain several different watermarks, and some almost as many different watermarks as sheets' (Stevenson 1948–9: 151). It is unlikely that any exemplar of an early printed book would have paper that exactly matched another exemplar (Stevenson 1951–2b: 90–1). Therefore, several exemplars of an individual play text need to be consulted to get a sense of watermark distribution. Stevenson's pioneering work shows that watermarks can be put to a variety of potential uses: 'A generation of scholars has used inconsistency in watermarks to spot cancels, inserted sheets, mixed issues, standing type, made-up, copies, facsimiles, and other irregularities' (Stevenson 1948–9: 182). For instance, if pages within a single gathering have a different watermark, then more than one sheet of paper was used to make up that gathering. That would be expected in folio gatherings, but unexpected in quartos or octavos. Therefore, watermarks can be used to ensure that a copy is made up the way that it is meant to be, and not a potentially corrupt copy. Paper can also assist with dating evidence: Greg used watermarks to spot that the Pavier quartos of 1619 were misdated, for instance (Greg 1908). More recently,

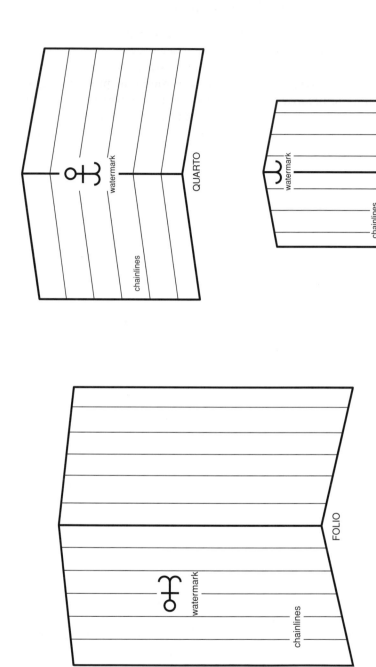

Fig. 22. Chainline and watermark positioning in folio, quarto, and octavo.

Carter Hailey has used paper evidence to date the fourth quarto of *Hamlet* and the fourth quarto of *Romeo and Juliet* (Hailey 2007). In addition, if matching individual sheets of paper are found across several different texts, then those play texts were likely to have gone through the press at roughly similar times. The premise would be that a batch of paper arrived and was then used in the various concurrent or consecutive projects in which a printer was engaged. Similarly, watermarks can assist in the determination of the printing order of formes in an individual volume. The editors of the Malone Society *Two Noble Kinsmen* trace the same batch of paper for gatherings B–L and part of M, but show that a different stock was used for half-sheet A:N, highlighting 'that the half-sheet A:N was indeed the last to be printed' (Proudfoot and Rasmussen 2005: viii). Watermark study is partially quantitative in its methods, and requires a lot of time; the Malone editors examined the watermarks of an exhaustive thirty-eight copies. As a starting point, it is valuable to chart the distribution of watermarks in a single copy to see if any patterns emerge that might deserve further scrutiny.

Further paper evidence might be derived from the chainlines, or the parallel impressions left in the paper from the chains of the paper mould. Stevenson notes that 'These wire and chain indentations are in effect watermarks; and in certain respects the chainmarks are easier to use than the designs called watermarks' (Stevenson 1954: 181). Chainlines offer one of the quickest ways for determining the format of early books, with those for folios and octavos running perpendicular to the text, and those for quartos running parallel to the text, as in Figure 22.

In the absence of watermarks, varying widths between chainlines can be used to identify separate stocks of paper. For quartos, chainlines can also help identify pages that are contiguous or not. If a full quarto sheet is folded, page one should be contiguous with page four, and page two should be contiguous with page three. Folio pages should be contiguous according to how the volume is made up, so for Shakespeare's 1623 folio in sixes it would be 1–6, 2–5, and 3–4. Contiguous quarto pages have their watermarks in line in the binding margins. So contiguous chain lines help determine if pages were printed together as a forme, which is not always clear, especially at the beginning or end of a given work. James Shirley's *The Witty Fair One* (1633), for instance, is made up as 4°: A² B–I⁴ K². A1–A2 and K1–K2 have chainlines that are contiguous, or run directly into one another. Therefore, both of these pages were set half-sheet imposition, instead of a single sheet intended for folding as A1, A2, K1[A3], and K2[A4]. On the other hand, Stevenson uses chainline evidence to determine that plays like Fletcher's

Monsieur Thomas (1639) use such folding-around of leaves to make up the volume, whereby the title page and the final page of the play are conjugate and wrapped around the other gatherings (Stevenson 1954: 194). The case of *Two Noble Kinsmen*, as above, also includes a title page printed on the same half sheet as the final page, 'folded back to create a cover for the quarto' (Proudfoot and Rasmussen 2005: v). Of course, any gathering might be made up of two pages set by half-sheet imposition. Or single pages can be inserted by the original printer as cancels, or in its subsequent history, that might be made 'perfect' by pages from another copy in 'mixed editions, sophistications, restorations' (Stevenson 1954: 183). Such unusual volume constructions can best be determined through chainline or watermark evidence, unless the volume is disbound and the physical binding edges of the paper can be examined as well.

Further evidence from paper can be gleaned from measuring the page, as Tanselle argues (Tanselle 1971). Dimensions of the paper itself relate largely to format, and will vary from copy to copy, depending upon how much trimming was done by the binder(s) who have worked on it, and according to paper shrinkage. Bibliographers interested in paper size will typically examine as many exemplars as possible to find the largest surviving pages. Multiplying that size by two for folio or four for quarto, for instance, would theoretically give the dimensions of a sheet that is slightly smaller than was the original, unfolded and uncut sheet.

These dimensions will rarely be very helpful in themselves, but might point to variations from copy to copy. Occasionally, books are printed on two different sizes of paper from the same (or slightly varied) setting of type, as in the case of Jonson's large and small first folios of 1616. Jonson had several presentation copies printed on large paper, as more prestigious gifts to patrons. The differentiation of large and small paper copies has proved important, as Jonson's twentieth-century editors were convinced that large-paper variants must have more authority, whereas Kevin Donovan has demonstrated that for some sheets the large paper copies are the least corrected, as they were the first to be printed (Donovan 1987). Similarly, James Shirley's *Gentleman of Venice* and *Politician*, both 1655, were printed as quarto and octavo, with the octavo format sheets being the first to go through the press (Fehrenback 1971). Differentiating these play texts on the basis of paper size, especially for the Jonson, is an important first step towards describing a given exemplar. Paper size differences within a copy can disclose that it is a made-up volume from different copies. For instance, in Shirley's *The Young Admiral* held at Meisei University Library, Tokyo (MR1065), quire E is 12 millimetres taller than the surrounding quires. Almost certainly, that quire came from another copy of the quarto that was cannibalised to make one, more complete version. Measurements are unlikely to disclose such variance on a local level, but across several exemplars they can be revealing.

A final piece of information that can be gleaned from paper is type impression. The physical indentations left by type can disclose whether the inner or outer of a sheet was set first. Type impression is determined via raked lighting and/or viewing a page at an angle. 'In a crisp, unpressed copy it is usually possible to recognise the first forme by the indentations of the second – a little hillock with ink on its surface occurs wherever a letter in the first-forme page has been indented by a letter of the second forme' (Povey 1960: 189). Special lamps can be constructed to aid in the process, so that a shadow is cast by the tiny 'hillock' on the first forme (Povey 1960). This technique is used purely to establish printing order, but if two presses are working at once on both sides of the same forme, it may be that the order varies from exemplar to exemplar (making this technique also suitable for detecting two presses at work). However, such raised ink formations can be difficult to detect, as Antony Hammond points out (Hammond 1986: 156).

Techniques of paper analysis are often ignored in critical editions of early modern drama. The work requires consultation of a large number of surviving copies, and it is often difficult to seek watermarks, chainlines, and type impressions. However, they provide the most certain evidence towards the make up of a volume and the printing order of its formes.

Compositor identification: spacing, spelling, and punctuation

As Chapter 1 makes clear, many of the textual properties associated with early play texts derive from compositors. Evidence suggests that compositors were willing to change spelling, spacing, and punctuation to deal with the complex business of translating a manuscript play into a printed text with pre-defined spacing limitations. These features can also be used to separate one compositor from another, on the basis that compositors would develop distinguishable habits. It is important to note, however, that compositors might divide their labour by forme, page, or even part-page, so finding the divisions might require working on units of text that are smaller than page-level.

A small industry of scholars in the twentieth century worked to determine the compositors of Shakespeare's 1623 folio. Paul Werstine notes that, 'Recent qualitative study of the compositors' work has justified the labour expended in compositor identification, since accuracy in transmission has been shown to vary widely from one workman to another' (Werstine 1982: 206). In other words, a sense of how accurate or inaccurate a compositor was by habit might justify the degree of security an editor or a reader feels towards the printed text. Charlton Hinman's 1963 study of the compositors of Shakespeare's 1623 folio was based largely on the kinds of type-identification evidence discussed above. However, compositors do not necessarily consistently use separate cases of type, and type can be deployed on concurrent projects in ways that disrupt the reliability of such evidence.

Spelling, punctuation, and spacing evidence can be helpful in separating the habits of multiple compositors. T. H. Howard-Hill's study of 'The Compositors of Shakespeare's Folio Comedies' examines such evidence as the: 'spacing after commas in short lines, and at the ends of lines, their typographical arrangement of turned-over verse lines, their preferences in dealing with *'ll* and *th'* elisions, and some fairly common spellings supplementing the familiar *do*, *go*, and *here*' (Howard-Hill 1973: 61). Almost any evidence of this type can be brought to bear on the question, but Howard-Hill here outlines good places to start. If the old-spelling text is available electronically (as many of the texts in EEBO are, for instance), then it can be worth running it through concordance software to determine the range of available spellings, although this evidence would be indicative only, as accurate old-spelling e-texts are difficult to find. As Howard-Hill notes, words that can optionally end with an extra 'e' (like 'mee', 'goe', 'hee') can disclose variance, as can words that would today be contractions (like 'Ile' or 'I'll'). Capitalisation is also often a feature that might separate compositors, and speech prefixes and other names might be abbreviated differently, too. As compositors had latitude to change the spellings of words in their source manuscripts to fit the measure of a line, sometimes individual compositors will spell a single word in multiple ways. For instance, the compositor of Shirley's *The Traitor* (1635) spells 'humbly' in the modern way and 'hūbly' on signature H2. The shortened version of the word clearly relates to the cramped spacing of its line. On the other hand, the same compositor on the same page offers both 'He' and 'Hee', seemingly independent of any spacing considerations. Nonetheless, patterns of spelling, especially for common words, can help point to individual compositors.

Patterns in the use of punctuation can also assist towards compositor identification. Antony Hammond's 1986 study of *The White Devil*, for instance, notes that: 'The semi-colon is used only 25 times up to E4ᵛ, and 14 pages lack it altogether; from F1ʳ on it is used 5.4 times as often: 220 occurrences altogether, and only three pages are without one' (Hammond

Table 3. *Compositor divisions and turned-over lines in* The Winter's Tale

COMPOSITOR	A	B	C	D
PAGES	1	14	2	20
OCCURRENCES	1	20	2	94

(Howard-Hill 1973: 71).

1986: 143). Such an abrupt change in frequency would seem to highlight a change of compositor. Dashes, colons, exclamation marks, and question marks are useful types of punctuation for comparison, as is the overall frequency of punctuation (of any type) per line. As most play-text manuscripts were lightly punctuated, punctuation, perhaps more strongly than spelling, is a marked characteristic of the compositor.

A final pointer towards compositor identification is the use of indentation or other distinctive spacing. Indentations (for speech headings, stage directions or other recurrent features of a dramatic text) are usually consistent, to create a visually appealing page. But such consistency can slightly vary, according to compositor habit. For instance, one compositor might indent four millimetres before a speech prefix, while another might indent six millimetres. Howard-Hill identifies as a spacing issue how compositors deal with turn-overs in verse lines (as discussed in Chapter 2). He notes a distinguishable pattern of those who, 'unable or unwilling to set it as a turn-down or turn-up at the right margin of the column, have carried the remaining part of the line on to the next line' and plots the occurrence of indented turn-overs in *The Winter's Tale* as shown in Table 3, above. The propensity of such turn-overs is clearly much higher in those folio sections associated with compositor D. Such distinctive use of space can therefore be a habit that distinguishes one compositor from another.

Compositor identification based upon recurrent type, spelling, punctuation, or spacing is not always a rewarding process. It is perfectly feasible to find that one compositor set all of a given play text, especially as they are relatively short books. Longer projects, such as folio collections, are much more likely to have complex patterns of compositors at work. However, a sense of the habits of compositors working for a given printer can extend across multiple volumes, so compositor research, and especially the identification of habits unique to a given compositor, can impact more widely upon other play texts or books from the period.

Stop-press correction

Printers in this period made corrections as they went along, as discussed in Chapter 1, and they did not separate corrected or uncorrected sheets. Therefore any given exemplar might be different from another, and these differences can be at the level of formes. In order to determine the most-corrected state of a given edition, multiple surviving exemplars must be compared, letter by letter.

Such collation may be done: (1) by eye-balling differences; (2) by using manual techniques, like same-size transparency overlays; or (3) by using optical collation machines (such as the Hinman, McLeod, or Hailey models). These methods are ordered above from least to most accurate, but also from most to least portable. No process is a hundred per cent accurate, but accuracy increases as the number of copies inspected increases. Transparencies offer a good compromise in terms of being inexpensive and portable, but they are slow to disclose changes in punctuation. They also disguise 'corrections' made by earlier readers, and they pick up smudges, spotting, or foxing that can make determining variants difficult. In terms of accuracy, transparencies do not easily show absent text (such as added marginal stage directions). Eye-balling is arguably more accurate than transparencies if done very slowly, but those editions that have relied upon eye-balling, like the Oxford *Ben Jonson* (Herford and Simpson 1925–52), usually were able to consult only a handful of copies. Collation machines offer high levels of accuracy, by allowing two copies to be seen stereoscopically by two eyes. The history of such machines, which date back to the 1940s, begins with Charlton Hinman's optical collator, which 'stands nearly six feet tall and weighs over 400 pounds' (Smith 2002: 135), and which was famously used on the Shakespeare first folio. Although Randall McLeod and R. Carter Hailey now make much smaller and less expensive machines, not very many collators of any manufacture are available for scholarly use. Such machines also benefit from equal eyesight in both eyes.

The standard collation figure for most critical editions today is at least twenty exemplars (if that many survive), and these somewhat larger collation projects can show that variants sometimes exist in a small number of copies. Once variants are spotted, they should be recorded in tabular form. Variant sheets can exist in several different states, disclosing multiple stages of correction. An extracted table of variants from Shirley's *The Traitor* (1635), for instance, shows four different states for gathering F (outer) (see Table 4).

Table 4. *Stop-press correction in* The Traitor, *F (outer)*

		State 1	State 2	State 3	State 4
F(o) sig. F1	line				
	1	*leade*	*lead*	~	~
	6	*pesons*	*persons*	~	~
F3					
	33	yon	~	you	~
F4v					
	37	but but	~	~	but

In each of the four states, the forme of four quarto pages had to be unlocked, and the corrected type removed, added, or replaced. So such corrections must be tracked at the level of the forme, and not the page, even if not all pages are affected by each stage of correction. The tilde '~' is used when a variant remains the same in the newly corrected forme. In this example, the first stage of correction changed 'leade' to 'lead' and corrected 'pesons' to 'persons', as fairly minor changes. The turned letter in 'yon' (for 'you') was not spotted until later in the print run, and received a separate correction in the forme. Finally, the duplication of 'but' was corrected at still a later stage, giving a fourth and final, and most-corrected (known) state. These stages of correction were disclosed after comparing only eleven surviving copies, so more variants to F (outer) might be detected with future research. All of the errors might have been corrected by an experienced editor in producing an edition, but it is better to find them corrected at the press than need to conjecture because of insufficient collation. The table above necessarily uses the terminology 'state 1', 'state 2', et cetera, instead of 'corrected' versus 'uncorrected', because there is more than one stage of correction. Where there is only one moment of correction for a specific variant, then 'corrected' and 'uncorrected', sometimes abbreviated to 'corr.' or 'uncorr.', or even 'c' or 'u' can be used instead. But scholars should be wary of these terms, as 'correction' is not always possible to determine. Any table of variants should be accompanied by an indication of where those variants occur in the surviving copies. In the case of *The Traitor*, the collation was conducted in the Huntington Library, San Marino, the Clark Library, UCLA, Meisei University Library, Tokyo, the Cambridge University Library, and St Catharine's College, Cambridge. Variants are distributed as follows (see Table 5).

Table 5. *Distribution of variants in* The Traitor, *F (outer)*

	State 1	State 2	State 3	State 4
F(o)	Huntington Lib. 1	Clark Library, Meisei Univ. Lib. 1, Meisei Univ. Lib. 2, Meisei Univ. Lib. 6	Cambridge Univ. Lib., Huntington Lib. 2, Meisei Univ. Lib. 3, Meisei Univ. Lib. 4, St Catharine's College, Cambridge	Meisei Univ. Lib. 5

Such a list can help determine the incidence of correction (and therefore how early in the print run it might have happened).

Further differences between formes over the course of a print run emerge unintentionally, and these are known as 'mechanical' or 'accidental' variants, as opposed to stop-press corrections. Usually, these variants occur when loose type in the forme shifts around or is pulled. Chiaki Hanabusa records two such shifts in D1^v of *The Famous Victories of Henry the Fifth* (1598): 'belée ue,' or 'b eléeue,' and 'sayin gs,' or 'sayi ngs' (Hanabusa 2007: viii). Only two exemplars of this play survive, but if more were available, it is likely that the letters would have shifted around in various configurations, so that gaps appeared at other points in the line. Such looseness in the forme can lead to letters shifting up and down, as well as left or right. Pulled type (including not just characters but also spaces and quads) can also result from the type not being sufficiently tight in its forme. Sometimes accidentals are a product of a forme being loosened during stop-press correction. In these cases, such movement of type may be recorded as part of the list of stop-press variants. Other accidentals that occur during the print run should be noted in a separate list, but not included as part of the stop-press changes, as accidentals and stop-press corrections are different categories of data that can be used to deduce different conclusions about patterns of proofreading.

Uncorrected errors should also be recorded separately as part of the collation process, as they might also be taken to indicate the 'care' of a printer towards the production of the text. Uncorrected errors clearly point to places that need to be emended in any critical edition. Such errors can include turned letters and obvious misspellings. Setting verse as prose or vice versa can also be seen as an uncorrected error, but this feature might be as indicative of a difficult manuscript as of a negligent printer. A sample of uncorrected errors of Shirley's *The Traitor* (1635), including the signatures and line numbers of occurrence, follows:

B4v, 15] meee
C1, 33] yonr
C1v, 19] overthrw
D3v, 10] cut [for 'but']
E4, 4] *Dep..*

It is possible that such uncorrected errors were subject to emendation in copies that do not survive or have not been consulted.

The bulk of the textual work on an edition usually relates to stop-press collation. Very few play texts have had all of their surviving exemplars collated; texts are usually geographically dispersed in such a way as to make collation expensive and time-consuming. Although digital images may be used with modern collation machines, which helps speed up the process, the digital photographs themselves are expensive. Even the most examined of Shakespearean play texts, those in the folio of 1623, have not been subject to a complete collation. Such efforts on these and other plays will be an important task for future scholarship.

Reader annotations

A final element of a play text to note is the presence of reader annotations. These can vary from the unhelpful punctuation changes to Shirley's *Royal Master* discussed earlier in the chapter to substantive emendations. Marks of ownership or marginal comments should therefore be briefly recorded. Although such comments are not necessarily worthy of discussion, they can help in studies of the reception of a given play text. Occasionally, insightful editorial interventions emerge in marginal comments, and these can be read as part of a volume's editorial history. For instance, the editor F. G. Waldron's personal copies of his 1783 edition of Jonson's *The Sad Shepherd* are held in the British Library (BL C.45.c.4 and 643.g.15). Both of these copies are extensively annotated by Waldron with helpful emendations to the play. Rarely are such annotations as valuable, but they can charmingly highlight that play texts from this period have enjoyed a great variety of readers.

This chapter has been concerned to outline different ways of 'reading' Shakespearean play texts. These ways include the technical and the more literary, but they are not mutually exclusive, and indeed editors of critical editions must be practitioners of both. Reading play texts in the original is a radically different experience from reading them in modernised editions. For more canonical texts, four hundred years of improvements has altered their literary character for the 'better', by erasing mistakes and inconsistencies. The fruits of that four-hundred-year history will be the subject of the next chapter, which considers contemporary editorial practice on early modern drama.

FURTHER READING

Bowers, Fredson 1949. *Principles of Bibliographical Description*. Princeton University Press

English Short Title Catalogue 2010. London: The British Library Board, http://estc.bl.uk

Gaskell, Philip 1972. *A New Introduction to Bibliography*. Oxford University Press

Goldberg, Jonathan 1986. 'Textual Properties', *Shakespeare Quarterly* 37: 213–17

Greg, W. W. 1939–59. *A Bibliography of the Early Printed Drama*, 4 volumes. London: Bibliographical Society

McGann, Jerome J. 1983. *A Critique of Modern Textual Criticism*. University of Chicago Press

(ed.) 1985. *Textual Criticism and Literary Interpretation*. University of Chicago Press

Roberts, Sasha 2003. *Reading Shakespeare's Poems in Early Modern England*. Basingstoke: Palgrave

CHAPTER 4

Reading modern editions

This chapter considers how the conventions of reproducing and editing Renaissance drama shape an understanding of the plays, and how those reading competing editions are likely to experience markedly different versions. The bulk of the chapter is devoted to modernised editions and how editorial policy affects the texts, but some consideration is given to old-spelling editions, which have recently come back into favour. The discussion especially focuses upon stage directions, which tend to offer the most striking variations across editions. It will also consider spelling and punctuation, emendation, act and scene divisions and locations, commentary, and collation lines. The chapter closes with a consideration of electronic editions.

A great deal of editorial history has passed in the four hundred years of Shakespeare's textual heritage. It is not the purpose of this book to trace the trajectory from Shakespeare's original printed texts to the present. Andrew Murphy's *Shakespeare in Print* (Murphy 2003) already performs that function admirably. Styles of editing in the eighteenth and nineteenth centuries were radically different from the bibliographically-informed editing that emerged in the twentieth century. This chapter focuses on the editions that are used by contemporary scholars when reading and citing Shakespeare and other early modern dramatists. Some of these, especially multi-volume editions of collected works, did not have large print runs and are available only in libraries. The magisterial collected works of *Ben Jonson*, edited by C. H. Herford and Percy and Evelyn Simpson (Herford and Simpson 1925–52), for instance, is now available only in libraries or second-hand, at considerable expense, but the edition remains at present, or at least until the new *Cambridge Jonson* is published, the only resource for scholars interested in, say, *The Case is Altered*. Similarly, Fredson Bowers's *The Dramatic Works in the Beaumont and Fletcher Canon* (Bowers 1966–96) is financially out of reach for many of even the most dedicated scholars. Collected works of non-Shakespearean drama have largely become

library-only editions. This chapter therefore focuses mostly on the inexpensive editions of Shakespeare that define the field.

MODERNISATION VERSUS OLD SPELLING

The first choice an editor must make about a play text is whether to present
it with modernised spelling and punctuation or to preserve those forms as
originally printed. As well as being the most significant decision an editor
must make, it unfortunately is the most contentious, with entrenched
defenders of each possibility. It is also a choice that must be made by the
reader.

The norm for the first half of the twentieth century was to modernise
Shakespeare and produce old-spelling editions of his contemporaries. In
1960, John Russell Brown wrote an important critique of this practice in
'The Rationale of Old-Spelling Editions of the Plays of Shakespeare and
His Contemporaries' (J. R. Brown 1960). For Brown, one of the chief
problems of old-spelling editions is that they preserve little information
that is bibliographically valuable, such as the categories of data outlined
in Chapter 3. Such information can partially be recovered in facsimile,
and is fully obtained only in original exemplars. But old-spelling texts
often change the lineation, spelling, and punctuation of their source texts,
as Brown complained of Fredson Bowers's *Dramatic Works of Thomas
Dekker*: 'the editor's silent alterations disregard the lining of prose, destroy
the evidence that any verse-line is a full line of type, expand contractions,
regularize the position and typography of stage-directions and speech-
headings, and emend "faulty punctuation" at the end of complete speeches'
(J. R. Brown 1960: 58). In other words, old-spelling texts cannot be trusted
to represent the text as originally printed. Brown went on to argue that
compositors changed (or might have changed) spelling and punctuation
to such an extent that authorial habits were largely irrecoverable, and
that even such traits as apparently Elizabethan spelling, punctuation, and
pronunciation could not be consistently reconstructed, as they were too
variable or now lost. Brown therefore favoured modernisation, because:

A perversion of Elizabethan English is inevitable in both old-spelling and modern-
spelling texts, and so it may seem advisable to choose that kind of edition which
dispenses with the risky impression of the 'real' thing, to avoid a text which is
anachronistically unusual and full of minute distinctions which the inexperienced
reader might easily observe too curiously and the experienced one must ignore or
else seek more information to interpret. (J. R. Brown 1960: 61)

Modern spelling is thus less misleading, because it does not attempt to recover the irrecoverable.

Arthur Brown had in 1956 attacked modernised editions, and in 1960 offered a rejoinder to John Russell Brown's article. Arthur Brown's 1956 piece specifically targets editions like the Arden and New Cambridge Shakespeare, which unite modernised texts for undergraduates with full textual apparatuses: 'Any attempt to pour the dry wine of bibliography down [an undergraduate's] throat will only succeed in choking him, and any attempt to weaken the draught by watering it down will only give him a totally false impression of his capacity to absorb the stuff' (A. Brown 1956: 18). Brown continues by noting that modernisation forces an editor to make decisions (like whether a word with a terminal 's' is possessive, plural, or a contraction for 'is') that the old-spelling text leaves open to interpretation (20). For Brown, modernised editions are also more willing to include conjectural readings: 'We are still carrying far too much dead wood in the way of conjectural emendations from the later folios and the eighteenth century editors, and certainly our semi-popular editions should not be made the vehicle for these' (A. Brown 1956: 23).

These two arguments set out the grounds for the debate, which has changed little in the past fifty years. The imagined reader's knowledge of textual matters is the main consideration, and the distinctions between a student readership and a scholarly one frame most of the justifications for either side. The market continues to be driven by students, not scholars, as Randall McLeod points out:

The creations of photofacsimiles did not bring about the revolutions, even in academic criticism, of which it was capable. This need not wholly surprise us, as many Renaissance scholars function at some distance from editing contemporary texts, and are tied, moreover, to students for whom popular editions are traditional. In fact the tradition of editing Shakespeare is largely maintained by pedagogy, in which the teacher's role mediates the students' confrontation with art, and shapes it according to various intellectual and social paradigms, which impose ideal order on recalcitrant facts. (Randall 1981–2: 38)

Modernisers see modernisation as essential to student understanding, and make the point that much of an original text includes the spelling and punctuation of irrelevant mediaries. This case has been made most strongly in Wells and Taylor's *Modernizing Shakespeare's Spelling with Three Studies in the Text of* Henry V (Wells and Taylor 1979) and Wells's *Re-Editing Shakespeare for the Modern Reader* (Wells 1984), which remain the seminal texts in the field. Those defending old spelling point out that it brings the reader closer to the time of composition and first reception, and the most recent defence of the practice (largely from a historian's perspective) is Michael Hunter's *Editing Early Modern Texts: An Introduction to Principles and Facts* (Hunter 2007), which excludes (albeit briefly) the possibility of modernised spelling in serious scholarly work, by referring with derision to the 'vogue for modernisation' (91).

The tension between the forces of sales on the one hand, and scholarly depth on the other, drives current discussion. Major scholarly editions will be published only by a handful of presses, and even then infrequently, so that editions of non-Shakespearean drama can lay the foundations of scholarly reading for decades. Therefore, there is often very little choice when reading the works of minor dramatists. Shakespeare is available in old and modernised spelling in the Oxford Shakespeare, for instance, in libraries if not bookshops. Jonsonians can choose the old-spelling Oxford edition or the modernised Revels series for most plays (and the forthcoming *Cambridge Jonson* will be modernised). But those wanting a complete Beaumont and Fletcher will need to rely on Bowers's old-spelling edition, and Middleton's complete works is now available only in modernised spelling. Although the debate is clearly unsettled, the fact remains that compromises are entailed in either choice.

The major problem with old-spelling editions is the differentiation between 'edition' and 'reprint'. Editions involve editorial judgement, and that judgement invariably distances the resultant text from the original. Old-spelling editions can fool readers into thinking that all parts of a text are 'original', as John Russell Brown asserted in 1960, but even now editorial changes in old-spelling editions are commonplace. Fredson Bowers has written the most comprehensive statement on editing drama in old-spelling. He sees emendation as a crucial editorial tool:

> If we take diplomatic reprints not as a base but as a point of reference, the problem may be approached by inquiring in what respects the original copy-texts may be adjusted without harm to their essential quality. The first requirement of an old-spelling edition is that it be critically edited . . . For some interested users the unwavering reproduction of the text's original form in all its defects may make the reading more difficult than the effort is worth as against the ease of a modernized version. On the contrary, a critical editor tries to identify and exorcise error in an attempt to reconstruct what may be thought to represent the authorial inscription before corruption by scribe or compositor. The heart of a critical old-spelling edition, therefore, lies in the process of emendation. (Bowers 1987: 199–200)

In other words, old-spelling editions should not attempt to preserve the original as a transcription might, and therefore they are a half-way compromise between editing for a reader and the originals. Although a collation line might point to such changes, the text as printed always has authority over such notes in the process of reading. Variability in practice will mean that readers never know exactly how close to the original an original-spelling text might be: 'The line to be drawn between required, useful, and superfluous additions to the copy-text directions is much a matter of editorial taste' (Bowers 1987: 205). Bowers, for instance, recommends emending 'Exit' to 'Exeunt' when it appears that more than one character leaves the stage. The question then arises as to how far such changes to stage directions constitute an alteration to the fabric of the play, or are themselves acts of interpretation. In fact, Bowers asserts that more liberal changes may be made to non-spoken parts of a text: 'the alterations within dialogue assume an importance superior to the alterations that may be made in the framework, chiefly the stage-directions, speech-prefixes, and the division into acts and scenes' (Bowers 1987: 202). Therefore 'old-spellingness' should be a trait of the spoken text alone. Bowers further advocates regularising character names, so that: 'When titles differ whether through authorial negligence or mixed authorship, one or other form must be regularized to avoid confusion' (Bowers 1987: 207). The Oxford Shakespeare's old-spelling text adopts these recommendations, so that, as David Bevington points out, making Winchester in *1 Henry VI* consistently move from bishop to cardinal necessitates several alterations to the original text:

Later in the play he is elevated to a cardinal's degree, and so the Oxford editors demote him to bishop in I.iv . . . Line 19, 'The Cardinall of Winchester forbids,' becomes 'My lord of Winchester forbids,' significantly changing the meter along with the fact. The line marked 36 in most editions, 'Ile canuas thee in thy broad Cardinalls Hat,' is omitted entirely. 'Thy Scarlet Robes' becomes 'Thy purple robes' a few lines later, and then 'Vnder my feet I stampe thy Cardinalls Hat' becomes 'Under my feet I'll stamp thy bishop's mitre'. (Bevington 1987: 506)

Once such changes are made, it is easy to see arguments in favour of a modernised Shakespeare, as this text is in no sense 'original'. The visual elements of such editions are not in keeping with early modern play texts either, losing the typography, layout, intial-letter illustrations, and paratexts like catchwords, running titles, and signatures. As Bevington asks of another original-spelling series: 'What do these texts provide that one cannot better obtain from a good photographic copy of an early printed text?' (Bevington 1996: 331).

A further problem with old-spelling texts relates to availability and usability. Bevington notes in his review of the Oxford Shakespeare old-spelling text that: 'It will surely become the basis of a great deal of further work' (Bevington 1987: 501). Unfortunately, it is now out of print and has been rarely cited by scholars. When first published it cost nearly three times as much as the modernised text. Old-spelling texts are caught in a perpetual cycle whereby they are too expensive to be purchased by individual scholars and students and therefore they remain unused. Their limited print runs ensure that the cost per volume is high. Ambitious old-spelling projects for Beaumont and Fletcher and Webster remain outside the classroom, and they are rarely cited in academic critical work on those dramatists.

Current old-spelling projects on Ford and Heywood are in preparation, so this trend might be reversing. Such ongoing old-spelling editions point to the fact that scholars have no unequivocal position in favour of modernised spelling. In fact, modernised editions present several difficulties of their own. Firstly, there is no such thing as *a* modernised edition. There are many different formats and methodologies behind such editions, and as Wells and Taylor argue, the effort required to produce a modernised edition is so enormous as to often be impossible within the confines of a small editorial team:

> Those who prepare such editions should, ideally, examine all the available docu-
> ments; familiarize themselves with any aspect of textual transmission or theatrical
> practice which might affect individual texts; acquire a comprehensive knowledge
> of the verbal usage of the author and the period; and scrutinize the available text(s)
> in detail with all this information in mind, simultaneously and comprehensively.
> This ideal is, of course, unattainable; but editors nevertheless try to attain it,
> individually and collectively. (Wells and Taylor 1997: 6)

The editing of Shakespeare is now a highly time-consuming process that requires careful consideration of scores of historical editions. Even non-Shakespearean drama often has an advanced textual and editorial history. Those plays that have no such history often require even more effort, as an editor is forced to undertake a full bibliographical analysis alone. Not only is editing time-consuming, editors come at texts from very different stand-points, or apply only a selection of bibliographical and editorial techniques. Therefore, editions are often shaped by personal editorial judgements. John Jowett notes that, 'Put simply, editing entails establishing the most author-itative source text and following it. Beyond this, it entails making certain kinds of alteration to the text on the basis that this document, from the viewpoint of the modern reader, is obfuscatory, misleading, or wrong' (Jowett 2000: 127). These 'certain kinds of alteration' have never been codified in an agreed way, explaining why editions have extraordinary variance over even very stable passages from a single copy text.

EDITING AND THE TRANSMUTATION OF COPY TEXT

A brief passage from *Pericles* (1609) as edited in some collected and single-volume editions of recent decades will exemplify the range of possible re-interpretation that might be applied to a fairly straightforward extract. This passage from the first quarto includes two lines from the end of Gower's second chorus, a brief stage direction, and the opening lines of Pericles' subsequent speech:

And heere he comes: what shall be next,
Pardon old *Gower*, this long's the text.
        Enter Pericles wette.
    Peri. Yet cease your ire you angry Starres of heauen,
Wind, Raine, and Thunder, remember earthly man...
              (*Pericles* 1609: C1v)

What follows are six extracts based on the same selection of text from six different editions of the past three decades.

NEW PENGUIN SHAKESPEARE, ED. PHILIP EDWARDS (1976)

      And here he comes. What shall be next,
40   Pardon old Gower – this longs the text.   *Exit*

II.1   *Enter Pericles, wet*
    PERICLES
      Yet cease your ire, you angry stars of heaven!
      Wind, rain, and thunder, remember earthly man...

OXFORD SHAKESPEARE COMPACT EDITION, ED. STANLEY WELLS *ET AL* (1988)

     ⌈*Enter Pericles wet and half-naked*⌉
And here he comes. What shall be next
Pardon old Gower; this 'longs the text.   *Exit*

     ⌈*Thunder and lightning*⌉
PERICLES
      Yet cease your ire, you angry stars of heaven!   41
      Wind, rain, and thunder, remember earthly man...

THE NEW CAMBRIDGE SHAKESPEARE, ED. DOREEN DELVECCHIO
AND ANTHONY HAMMOND (1998)

And here he comes; what shall be next   39
Pardon old Gower, this longs the text.   [*Exit*]

[2.1] *Enter* PERICLES *wet*
PERICLES Yet cease your ire, you angry stars of heaven!
Wind, rain, and thunder, remember earthly man . . .

THE NORTON SHAKESPEARE, ED. STEPHEN GREENBLATT *ET AL* (1997)

Enter PERICLES *wet* [*and half-naked*]
And here he comes. What shall be next
40   Pardon old Gower; this 'longs the text.   [*Exit*]
[*Thunder and lightning*]
PERICLES Yet cease your ire, you angry stars of heaven!
Wind, rain, and thunder, remember earthly man . . .

THE ARDEN SHAKESPEARE, ED. SUZANNE GOSSETT (2004)

And here he comes. What shall be next,   40
Pardon old Gower: this 'longs the text.   [*Exit.*]

[2.1]   *Enter* PERICLES *wet.*
PERICLES
Yet cease your ire, you angry stars of heaven!
Wind, rain and thunder, remember earthly man . . .

THE RSC SHAKESPEARE, ED. JONATHAN BATE *ET AL* (2007)

And here he comes: what shall be next,
Pardon old Gower, this 'longs the text.   [*Exit*]

[Act 2 Scene 1]   *running scene 5*
Enter Pericles wet
PERICLES Yet cease your ire, you angry stars of heaven!
Wind, rain and thunder, remember earthly man . . .

There is striking uniformity in the overall shape of these edited passages,
but none of them, even over so short an extract, is identical. All offer aids
to the reader, like line numbers and scene divisions, but such divisions
change from edition to edition. Editorial consensus places a scene break
between the speeches of Gower and Pericles, but Oxford (and the Norton,
which follows the Oxford) print one continuous scene. Such line-number
and scene variation makes the citation of a passage from one edition to the

next difficult. Heavy breaks impose a more distinct division, and perhaps a place for pausing, in the reading text. The RSC Shakespeare uniquely includes intrusive breaks in a larger fount and more subtle 'running scenes'.

Surprisingly, given the relatively simple lexis of the passage, no two editions are punctuated in the same way. The comma after 'rain' reflects differences between US and UK punctuation, and is of minor concern. All editors choose to add an exclamation mark after 'heaven', which might be taken as an obvious choice. But A. R. Braunmuller warns that such pointing, 'is a mark of high importance to the reader, to the actor conceiving a speech, and to the director imagining a performance, but it is also, of course, a mark that hardly appears in the First Folio or in many quartos of Shakespearean texts' (Braunmuller 2006: 137). Clearly, Pericles could enter exhausted from his swim and without as much exclamation as editors have imposed here. In the light of this consistency over one of the most rarely used marks of punctuation, it is interesting that all editors point Gower's independent clauses differently. Gower speaks three of them, and modern punctuation would typically separate independent clauses with full-stops. In these extracts, no editor chooses to rely on full-stops alone, and colons, semi-colons, and dashes are more in favour. Such punctuation shows editors 'performing' Gower's lines for him, by imagining the briefer pause implied by the semi-colon, or the logical continuation implied by the colon, or the break in the train of thought implied by the dash. The RSC Shakespeare retains this rhetorical mode so far as to disrupt a grammatical one: the phrase 'what shall be next, / Pardon old Gower, this 'longs the text' is clearly two independent clauses, so separating them with a comma yields a run-on sentence. (The force of the phrase is one of continuity, so it is an easy mistake to make.) In all of these texts, the editors have avoided the most straightforward punctuation. As they have also not replicated each others' more complex choices, the implication is either that English has an extraordinary variety of options, or that editors, in imagining performance, use more rhetorical pointing. Perhaps the chorus figure that Gower occupies is in some respects proximate to that of editor. Another important punctuation choice concerns the quarto's 'long's', and it is a decision that changes the meaning of the word. In the quarto, Gower is asking for pardon because 'this long [is the] text'. In other words, the text is at an end, so he asks pardon for ending abruptly. Most of the editors change this to the more obvious meaning, ''longs', an abbreviated form of 'belongs'. Gower would then be asserting that the action proper belongs to 'the text' – that is, the dialogue of the play. But putting this distinction between chorus and dialogue in these terms is strange, as of course Gower himself is speaking 'text'. Edwards's earlier Penguin edition prints 'longs', which presumably is a truncation of 'belongs', although that sense is not recorded in the *Oxford English Dictionary*, or perhaps means 'is owing to', a sense that was available in the period. So in addition to changes brought about by a sense of the timing and phrasing of delivery, editors of this passage have also punctuated to pin down the meaning of a word that in old spelling might have multiple valences.

The stage action is similarly affected by such editorial decisions. All editors have Gower exit, for instance. Some of the editions signify the editorial nature of that addition clearly by using square brackets. Gower probably exited in the original productions, as he does not speak in the middle of the acts. But interestingly, some successful modern productions of *Pericles* have kept Gower on stage throughout the play (Giddens 2009). Similarly, having choral figures remain onstage was available as a possibility in early modern drama, as in the anonymous *The Taming of a Shrew* (1594). Performance history has been open to ignoring the editorial direction for Gower's departure, but critics reading the play need to be similarly willing to doubt directions contained within square brackets. Entrances and exits, in particular, shape the effect of a scene, as who is on stage is always one of the primary considerations: 'To an actor, the world is divided into two places: on stage, and off' (Hammond 1992: 83). The Oxford and Norton texts therefore change the relationship of Gower and Pericles significantly by having Pericles enter two lines earlier than the quarto placement. Chapter 2 explored how stage-direction time might extend beyond a specific point in a series of spoken words, so it is entirely possible that the quarto's direction is misplaced, or that the entrance of Pericles and exit of Gower overlap. Equally, Shakespearean plays frequently have characters 'see' – and sometimes hear – an entering character before they are onstage. Margaret Jane Kidnie has interestingly experimented with typographical arrows to indicate a time span for possible entries in these cases (Kidnie 2004: 170–1). Pericles does not literally have to be onstage before Gower says, 'And here he comes'. The Oxford editors express doubt over the placement of this direction through their use of 'broken brackets', which 'indicate directions (and speech-prefixes) whose substance and/or location are, in the editors' opinion, not confidently to be inferred from the dialogue, however likely they may appear' (Wells and Taylor 1997: 155). Although the distinction between full brackets and broken ones is potentially useful, it is difficult to pay more attention to the punctuation of stage directions than to their content, and Leslie Thomson has pointed out that the Oxford

Shakespeare is not always clear in how they are deployed (Thomson 1988). Such a range of broken and unbroken brackets also seems to make the editorial voice intercede more strongly than before. Perhaps unsurprisingly, broken brackets have not been widely adopted, although the New Folger Shakespeare, edited by Barbara A. Mowat and Paul Werstine, has continued to adopt an even more elaborate system of sigla. The Oxford editors' second interpolation in this stage direction has Pericles enter partially undressed. We learn that Pericles needs clothing later in the scene, so it is entirely sensible to have him in some form of undress. But perhaps 'half-naked' is too specific. The Oxford edition's final addition is the call for '*Thunder and lightning*'. Pericles enters shouting at the 'Wind, rain and thunder', so the scene should have them if technologically possible (as thunder and lightning were), but then again, there is no mention made of lightning, however logically it precedes thunder. Fireworks were probably not required for storms, but they were extensively used (Jones 2009), and lightning is certainly mentioned in the opening direction of *The Tempest*.

These variances over even a simple passage – two actors who appear alone onstage – highlight the radical potential for editorial stage directions to alter the action. As Antony Hammond notes, 'Even the most conservative of editors may turn out to be prepared to add or alter directions without any *textual* authority, relying rather on his sense of theatrical necessity' (Hammond 1992: 71). Editors have a powerful influence on a reader's conception of the action. Yet as Chapters 2 and 3 have shown, dramatic texts by their nature have usually excluded stage directions altogether. In response to this problem, editors have filled in the gaps that copy texts leave behind. As M. J. Kidnie points out, however, such editorial enhancement is based upon two assumptions: 'first, that where an editor interpolates modern stage directions, there is specific stage business to which the main text obviously gives rise; and, second, that this stage business can be known with confidence by the editor and conveyed to the reader by means of the dramatic text' (Kidnie 2000b: 465). At the most basic level, 'any alteration an editor may choose to make to the staging of a script will inevitably embed critical interpretation in the dramatic text' (Kidnie 2000b: 467). Kidnie sees no simple solution to this problem, but does suggest that, 'editors might resist modifying or supplementing extant stage directions altogether, asking readers to interact with the dramatic text as necessarily unfixed and unstable' (Kidnie 2000b: 470). Kidnie in a later piece argues that editors should be concerned with, 'how we might translate the stage directions of early modern scripts in such a way as to make readers aware of textual indeterminacy' (Kidnie 2004: 163). Despite this increasing editorial responsibility, readers of modern editions must be especially sceptical when it comes to any stage directions, original or modernised.

The various editions of *Pericles* do not seem to imply, however, that such caution would be needed for the spoken dialogue of a play. Modernisation has little effect on most words in early modern play texts when they are said aloud. Orally, 'he' and 'hee' are the same, and the distinction between a full-stop and a semi-colon is not an obvious one. Although *Pericles* as a whole requires much relineation, and resetting verse and prose as Chapter 3 notes, most editions change the actual words very little: word-for-word consistency easily exceeds ninety-nine per cent. But it is worth keeping David Bevington's caution in mind when studying the text of a play: 'In these texts you can never be sure just whose words you may be reading' (Bevington 1987: 507). Although Bevington here is referring specifically to the old-spelling and modernised Oxford Shakespeare, those words of warning must shape the reading of any modernised edition.

EDITORIAL PRINCIPLES AND TEXTUAL APPARATUS

The unfortunate solution for a literary scholar must rest in two distinct practices. The first of which is similar to that required for reading play texts in their original format: texts must be researched. As Bevington recommends: '*caveat lector*: know your play, know your editor, know whether you can sympathize with the editorial philosophy or not, and fasten your seat belts accordingly' (Bevington 1987: 511). Readers must also pay some attention to the textual apparatus.

Unfortunately, the 'editorial philosophy' and the textual apparatus are not always easy to detect, and sometimes both are altogether absent. The Oxford Shakespeare prints them in a separate volume that costs much more than the text itself. Although its *Textual Companion* (1987) can be lauded for explaining textual principles fairly clearly (and those principles were elaborated elsewhere in several contemporary publications, including Stanley Wells's *Re-Editing Shakespeare for the Modern Reader* (Wells 1984)), not all editions are so forthcoming. The starting point for any editing endeavour might be a set of editorial guidelines, as Stanley Wells argues: 'The first and perhaps most important task of a General Editor is to lay down the principles to which he and his publisher wish his edition to conform' (Wells 2006: 39). Yet, those guidelines are often very brief, and they are very rarely made public. In fact, the presence of guidelines is often overstated, as many series make do without them, or, having them, rely on sketchy advice. The general editors therefore must ensure conformity with a series of brief or unspoken ideas about editing, but this is not a straightforward task: 'To persuade editors actually to absorb and act upon the advice they are given – especially if, as is likely to happen, they have already edited for a series with different procedures and so think they know already how it should be done – is not always easy' (Wells 2006: 45). Editing is a deeply personal activity, and therefore describing one's methodology is tricky. Even those series with stringent guidelines, like the forthcoming *Cambridge Jonson* (with nearly two hundred pages of helpful advice to its editors), have local variation amongst the contributing editors.

Textual philosophies are also difficult to detect because the editorial voice is frequently a confident one. Such confidence might undermine methodological considerations. Typical of this editorial style are statements that leave little room for doubt, like this one from Karl Klein's New Cambridge Shakespeare edition of *Timon of Athens*:

the nature of the manuscript copy used by the compositors must remain speculative. Nevertheless, evidence of various kinds leads to the likelihood that the text of *Timon* printed in the First Folio is based on authorial manuscript – but authorial fair copy and not marked up for theatrical performance – with perhaps a part transcribed by a scribe. (Klein 2001: 181)

The nod towards doubt here is overtaken by the very assertive and specific account of the origins of the underlying manuscript. Although this kind of editorial confidence has slowly given way to an acknowledgment of degrees of uncertainty in editorial practice, most editions adopt a kind of eclectic practice, whereby decisions are made moment by moment and with little explanation. In one line of a play, the copy text might be the folio, in another the quarto, in a third an eighteenth-century editor, in a fourth the editor's original emendation. Clearly, in these instances the philosophy is not based upon a logically consistent position with respect to the copy text, except that the copy text might be adjusted as the editor sees fit. The Arden edition of *Timon of Athens* has already been highlighted as having one of the briefest textual essays in the series. But that essay also gives one of the most helpful accounts of editorial practice:

The present, modernized edition is necessarily based on the Folio version, defective as it may be, but has been emended in places where F readings seem deficient or wrong. All such changes to the original are products of editorial judgement and therefore subject to scrutiny; for this reason they are recorded in the textual notes, which appear in small print at the bottom of each page, below the commentary. (Dawson and Minton 2008: 146)

All responsible editions include such collation notes, and those that record them on the same page as the relevant text facilitate an understanding of local decisions. Such notes permit the reader to reconstruct an editorial philosophy when none is directly given. But more importantly, such notes should allow the reader to reconstruct the primary material behind an individual editorial decision.

Thomas L. Berger has famously called the collation line the 'band of terror'. The terror comes in part from the complexity of the sigla used in these lines, and in part from a lack of agreed consistency across different editing series. It is worth considering a few examples of how they vary across editions, and how these instances are read. The following is an extract from the Arden Shakespeare series, a by-word for complexity and fullness in both textual and critical notes. The passage includes text and collation from Dawson and Minton's edition of *Timon of Athens*, Act IV, Scene III, but does not fully replicate the *mise-en-page*:

FLAVIUS   Have you forgot me, sir?
TIMON
          Why dost ask that? I have forgot all men.
          Then, if thou grant'st thou'rt a man, I have forgot thee.
FLAVIUS
          An honest poor servant of yours –   470
TIMON
          Then I know thee not.
          I never had honest man about me, I; all
          I kept were knaves to serve in meat to villains.
FLAVIUS
          The gods are witness,
          Ne'er did poor steward wear a truer grief   475
          For his undone lord than mine eyes for you.
TIMON
          What, dost thou weep? Come nearer then. I love thee
          Because thou art a woman and disclaim'st
          Flinty mankind, whose eyes do never give
          But thorough lust and laughter. Pity's sleeping.   480

469   grant'st] *Capell;* grunt'st *F;* grantest *Pope* thou'rt] *(*th'art*)*
472   me, I; all] *Capell;* me, I all *F;* me, I, all *F4;* me; ay all *Knight*
477   nearer then. I] *Oxf subst.;* neerer, then I *F* 480 thorough]
        *(*thorow*);* or through *Pope*

This passage contains no stage directions (in this edition at least), and the collated changes refer purely to the dialogue. The editors' collation notes start with line numbers ('469') and lemmas ('grant'st'), or the text to which the notes refer. Then that information is separated from the rest of the notes by right square brackets. The information that appears immediately after the bracket is the original source of the reading. In the case of 'grant'st' for line 469, Edward Capell's 1767–8 edition is the source of the emendation. After an italic semi-colon, we learn that the folio reading ('*F*') is 'grunt'st'. A second italic semi-colon separates yet another reading, the extra-metrical 'grantest' suggested by Alexander Pope's 1723–5 edition. Arden Shakespeares do not offer historical collations, so the point here is to highlight the first editor to suggest a given reading, and other convincing possibilities. The next collation note refers to 'thou'rt' on the same line (hence there is no line number). The italicised brackets surround the original folio reading, and highlight that the editors do not see this change as substantive. It is simply a modernisation of the contraction. Knowledge of this basic format permits the reading of all of the collation notes on this page. The note for line 472 is more complex in dealing with punctuation. It provides alternative readings from four different sources: Capell, the first folio, the fourth folio, and Charles Knight's 1839–42 edition. Collation notes that deal with punctuation and changes to lineation are usually more complex than those that deal with individual words, for reasons explored above regarding the vast array of different choices editors can make with respect to these issues. If an edition is original in suggesting an emendation, it will, in the Arden series, follow the right square bracket with the phrase '*this edn*'. But as Eric Rassmussen has repeatedly shown in his reviews of editions for *Shakespeare Survey*, such claims for editorial originality are not always to be trusted.

The policies of the Arden series with respect to naming conventions and textual notes are widely accepted by scholars in editions of Shakespeare and his contemporaries, but it is worth considering in addition some slight variations. For instance, this Arden volume includes a separate 'Appendix 4: Changes to lineation', where the following notes concern the extract above:

469]   *Capell; F lines* man. / thee. /
471–4]   *F; Kittredge lines* not. / I. / villains. /
477]   *Rowe; F lines* weepe? / thee /

Clearly, much lineation confusion exists in the folio here. Whereas the editors accept the lineation from F of lines 471–4, and reject George Lyman Kittredge's proposed relineation, they change F at 469 and 477, accepting the proposed line divisions of Capell and Rowe respectively. Not all Arden editions include such an appendix. Some incorporate such lineation changes into the collation line at the bottom of the page. Learning the format of one play in a series will not necessarily provide a blueprint for others.

The Oxford Shakespeare individual edition of the play, edited by John Jowett (2004), similarly includes lineation changes in an appendix that must be consulted separately. Interestingly, the collation at the bottom of the page for this same passage (which is remarkably similar in its modernisation) reads as follows:

474   grant'st∧ thou'rt a man,] POPE; grunt'st, th'art a man. F 479
Ne'er] F (Neu'r) 480.1 *He weeps*] BEVINGTON; *not in* F

The format of the collation, in the use of small capitals and italicisation, is slightly different from the Arden edition, but it is put together on much the same organising principle of right square brackets and semi-colons. The main difference between Jowett's text and the Arden edition is the inclusion of David Bevington's suggested stage direction at line 480 (which is implied by the dialogue). However, each edition includes a note that is missing from the other, even though they have much the same text. Jowett makes no mention of the additional terminal punctuation that separates 'nearer then; I' in his edition, but that is rendered as 'neerer, then I' in the folio. The Arden edition does collate this change, which is a substantive introduction of a separate independent clause. On the other hand, Jowett collates his change from the folio's 'Neu'r' to 'Ne'er', yet the Arden edition, which makes the same change, ignores this variation. Perhaps the most interesting distinction between the two editions is that they name a character differently. In the Arden text, as above, Flavius is the steward's name; whereas the Oxford edition calls him 'Steward'. This situation is explained in the Arden edition's notes on the 'List of Roles': 'Flavius Timon's steward is not mentioned in the cast list in F, although he is one of the major characters in the play. He is given the name Flavius only in 1.2, and is called simply "Steward" throughout the rest of the drama' (157).

Collation lines are, at least in part, subject to editorial judgement and whim. It is impossible to locate such judgement within the scope of a series, as editorial decisions are highly localised, and indeed there might be detectable variation within a single text. Further, finding relevant textual notes in these editions is difficult. The Oxford Shakespeare, with its separate and expensive *Textual Companion*, has already been mentioned. The Oxford *Ben Jonson*, edited by Herford and the Simpsons, also keeps its textual notes in separate volumes. But as it was published over twenty-seven years, corrections trickle throughout the series, too, so that many volumes might need to be checked to determine the editors' final textual reading. As such expensive multi-volume editions now reside almost exclusively in libraries, the process of searching for such variants becomes even more inconvenient. Even the Arden *Timon* extracted above has three locations for relevant notes: the bottom of the page, the appendix of lineation changes, and an earlier commentary note about Flavius.

The best editions for scholars present textual variants in one location, preferably on the page. But even editions that purport to do so are likely to offer a textual note only on the first occurrence of an emendation in the play, so care must be taken over local notes further into the edition. For instance, my textual note to 'The Persons of the Play', in the forthcoming edition of Jonson's *The Sad Shepherd* for the *Cambridge Jonson* offers '**14** EGLAMOUR] F2 *(Aeglamour), spelling used throughout* F2' (Giddens and Barton forthcoming). Like the Arden *Timon*, therefore, I mention the character's changed spelling once, so it would be easy to miss later in the text. However, one version of the truth is probably better for research purposes than the multiple versions of the truth that emerge when editions rely upon several different tables to convey textual information. Penguin edition, especially, can present multiple tables that must be collated to garner a full range of what the editors think about the text. In particular, changes to stage directions are separated from changes to dialogue. Stanley Wells says of the notes to the Penguin Shakespeare: 'Wishing the editions to have full scholarly respectability we felt that textual notes were needed, but that if they were to be of any value they should be presented with more concern for the understanding of the non-specialist reader than in the Arden edition' (Wells 2006: 43). Therefore the Penguin textual notes are deliberately curtailed to only the most essential information.

More difficult are editions that half-present textual information without signalling their different intentions. In other words, they appear to have full textual notes, but upon further examination one finds them highly selective. Although the RSC Shakespeare, edited by Bate and Rasmussen, includes 'Textual Notes' at the end of every play, a glance at their brevity shows that either the editors have been very textually conservative and have preserved their copy text (generally the folio), or that they have not recorded a great number of changes. The section of *Timon* extracted above in their edition has accepted a handful of changes from editorial history, but the one relevant note for the section is '**479 grant'st** = Ed. F. = grunt'st'. This edition makes no attempt at a full collation, and like the Penguin series does not credit the originator of a reading. The Penguin and RSC editions are closely tied to the theatre and student markets. Relatively blank pages allow actors and students to pencil any necessary notes into the margins, and perhaps such readers do not require extensive textual history.

As a counterpoint to these textually stripped editions, variorum editions attempt to record every suggested textual variant. The New Variorum Shakespeare series was begun by Horace Howard Furness in the nineteenth century, and work on the variorum editions continues today under the Modern Language Association. Such editions are very helpful when newly published, but because of the accelerated pace of publication of and on Shakespeare, they tend to date quickly. Further, if standard collations are complicated enough, negotiating every variant reading from centuries of conjecture can make for very difficult reading.

COMMENTARY, INTRODUCTIONS, AND THE CRITICAL APPARATUS

This book is about reading Shakespearean play texts (not reading readings of such texts), yet as the book has shown throughout, editing is an act of interpretation. Therefore a brief word can be given to the kinds of non-textual apparatuses that surround editions. Just as editing itself was meant to be based on self-denying ideals of authorial intention and 'correction' of any errors introduced by others, the critical apparatus of introductions and commentary has long been based upon a balanced editorial voice. The Guidelines to the *Cambridge Jonson*, for instance, advise editors that: 'Introductions should be primarily factual, including in the relatively brief space available the information that is critical to any edition. At the same time you will want to indicate major areas of critical debate, and to provide an engaging discussion aimed at further critical inquiry' (Bevington, Butler, and Donaldson 2001: 36). Similar advice usually applies to commentary notes. The major varying factors in critical editions relate to the space that might be given to such critical material. The single-volume Oxford Shakespeare devotes only one page per play for short introductions. The Arden *Timon of Athens* has 151 pages of introductory material and 92 pages of appendices. The Oxford individual edition of the same play has an 157-page introduction and 34 pages of appendices. Clearly, as Stanley Wells admits, the Oxford series was designed to 'rival the Arden' in terms of critical breadth (Wells 2006: 47). Both series now include introductions that are effectively books on the plays: 'There are times when I have observed with a sigh that an editor, having failed, for example, to observe the proposed word limits, has written a monograph rather than an Introduction, but not had the heart to wield the blue pencil too drastically' (Wells 2006: 48). New Cambridge Shakespeare editions are generally shorter. Its *Timon of Athens* has a sixty-six-page introduction and a brief appendix. Such variability also characterises commentary notes. The opening stage direction and first six lines of the second scene of the play show how the major editions have varying space for commentary. Although the New Cambridge Shakespeare gives around 150 words to elucidate the passage, both the Arden and the Oxford Shakespeares provide over five hundred words each. Fewer words are usually permitted in the commentaries of complete works, so that the RSC Shakespeare, for instance, gives sixteen words to the commentary for this extract, and the Norton Shakespeare, edited by Stephen Greenblatt *et al*, offers only ten words. This range also applies to non-Shakespearean editions, with the Revels series modelling itself on the Arden in terms of space for commentary and introductions, and the New Mermaids series being much more concise. It should be noted, however, that variants within series mean that such conclusions must be reached on a play-by-play basis.

The degree to which a reader desires such comprehensive commentary is largely a matter of personal taste. However, it is important to recognise that despite having similar aims as to what should be glossed: 'editors inevitably vary considerably in what they see as important or as necessary to explicate in relation to their perception of the nature and theatrical significance of a play by Shakespeare' (Foakes 1996–7: 327). Foakes compares the first commentary note in six editions of *King Lear* to show that the variance can be striking. Some differences emerge owing to the changing focus of criticism across time. Interest in staging has grown, for instance. Other differences are clearly owing to the proclivities of the individual editors. As the primary purpose of commentary is to explain the meaning of difficult words or passages, it is surprising that editors often identify entirely different words as needing a gloss. The following passage is taken from the Arden edition of *Timon of Athens*:

TIMON   Give me breath.
    I do beseech you, good my lords, keep on,
    I'll wait upon you instantly.
              [*Exeunt Timon's train and Alcibiades.*]
    [*to Flavius, who comes forward*] Come hither. Pray you
    How goes the world, that I am thus encountered
    With clamorous demands of broken bonds
    And the detention of long-since-due debts
    Against my honour?
FLAVIUS [*to Servants*]   Please you gentlemen,
    The time is unagreeable to this business.
            (Dawson and Minton 2008: 2.2.35–42)

Table 6. *Words glossed in* Timon of Athens, *2.2.35–42*

Oxford	Arden	Cambridge
Give me breath	Give me breath	[no gloss]
good my lords	[no gloss]	[no gloss]
keep on	[no gloss]	keep on
wait upon you instantly	I do . . . instantly	I'll . . . you
How goes the world	[no gloss]	[no gloss]
thus encountered	[no gloss]	[no gloss]
of	[no gloss]	[no gloss]
broken	broken bonds	demands . . . bonds
detention	detention	detention
Against	Against my honour	Against my honour
unagreeable	unagreeable	unagreeable

These eight lines would not seem to offer much scope for variation in the selection of material towards commentary. Yet the table of lemmas in the Oxford, Cambridge, and Arden editions (see Table 6) show clear distinctions.

Some individual words, 'detention', 'Against', and 'unagreeable', are glossed in each of the editions. The Arden and Cambridge editions are very similar in the choices of difficult passages, although the exact words chosen for elucidation differ. The Oxford edition here offers many more commentary notes. The three editions provide very different experiences to readers, in terms of the extent of help offered. Arguably, the Arden and Cambridge editions better suit a more able readership, but all three editions are targeted towards undergraduate classrooms. Different Shakespeare plays across the series would yield different results. Equally, the quantity of glosses is not fully indicative of an edition's quality. Glosses that paraphrase longer passages can be much clearer than several separate glosses of individually difficult words. So too, lengthy commentary can reflect an editor's interpretative peculiarities instead of information that a reader requires to comprehend a given passage. An undergraduate reader should be able to understand all of a text that has been usefully annotated. Any information in addition to that basic level is very much a matter of personal judgement. Currently, 'verbal parallels', quotations from the period that reflect a meaning readily found in the *Oxford English Dictionary*, or lengthy discussions of source material are generally discouraged by series editors. But in previous decades that kind of information was readily found in editions. Research is needed on what information needs to be glossed for today's undergraduates, and how readers from different parts of the world require different information in commentary notes.

This chapter has deliberately focused on the Oxford, Cambridge, and Arden Shakespeare series, because these are the critical editions that offer the most extensive apparatus. For those readers who desire less commentary or more pithy introductions, there are a host of competing editions. All critical editions have been increasingly attuned to performance history, and some editions have been developed alongside close relationships with specific theatre companies. Editions change over time, and it is important to note that many of those still sold in bookshops today are over twenty years old. But as Jonathan Goldberg argues, this multiplicity and historical difference provides for a lively field:

no two editions of Shakespeare are identical. There is no Shakespeare, no single Shakespeare, that is, but only a divided kingdom. If that is the case, free play is not irresponsible, but, rather, a critical position more responsive to the radical historicity of the texts that we miscall Shakespeare's but which are and have always been the product of textual and critical interventions. (Goldberg 1986: 214)

In part the strength of Shakespeare and other great dramatists from the period lies in their adaptability. Modernisation and heavy annotation encourages this flexibility with respect to changing cultures of reading. Partially for this reason, too, there is no global Shakespeare edition. Stanley Wells argues that, 'there has never been a multi-volume American edition of Shakespeare with textual and overall scholarly aspirations comparable to those offered by British publishers' (Wells 2006: 41). More striking is the fact that the markets for Shakespeare editions are very different in the US and UK. Sales figures are of course variable and difficult to come by, but it is clear from the Sales Rank figures of Amazon.co.uk that the new Bate and Rasmussen RSC Shakespeare is currently ahead in the UK market. The Riverside and the Norton Shakespeares tend to lead the US market. A similar split emerges over single-play editions, with the US favouring the New Folger Library Shakespeare and Signet Classics, and the UK pre-ferring the Oxford, Cambridge, Arden, and Penguin editions, alongside editions specially catering to schools, like the Cambridge School Shake-speare. Therefore students and scholars working in different countries are likely to have different experiences of Shakespeare. Such distinctions are less prevalent in non-Shakespearean drama, where the choices are notably reduced.

No Shakespeare series has a clear lead in terms of its critical content. In fact, there is little consistency within a single series. David Scott Kastan argues that, 'several editions are all too much alike, the text in modernized spelling with more or less annotation depending on whether it is intended for a scholastic market, for universities, or for the general reader' (Kastan 2001: 123). This chapter has shown that in text, collation, and commentary, editions depart more radically from each other than this statement implies. Most editors have devoted years to a play to produce a truly critical edition, and that is certainly evident across the Arden, Cambridge, and Oxford series. Such effort has intrinsic value:

A text reconstructed by a person who is immersed in, and has thought deeply about, the body of surviving evidence relevant to a work, its author, and its time may well teach the rest of us something we could not have discovered for ourselves, even if the reconstruction can never be definitive – and even if, indeed, it places us in a position to criticize its own constitution. (Tanselle 1994: 5)

Critical editions offer shortcuts to a fuller knowledge of the copy text(s), performance history, and history of relevant criticism of a given play. They are invaluable in saving much critical work, and providing a springboard towards approaches that seek to focus on issues outside of the textual intricacies of a play text. It is true that such editions come with in-built critical distortions, and that they are as much products of their time as Shakespeare's. Paul Werstine notes that: 'much of the enduring mystery that is *Hamlet*/Hamlet has been produced through the editorial construction of *Hamlet* as the combination of the second-quarto (Q2) and Folio (F) versions' (Werstine 1988: 2). But as Jonathan Goldberg argues, and as Chapters 1 and 2 of this book have shown, all plays from the period are reconstructed: 'There never has been, and never can be, an unedited Shakespearean text. Textual criticism and post-structuralism agree therefore: we have no originals, only copies' (Goldberg 1986: 213–14). Such textual multiplicity leads to the unparalleled choice afforded to readers of Shakespeare, with varying editions stretching back over four hundred years.

ELECTRONIC EDITIONS AND EDITING

Unlike its print counterpart, the history of electronic editions of Shakespeare and his contemporaries has not been a happy one. But this lack of success is not owing to a lack of scholarly enthusiasm. It is probably fair to say that scholars, publishers, and funding bodies have underestimated the effort and financial resources required to produce electronic editions of Shakespearean drama. Both the National Endowment for the Humanities in the US and the Arts and Humanities Research Council (formerly

Board) in the UK have invested large sums in support of electronic editing projects on both sides of the Atlantic. These projects, at least with respect to Renaissance drama, have not yet yielded the kinds of results that must have been expected with such large investment. Several projects have either failed or been very slow in coming, which is understandable considering the vast encoding and checking work required.

Electronic texts have had their biggest impact on the field through EEBO, which paradoxically carries the reader, via several-times-mediated facsimile, to the original. The old-spelling searchable texts provided by the Text Creation Partnership offer a powerful research tool, but one that has been received with limited enthusiasm in the light of imperfect accuracy. The potential of hypertext lies in the ability to add complex layers of editorial material to a text. Such material might disclose variant readings for a particular passage, arising both from the originals and from editorial history. Electronic editions obviously permit multimedia encounters with the performed text, through audio or video. The main advantage they hold is through the theoretical fantasy that they have no limits:

For a Shakespeare edition, one could have an edited text (or indeed more than one), as well as digital facsimiles of all early printings; and additional resources could be included, like source texts or concordances, theater reviews, illustrations, audio clips, and even film versions, all of which can be linked to allow easy movement back and forth between them. (Kastan 2001: 127)

Hypertext allows textual information to be available more efficiently and in an easier-to-read format, but it has not yet, nearly a decade after Kastan writes, been successful in providing such abundance for more than a scene or two of a Shakespearean play text, as in MIT's *Hamlet on the Ramparts*. Non-Shakespearean texts have fared better. The *Richard Brome Online* project beautifully integrates modernised texts with transcriptions of the originals. It also offers innovative video footage of professional actors exploring extracts from the plays.

Hypertext is theoretically about the reader being able to navigate across a range of material without being constrained by a linear mode of encountering the text, and *Richard Brome Online* achieves that aim well. But such reader-led approaches are also subject to some of the ideological constraints that have been held to shape printed editions. *ArdenOnline* even encoded the words of male and female characters differently, for users interested in searching 'sexed' discourse from the period. Such encoding, like other forms of editorial apparatus, reflects the cultural conditions of its time of production. Unfortunately *ArdenOnline* lasted for only one year

(1999–2000), as the publishers could not make sufficient profit to keep it running (Holland and Onorato 2008: 248). None of the other major Shakespeare publishers have been able in the succeeding decade to replace the ambition of a complete modernised electronic Shakespeare, although the dedicated scholars behind the *Internet Shakespeare Editions* make it likely for the near future.

Publishing endeavours in electronic non-Shakespearean drama have been equally subject to difficulties. The electronic Oxford Middleton, announced as forthcoming by John Lavagnino (with Gary Taylor) in 1991, has not been released. A project with which I am associated, *The Cambridge Edition of the Works of Ben Jonson*, has an ambitious electronic edition and has also been subject to delays. The business of textual encoding in XML is time-consuming and best done with a large team. In addition to the time required, electronic texts come into difficulties because publishers have not come up with user models that lead to profit. Further, the economic circumstances of electronic publishing limit the amount of costly multimedia material that might be included in such projects, so that many of the benefits of hypertext editions are unavailable from the beginning.

Scholars have sought to work around these limitations in a variety of ways. Most of them have been initially divorced from the involvement of publishers. Both the Richard Brome project and the *Complete Works of James Shirley* have been generously funded by the Arts and Humanities Research Council, so that their electronic texts will be effectively self-published and hosted by the university homes of the projects. The *Internet Shakespeare Editions* are similarly self-published (Best 2008: 221). These projects, although some started life as electronic only, will also be published in print by established presses. But because the presses did not control the copyright of the electronic texts from the beginning of the projects, all three aim to offer their material online and free of charge. Currently the market seems to demand fairly inexpensive or free digital content, while being happy to pay for print materials. John Jowett notes that: 'The extent to which scholarly electronic editions will transform Shakespeare study remains to be seen, but at the end of the twentieth century its role remained, at most, supplementary to the print edition' (Jowett 2006b: 4). That supplementary role seems unlikely to change in the near future. Yet already there are hints at what might come. Michael Best notes that there are, 'over 15,000 pages of scanned artefacts of performance' in the *Internet Shakespeare Editions* (Best 2008: 228). Hypertext is ideally suited to the abundance of textual and performance material that has surrounded Shakespeare for the past four centuries.

No one in the mid-1990s could have imagined that electronic editions would have moved so slowly or proven so difficult to publish (Holland and Onorato 2008). Even as recently as 2001, David Scott Kastan predicted that, 'Soon the new medium will be as unavoidable, and thus as invisible, as the one it is, if not replacing, at least competing with as the dominant environment for the written word' (Kastan 2001: 116). Although that might be true with respect to the replacement of letters by emails, it certainly does not yet apply to digital editions of Shakespeare. Despite the relative failure of scholarship to produce reliable critical editions of Shakespeare and his contemporaries in affordable online editions, there is an unprecedented availability of Shakespearean play texts. The number of photo facsimiles available online is increasing, and it is perhaps through this very old-fashioned form of textual reproduction that the new technologies prove most helpful. Digital content has evolved in other ways that scholars have not predicted. The 'Shakespeare' application developed for Apple iTunes by Readdle.com has already had over one million downloads (in less than two years), making it easily the most popular edition of the complete works of Shakespeare. Electronic editions of Jonson, Ford, Shirley, and Brome are venturing in their own independent directions. The profession has not decided, and indeed may never decide, what kinds of digital scholarly editions are most appropriate for classroom use. Whichever format first manages to be widely used on the internet is likely to be the global Shakespeare used by all. As Christie Carson argues: 'The model most widely adopted for the digital edition will determine the form and availability of Shakespeare's texts, inevitably privileging specific contexts' (Carson 2006: 168). The wide acceptance of an internet Shakespeare will depend upon teachers and lecturers setting such e-texts as required texts, and perhaps on the very unlikely scenario of them being permitted in open-book examinations.

But whatever the future of the print and digital edition, it will always be based upon the original play-texts.

FURTHER READINGS

Bowers, Fredson 1987. 'Readability and Regularization in Old-Spelling Texts of Shakespeare', *Huntington Library Quarterly* 50: 199–227

Galey, Alan and Siemens, Ray (eds) 2008. 'Reinventing Shakespeare in the Digital Humanities', special issue of *Shakespeare* 4

Holland, Peter (ed.) 2006. 'Editing Shakespeare', *Shakespeare Survey* 59
    (ed.) 2009. 'Close Encounters with Shakespeare's Text', *Shakespeare Survey* 62

Kidnie, Margaret Jane 2009. *Shakespeare and the Problem of Adaptation.* Abingdon and New York: Routledge

Massai, Sonia 2007. *Shakespeare and the Rise of the Editor.* Cambridge University Press

Schreibman, Susan and Siemens, Ray (eds) 2008. *A Companion to Digital Literary Studies.* Oxford: Blackwell

Bibliography

All citations of early play texts refer to the copies in Early English Books Online (EEBO), http://eebo.chadwyck.com/, unless otherwise stated. References to manuscripts or other printed material are given parenthetically within the text.

Barnard, John and McKenzie, D. F. (eds) 2002. *The Cambridge History of the Book in Britain*, volume IV, 1557–1695. Cambridge University Press

Bate, Jonathan and Rasmussen, Eric (eds) 2007. *William Shakespeare: Complete Works* (The RSC Shakespeare). Basingstoke: Macmillan

Bertram, Paul and Kliman, Bernice W. (eds) 1991. *The Three-Text Hamlet: Parallel Texts of the First and Second Quartos and First Folio*. New York: AMS

Best, Michael 2008. 'The *Internet Shakespeare Editions*: Scholarly Shakespeare on the Web', *Shakespeare* 4: 221–33

Bevington, David 1987. 'Determining the Indeterminate: The Oxford Shakespeare', *Shakespeare Quarterly* 38: 501–19

  1996. Review of Shakespearean Originals series, *Shakespeare Quarterly* 47: 330–34

Bevington, David *et al.* (eds) 2002. *English Renaissance Drama: A Norton Anthology*. London and New York: Norton

Bevington, David, Butler, Martin and Donaldson, Ian 2001. 'Guidelines for *The Cambridge Edition of the Works of Ben Jonson (CWBJ)*'. Privately circulated by Cambridge University Press

Blayney, Peter W. M. 1982. *The Texts of 'King Lear' and Their Origins*, vol. 1: *Nicholas Okes and the First Quarto*. Cambridge University Press

  1997. 'The publication of playbooks', in *A New History of English Drama*, John D. Cox and David Scott Kastan (eds). New York: Columbia University Press, 383–422

  2005. 'The Alleged Popularity of Playbooks', *Shakespeare Quarterly* 56: 33–50

Bowers, Fredson 1938. 'Notes on Running Titles as Bibliographical Evidence', *The Library* 4th series 19: 315–38

  1949. *Principles of Bibliographical Description*. Princeton University Press

  (ed.) 1953–61. *Dramatic Works of Thomas Dekker*, 4 vols. Cambridge University Press

  (ed.) 1966–96. *The Dramatic Works in the Beaumont and Fletcher Canon*, 10 vols. Cambridge University Press

1987. 'Readability and Regularization in Old-Spelling Texts of Shakespeare', *Huntington Library Quarterly* 50: 199–227

Braunmuller, A. R. 2006. 'On Not Looking Back: Sight and Sound and Text', in *From Performance to Print in Shakespeare's England*, Peter Holland and Stephen Orgel (eds). Basingstoke: Palgrave, 135–51

Briggs, Julia 2007. '*The Lady's Tragedy*: Textual Notes', in *Thomas Middleton and Early Modern Textual Culture*, Gary Taylor and John Lavagnino (eds). Oxford University Press, 621–6

Briquet, C. M. 1907. *Les Filigranes. Dictionnaire historique des marques du papier.* Paris: Alophonse Picard et fils

Brooks, Douglas A. 2002. *From Playhouse to Printing House: Drama and Authorship in Early Modern England.* Cambridge University Press

Brown, Arthur 1956. 'Editorial Problems in Shakespeare: Semi-Popular Editions', *Studies in Bibliography* 8: 15–26

1960. 'The Rationale of Old-Spelling Editions of the Plays of Shakespeare and His Contemporaries: A Rejoinder', *Studies in Bibliography* 13: 69–76

Brown, John Russell 1960. 'The Rationale of Old-Spelling Editions of the Plays of Shakespeare and His Contemporaries', *Studies in Bibliography* 13: 49–67

Burt, Richard 2007. 'Thomas Middleton, Uncut: Castration, Censorship, and the Regulation of Dramatic Discourse in Early Modern England', in *Thomas Middleton and Early Modern Textual Culture*, Gary Taylor and John Lavagnino (eds). Oxford: Clarendon Press, 182–94

Carson, Christie 2006. 'The Evolution of Online Editing: Where Will It End?', *Shakespeare Survey* 59: 168–81

Carson, Neil 1988. *A Companion to Henslowe's Diary.* Cambridge University Press

Cathcart, Charles 2009. 'Old Plays and the General Reader: an Essay in Praise of the Regents Renaissance Drama Series', *Early Modern Literary Studies* 14.3: 5.1–36, http://purl.oclc.org/emls/14–3/Cathrege.html

Clare, Janet 1990. 'The Censorship of the Deposition Scene in *Richard II*', *Review of English Studies* 44: 89–94

Cloud, Random 1982. 'The Marriage of Good and Bad Quartos', *Shakespeare Quarterly* 33: 421–31

Dawson, Anthony B. and Minton, Gretchen E. (eds) 2008. William Shakespeare, *Timon of Athens.* London: Cengage

DelVecchio, Doreen and Hammond, Antony (eds) 1998. William Shakespeare, *Pericles.* Cambridge University Press

Donovan, Kevin J. 1987. 'The Final Quires of the Jonson 1616 *Workes*: Headline Evidence', *Studies in Bibliography* 40: 106–20

Dutton, Richard 1991. *Mastering the Revels: The Regulation and Censorship of English Renaissance Drama.* London: Macmillan

Early English Books Online (EEBO) 2003–2010. Cambridge: Proquest, http://eebo.chadwyck.com/home

Edwards, Philip (ed.) 1976. William Shakespeare, *Pericles.* Harmondsworth: Penguin

Egan, Gabriel 2006. '"As it Was, Is, or Will be Played": Title-pages and the Theatre Industry to 1610', in *From Performance to Print in Early Modern England*, Peter Holland and Stephen Orgel (eds). London: Palgrave, 92–110

English Short Title Catalogue 2010. London: The British Library Board, http://estc.bl.uk

Erne, Lukas 2003. *Shakespeare as Literary Dramatist.* Cambridge University Press
2009. 'The Popularity of Shakespeare in Print', *Shakespeare Survey* 62: 12–29

Farmer, Alan B. and Lesser, Zachary 2007–10. *DEEP: Database of Early English Playbooks.* http://deep.sas.upenn.edu

Fehrenbach, Robert J. 1971. 'The Printing of James Shirley's *The Polititian* (1655)', *Studies in Bibliography* 24: 144–8

Foakes, R. A. 1985. *Illustrations of the English Stage, 1580–1642.* London: Scholar Press
1996–7. 'The Need for Editions of Shakespeare: A Response to Marvin Spevack', *Connotations* 6: 326–9
1997. 'Shakespeare Editing and Textual Theory: A Rough Guide', *Huntington Library Quarterly* 60: 425–42

Forker, Charles R. (ed.) 2002. William Shakespeare, *Richard II*. London: Thomson Learning

Gabrieli, Vittorio and Melchiori, Giorgio (eds) 1990. *Sir Thomas More: A Play by Anthony Munday and Others* (Revels Plays). Manchester University Press

Galey, Alan and Siemens, Ray (eds) 2008. 'Reinventing Shakespeare in the Digital Humanities', special issue of *Shakespeare* 4

Gants, David L. 1998. 'Patterns of Paper Use in the *Workes of Beniamin Jonson* (William Stansby, 1616)', *Studies in Bibliography* 51: 127–53

Gaskell, Philip 1972. *A New Introduction to Bibliography.* Oxford University Press

Giddens, Eugene 2003. 'The Final Stages of Printing Ben Jonson's *Works*, 1640–1', *Publications of the Bibliographical Society of America* 97: 57–68
(ed.) 2008. William Shakespeare, *Pericles*. London: Penguin
2009. 'Pericles: the afterlife', in *The Cambridge Companion to Shakespeare's Last Plays*, Catherine M. S. Alexander (ed.). Cambridge University Press, 173–84
2010. 'Editions and Editors', in *Jonson in Context*, Julie Sanders (ed.). Cambridge University Press, 65–72

Giddens, Eugene and Barton, Anne (eds) forthcoming. 'Ben Jonson, *The Sad Shepherd*', in *The Cambridge Edition of the Works of Ben Jonson*, David Bevington, Martin Butler, and Ian Donaldson (eds). Cambridge University Press

Goldberg, Jonathan 1986. 'Textual Properties', *Shakespeare Quarterly* 37: 213–17
2003. *Shakespeare's Hand.* Minneapolis and London: University of Minnesota Press

Gossett, Suzanne (ed.) 2004. William Shakespeare, *Pericles*. London: Cengage

de Grazia, Margreta 1991. *Shakespeare Verbatim: The Reproduction of Authenticity and the 1790 Apparatus.* Oxford: Clarendon Press

Greenblatt, Stephen *et al.*, (eds) 1997. William Shakespeare, *The Norton Shakespeare*. New York and London: Norton

Greetham, D. C. 1994. *Textual Scholarship: An Introduction*. New York and London: Garland

Greg, W. W. 1908. 'On Certain False Dates in Shakespearian Quartos', *The Library* 2nd series 9: 113–31, 381–409

(ed.) 1922. *Two Elizabethan Stage Abridgements: The Battle of Alcazar and Orlando Furioso*. Oxford: Malone Society

1923. 'The Handwritings of the *Manuscript*', in *Shakespeare's Hand in The Play of Sir Thomas More*, A. W. Pollard and J. Dover Wilson (eds). Cambridge University Press, 41–56

1928. 'Act-divisions in Shakespeare', *Review of English Studies* 14: 152–8

1931. *Dramatic Documents from the Elizabethan Playhouses: Stage Plots, Actors' Parts, Prompt Books*. Oxford: Clarendon Press

1939–59. *A Bibliography of the Early Printed Drama*, 4 vols. London: Bibliographical Society

1950–51. 'The Rationale of Copy-Text', *Studies in Bibliography* 3: 19–36

1954. *The Editorial Problem in Shakespeare: A Survey of the Foundations of the Text*, 3rd edn. Oxford: Clarendon Press

Gurr, Andrew (ed.) 2000. William Shakespeare, *The First Quarto of King Henry V*, New Cambridge Shakespeare: The Early Quartos. Cambridge University Press

Hailey, R. Carter 2007. 'The Dating Game: New Evidence for the Dates of Q4 *Romeo and Juliet* and Q4 *Hamlet*', *Shakespeare Quarterly* 58: 367–87

Hammond, Antony 1986. '*The White Devil* in Nicholas Okes's Shop', *Studies in Bibliography* 39: 135–76

1992. 'Encounters of the Third Kind in Stage-Directions in Elizabethan and Jacobean Drama', *Studies in Philology* 89: 71–99

Hanabusa, Chiaki (ed.) 2007. *The Famous Victories of Henry the Fifth* (Malone Society). Manchester University Press

Heawood, Edward 1950. *Watermarks, Mainly of the 17th and 18th Centuries*. Hilversum: Paper Publications Society

Helgerson, Richard 1994. *Forms of Nationhood: The Elizabethan Writing of England*. University of Chicago Press

Henslowe, Philip 1961. *Henslowe's Diary*, R. A. Foakes and R. T. Rickert (eds). Cambridge University Press

Herford, C. H. and Simpson, Percy and Evelyn (eds) 1925–52. *Ben Jonson*, 11 vols. Oxford University Press

Hinman, Charlton 1955. 'Cast-off Copy for the First Folio of Shakespeare', *Shakespeare Quarterly* 6: 257–73

1963. *The Printing and Proof-Reading of the First Folio of Shakespeare*, 2 vols. Oxford: Clarendon Press

(ed.) 1996. *The First Folio of Shakespeare: The Norton Facsimile*, second edition. New York: Norton

Holland, Peter (ed.) 2006. 'Editing Shakespeare', *Shakespeare Survey* 59
  (ed.) 2009. 'Close Encounters with Shakespeare's Text', *Shakespeare Survey* 62
Holland, Peter and Onorato, Mary 2008. 'Scholars and the Marketplace: Creating Online Shakespeare Collections', *Shakespeare* 4: 245–53
Honigmann, E. A. J. 1965. *The Stability of Shakespeare's Text*. London: E. Arnold
Howard-Hill, T. H. 1972. *Ralph Crane and Some Shakespeare First Folio Comedies*. Charlottesville: University of Virginia Press
  1973. 'The Compositors of Shakespeare's Folio Comedies', *Studies in Bibliography* 26: 61–106
  1988. 'Crane's 1619 "Promptbook" of "Barnavelt" and Theatrical Processes', *Modern Philology* 86: 146–70
Hunter, George K. (ed.) 1975. John Marston, *The Malcontent* (Revels). London: Methuen
Hunter, Michael 2007. *Editing Early Modern Texts: An Introduction to Principles and Practice*. Basingstoke: Palgrave
Ioppolo, Grace 2002a. '"The foule sheet and ye fayr": Henslowe, Daborne, Heywood and the Nature of Foul-Paper and Fair-Copy Dramatic Manuscripts', *English Manuscript Studies 1100–1700* 11: 132–53
  2002b. 'The Transmission of an English Renaissance Play-Text', in *A Companion to Renaissance Drama*, Arthur F. Kinney (ed.). Oxford: Blackwell
  2006. *Dramatists and their Manuscripts in the Age of Shakespeare, Jonson, Middleton and Heywood: Authorship, authority and the playhouse*. Oxford and New York: Routledge
Irace, Kathleen O. 1994. *Reforming the 'Bad' Quartos: Performance and Provenance of Six Shakespearean First Editions*. London: Associated University Press
Jackson, MacDonald P. 2003. *Defining Shakespeare: Pericles as Text Case*. Oxford University Press
Jenkins, Harold (ed.) 1982. William Shakespeare, *Hamlet*, Arden 2nd series. London and New York: Routledge
Jones, Gwilym 2009. '"Thus Much Show of Fire": Storm and Spectacle in the Opening of the Globe', in *The Spectacular in and around Shakespeare*, Pascal Drouet (ed.). Newcastle: Cambridge Scholars
Jowett, John (ed.) 2000. William Shakespeare, *The Tragedy of King Richard III*. Oxford University Press
  2003. 'Varieties of Collaboration in Shakespeare's Problem Plays and Late Plays', in *A Companion to Shakespeare's Works*, vol. 4, Richard Dutton and Jean E. Howard (eds). Oxford: Blackwell, 106–28
  (ed.) 2004. William Shakespeare, *Timon of Athens*. Oxford University Press
  2006a. 'From Print to Performance: Looking at the Masque in *Timon of Athens*', in *From Performance to Print in Shakespeare's England*, Peter Holland and Stephen Orgel (eds). Basingstoke: Palgrave, 73–91
  2006b. 'Editing Shakespeare's Plays in the Twentieth Century', *Shakespeare Survey* 59: 1–19
  2007. *Shakespeare and Text*. Oxford University Press

Kastan, David Scott 2001. *Shakespeare and the Book*. Cambridge University Press

Kidnie, Margaret Jane (ed.) 2000a. *Ben Jonson: The Devil Is an Ass and Other Plays*. Oxford University Press

    2000b. 'Text, Performance, and the Editors: Staging Shakespeare's Drama', *Shakespeare Quarterly* 51: 456–73

    2004. 'The Staging of Shakespeare's drama in print editions', in *Textual Performances: The Modern Reproduction of Shakespeare's Drama*, Lukas Erne and Margaret Jane Kidnie (eds). Cambridge University Press, 158–77

    2005. 'Where Is *Hamlet*? Text, Performance, and Adaptation', in *A Companion to Shakespeare and Performance*, Barbara Hodgdon and W. B. Worthen (eds). Oxford: Blackwell, 101–20

    2009. *Shakespeare and the Problem of Adaptation*. Abingdon and New York: Routledge

Klein, Karl (ed.) 2001. William Shakespeare, *Timon of Athens*. Cambridge University Press

Lavagnino, John 1991. 'Announcement of Middleton project', *SHAKSPER: The Global Electronic Shakespeare Conference* (2 October), www.shaksper.net/archives/1991/0241.html

Lesser, Zachary 2004. *Renaissance Drama and the Politics of Publication: Readings in the English Book Trade*. Cambridge University Press

Lesser, Zachary and Stallybrass, Peter 2008. 'The First Literary *Hamlet* and the Commonplacing of Professional Plays', *Shakespeare Quarterly* 59: 371–420

Levenson, Jill L. (ed.) 2000. William Shakespeare, *Romeo and Juliet*. Oxford University Press

Long, William B. 1997. 'Perspective on Provenance: The Context of Varying Speech-heads', in *Shakespeare's Speech-Headings*, George Walton Williams (ed.). London: Associated University Press, 21–44

McGann, Jerome J. 1983. *A Critique of Modern Textual Criticism*. University of Chicago Press

    (ed.) 1985. *Textual Criticism and Literary Interpretation*. University of Chicago Press

McKenzie, D. F. 1969. 'Printers of the Mind: Some Notes on Bibliographical Theories and Printing-House Practices', *Studies in Bibliography* 22: 1–75

McKerrow, R. B. 1911–13. 'Notes on Bibliographical Evidence for Literary Students and Editors of English Works of the Sixteenth and Seventeenth Centuries', *Transactions of the Bibliographical Society* 12: 213–318

    1913. *Printers' and Publishers' Devices in England and Scotland 1485–1640*. London: Bibliographical Society

    1927. *An Introduction to Bibliography for Literary Students*. Oxford: Clarendon Press

    1931. 'The Elizabethan Printer and Dramatic Manuscripts', *The Library* 3rd series 12: 253–75

    1938. Review of Shakespeare's *Titus Andronicus*: the first quarto, 1594, *Review of English Studies* 14: 86–8

    1939. *Prolegomena for the Oxford Shakespeare*. Oxford: Clarendon Press

1997. 'A Suggestion Regarding Shakespeare's Manuscripts', 1935, repr. in *Shakespeare's Speech-Headings*, George Walton Williams (ed.). London: Associated University Press, 1–9

2000. 'The Relationship of English Printed Books to Authors' Manuscripts during the Sixteenth and Seventeenth Centuries: The 1928 Sandars Lectures', Carlo M. Bajetta (ed.), *Studies in Bibliography* 53: 1–67

McKerrow, R. B. and Ferguson, F. S., 1932. *Title-page Borders used in England and Scotland 1485–1640*. London: Bibliographical Society

McLeod, Randall (1979). 'A Technique of Headline Analysis, with Application to *Shakespeare's Sonnets*, 1609', *Studies in Bibliography* 32: 197–210

(1981–82). 'Un "Editing" Shakespeare', *SubStance* 10: 26–55

McMillin, Scott 1987. *The Elizabethan Theatre and The Book of Sir Thomas More*. Ithaca: Cornell University Press

Maguire, Laurie E. 1996. *Shakespearean Suspect Texts: The 'Bad' Quartos and their Contexts*. Cambridge University Press

Marotti, Arthur and Bristol, Michael D. (eds) 2000. *Print, Manuscript, and Performance: The Changing Relations of the Media in Early Modern England*. Columbus: Ohio State University Press

Massai, Sonia 2007. *Shakespeare and the Rise of the Editor*. Cambridge University Press

Masten, Jeffrey 1997. *Textual Intercourse: Collaboration, Authorship, and Sexualities in Renaissance Drama*. Cambridge University Press

May, James E. 2001. 'Who Will Edit the ESTC? (and have you checked OCLC lately?)', *Analytical and Enumerative Bibliography* 12: 288–304

Mueller, Martin 2008. 'Digital Shakespeare, or towards a literary informatics', *Shakespeare* 4: 284–301

Murphy, Andrew (ed.) 2000. *The Renaissance Text: Theory, Editing, Textuality*. Manchester University Press

2003. *Shakespeare in Print: A History and Chronology of Shakespeare Publishing*. Cambridge University Press

Orgel, Stephen (ed.) 1987. William Shakespeare, *The Tempest*. Oxford University Press

2006. 'The Book of the Play', in *From Performance to Print in Shakespeare's England*, Peter Holland and Stephen Orgel (eds). Basingstoke: Palgrave, 13–54

Parry, Graham 2002. 'Literary Patronage', in *The Cambridge History of Early Modern English Literature*, David Loewenstein and Janel Mueller (eds). Cambridge University Press, 117–40

Pollard, A. W. 1907. 'The Objects and Methods of Bibliographical Collations and Descriptions', *The Library* 2nd series 8: 193–217

1909. *Shakespeare's Folios and Quartos*. London: Methuen

Pollard, A. W. and Redgrave, G. R. 1976. *A Short-Title Catalogue of Books Printed in England, Scotland, & Ireland and of English Books Printed Abroad, 1475–1640. 1926*; revised by W. A. Jackson, F. S. Ferguson, and Katharine F. Pantzer. London: Bibliographical Society

Povey, Kenneth 1960. 'The Optical Identification of First Formes', *Studies in Bibliography* 13: 189–90

Proudfoot, Richard and Rasmussen, Eric (eds) 2005. *Two Noble Kinsmen* (Malone Society). Oxford University Press

Rasmussen, Eric 1991. 'Setting Down what the Clown Spoke: Improvisation, Hand B, and *The Book of Sir Thomas More*', *The Library* 6th series 13: 126–36

Richard Brome Online 2010. Richard Cave (ed.) http://www.hrionline.ac.uk/brome

Riddell, James A. 1986. 'Variant Title-pages of the 1616 Jonson Folio', *The Library* 6th series 8: 152–6

Roberts, Jeanne Addison 1980. 'Ralph Crane and the Text of *The Tempest*', *Shakespeare Studies* 13: 213–33

Roberts, Sasha (2003). *Reading Shakespeare's Poems in Early Modern England*. Basingstoke: Palgrave

Schreibman, Susan and Siemens, Ray (eds) 2008. *A Companion to Digital Literary Studies*. Oxford: Blackwell

Sellers, Harry 1927. 'Bibliographica', *Year's Work in English Studies* 8: 360–7

Shaaber, M. A. 1944. 'The Meaning of the Imprint in Early Printed Books', *The Library* 4th series 24: 120–41

'Shakespeare in Quarto' 2010. London: The British Library Board, www.bl.uk/treasures/shakespeare/homepage.html

Slights, William W. E. 2001. *Managing Readers: Printed Marginalia in English Renaissance Books*. Ann Arbor, Mich.: University of Michigan Press

Smith, Steven Escar 2002. '"Armadillos of Invention": A Census of Mechanical Collators', *Studies in Bibliography* 55: 133–70

Spector, Stephen (ed.) 1987. *Essays in Paper Analysis*. Washington, DC: Folger Shakespeare Library

Stern, Tiffany 2004. *Making Shakespeare: From Stage to Page*. London and New York: Routledge

Stevenson, Allan H. 1948–9. 'New Uses of Watermarks as Bibliographical Evidence', *Studies in Bibliography* 1: 151–82

    1951–2a. 'Shakespearian Dated Watermarks', *Studies in Bibliography* 4: 159–64

    1951–2b. 'Watermarks Are Twins', *Studies in Bibliography* 4: 57–91

    1954. 'Chain-Indentations in Paper as Evidence', *Studies in Bibliography* 6: 181–95

Syme, Holger Schott 1998. 'Unediting the Margin: Jonson, Marston, and the Theatrical Page', *English Literary Renaissance* 38: 142–71

Tabor, Stephen 2007. '*ESTC* and the Bibliographical Community', *The Library* 7th series 8: 267–86

Tanselle, G. Thomas 1971. 'The Bibliographical Description of Paper', *Studies in Bibliography* 24: 27–67

    1989. 'Reproductions and Scholarship', *Studies in Bibliography* 42: 25–54

    1994. 'Editing without a Copy-Text', *Studies in Bibliography* 47: 1–22

Taylor, Gary 1993. 'The Structure of Performance: Act-Intervals in the London Theatres, 1576–1642', in *Shakespeare Reshaped, 1606–1623*, Gary Taylor and John Jowett (eds). Oxford: Clarendon Press, 3–50

    2006. 'Making Meaning Marketing Shakespeare 1623', in *From Performance to Print in Shakespeare's England*, Peter Holland and Stephen Orgel (eds). Basingstoke: Palgrave, 55–72

Taylor, Gary *et al.*, (eds) 2007. *Thomas Middleton: The Collected Works; Thomas Middleton and Early Modern Textual Culture*, 2 vols. Oxford University Press

Taylor, Gary and Warren, Michael (eds) 1983. *The Division of the Kingdoms: Shakespeare's Two Versions of King Lear*. Clarendon Press

Thompson, Ann and McMullan, Gordon (eds) 2003. *In Arden: Editing Shakespeare: Essays in Honour of Richard Proudfoot*. London: Thomson Learning

Thompson, Ann and Taylor, Neil (eds) 2006. William Shakespeare, *Hamlet* (Arden Shakespeare), 2 vols. London: Cengage

Thomson, Leslie 1988. 'Broken Brackets and Mended Texts: Stage Directions in the Oxford Shakespeare', *Renaissance Drama* 19: 175–93

Vaughan, Virginia Mason and Vaughan, Alden T. (eds) 1999. *The Tempest* (Arden Shakespeare). London: Thomson Learning

Vickers, Brian 2002. *Shakespeare Co-Author*. Oxford University Press

Waller, Frederick O. 1958. 'Printer's Copy for *The Two Noble Kinsmen*', *Studies in Bibliography* 11: 62–85

Wells, Stanley 1984. *Re-Editing Shakespeare for the Modern Reader*. Oxford University Press

    2005. *A Dictionary of Shakespeare*. Oxford University Press

    2006. 'On Being a General Editor', *Shakespeare Survey* 59: 39–48

Wells, Stanley and Taylor, Gary 1979. *Modernizing Shakespeare's Spelling with Three Studies in the Text of Henry V*. Oxford University Press

    1997. *William Shakespeare: A Textual Companion*, 1987; repr. with corrections. Oxford University Press

Weiss, Adrian 2007. 'Casting Compositors, Foul Cases, and Skeletons: Printing in Middleton's Age', in *Thomas Middleton and Early Modern Textual Culture*, Gary Taylor and John Lavagnino (eds). Oxford University Press, 195–225

Werstine, Paul 1982. 'Shakespeare First Folio Comedies', *Studies in Bibliography* 35: 206–34

    1990. 'Narratives About Printed Shakespeare Texts: "foul papers" and "bad" quartos', *Shakespeare Quarterly* 41: 65–86

    1996. 'Editing after the End of Editing', *Shakespeare Studies* 24: 47–54

    1998. 'Touring and the Construction of Shakespeare Textual Criticism', in *Textual Formations and Reformations*, Laurie E. Maguire and Thomas L. Berger (eds). Cranbury, N. J.: Associated University Press, 45–66

    1999. 'Post-Theory Problems in Shakespeare Editing', *Yearbook of English Studies* 29: 103–17

2009. 'The Continuing Importance of New Bibliographical Method', *Shake-speare Survey* 62: 30–45

Williams, George Walton 1958. 'Setting by Formes in Quarto Printing', *Studies in Bibliography* 11: 40–55

Wiggins, Martin 1997. 'Conjuring the Ghosts of *The White Devil*', *Review of English Studies* 48: 448–70

Index